Flexicurity Capitalism

Flexicurity Capitalism
Foundations, Problems, and Perspectives

Peter Flaschel
AND
Alfred Greiner

OXFORD
UNIVERSITY PRESS

Oxford University Press, Inc., publishes works that further
Oxford University's objective of excellence
in research, scholarship, and education.

Oxford   New York
Auckland   Cape Town   Dar es Salaam   Hong Kong   Karachi
Kuala Lumpur   Madrid   Melbourne   Mexico City   Nairobi
New Delhi   Shanghai   Taipei   Toronto

With offices in
Argentina   Austria   Brazil   Chile   Czech Republic   France   Greece
Guatemala   Hungary   Italy   Japan   Poland   Portugal   Singapore
South Korea   Switzerland   Thailand   Turkey   Ukraine   Vietnam

Copyright © 2012 by Oxford University Press

Published by Oxford University Press, Inc.
198 Madison Avenue, New York, New York 10016
www.oup.com

Oxford is a registered trademark of Oxford University Press

All rights reserved. No part of this publication may be reproduced,
stored in a retrieval system, or transmitted, in any form or by any means,
electronic, mechanical, photocopying, recording, or otherwise,
without the prior permission of Oxford University Press.

Library of Congress Cataloging-in-Publication Data

Flaschel, Peter, 1943-
  Flexicurity capitalism : foundations, problems and perspectives / Peter
Flaschel and Alfred Greiner.
    p. cm.
  Includes bibliographical references and index.
  ISBN 978-0-19-975158-7 (cloth : alk. paper) 1. Manpower policy. 2. Labor
policy. 3. Job security. 4. Capitalism–Social aspects. I. Greiner, Alfred. II. Title.
  HD5713.F53 2011
  330.12'2–dc22
                                                                2010014740

---

1 3 5 7 9 8 6 4 2

Printed in the United States of America
on acid-free paper

CONTENTS

	Notation	ix
	Introduction	1
1	Marx: Socially Acceptable Capitalism?	7
	1.1 Introduction	7
	1.2 The Minimum-Wage Debate	9
	1.3 Sustainable Social Evolution through an Unrestricted Reserve-Army Mechanism?	10
	1.4 Classical Growth Dynamics	12
	1.5 Hiring and Firing, Social Security, and Restricted Reserve-Army Fluctuations	15
	1.5.1 Human Rights: Basic Income and Minimum Wages	16
	1.5.2 Capital's and Labor's Responsibility: Minimum Wages and Basic Income Needs	17
	1.5.3 Capital's and Labor's Responsibility: Upper Bounds for Real Wage Increases	22
	1.5.4 Automatic Stabilizers: Blanchard and Katz Error-Correction Terms	23
	1.6 Conclusions	24
	Appendix: Wage Dynamics: A Specific Theoretical Foundation	26
2	Kalecki: Full Employment Welfare Capitalism?	27
	2.1 Introduction	27
	2.2 Economic and Political Aspects of Full Employment	29
	2.3 The Model	32
	2.4 The Implied Laws of Motion	36
	2.4.1 The DAD Module: Multiplier and Employment Dynamics	37
	2.4.2 The DAS Module: Real-Wage Dynamic and Capital Accumulation	38
	2.5 Steady-State Configurations and Reduced-Form Three-Dimensional Dynamics	39
	2.5.1 Balanced Growth in the Four-Dimensional Dynamics	39
	2.5.2 Reduced-Form Three-Dimensional Dynamics	41
	2.6 Feedback Structures	43
	2.6.1 Feedback Channels in KMGS Growth	43
	2.6.2 The Feedback Structure of the KGR Model of Capital Accumulation and Employment Dynamics	45

	2.6.3 A Feedback-Suggested Local-Stability Scenario	47
	2.6.4 Consensus-Based Economies: Attraction Toward Accepted Steady-State Positions	48
2.7	Local Instability and Global Boundedness	49
	2.7.1 Conflict-Driven Economies: Repelling Steady-State Configurations	49
	2.7.2 Kalecki-Type Upper Turning Points	50
	2.7.3 Goodwin-Type Upper Turning Points?	51
	2.7.4 Rose-Type Lower Turning Points	53
	2.7.5 Goodwin-Type Lower Turning Points?	54
2.8	Numerical Examples	54
2.9	Political Aspects of the Kaleckian Investment and Employment Cycle	58
	2.9.1 Monetary Policy	59
	2.9.2 Fiscal Policy	61
2.10	Conclusions	63

3 Schumpeter: Capitalism, Flexicurity, and Democracy? 66
  3.1 Introduction 66
  3.2 From Marxian Reserve Army to Schumpeter's Competitive Socialism and Beyond 68
  3.3 Flexicurity Capitalism: Budget Equations, Consumption, and Investment 74
    3.3.1 Full-Employment Capitalism: Ideal, Status-Quo, and Compromises 74
    3.3.2 Basic Principles and Problems 76
    3.3.3 Sectoral Accounts, Consumption, and Investment 77
  3.4 Dynamics: Stability and Sustainability Issues 82
    3.4.1 Stability of Balanced Reproduction 82
    3.4.2 Sustainability of Balanced Reproduction 84
  3.5 Pension Funds and Credit 86
  3.6 Education and Schooling 93
    3.6.1 The Educational System: Basic Structure and Implications 93
    3.6.2 Equal Opportunities and Lifelong Learning 97
  3.7 Challenge I: Keynesian Business Fluctuations 104
  3.8 Challenge II: Schumpeterian Processes of "Creative Destruction" 110
  3.9 The Future of Capitalism: A Brief Appraisal 114
  3.10 Elites in Flexicurity Societies 117
    3.10.1 Basic Aspects 117
    3.10.2 Elite Groups and Areas of Operation 120
    3.10.3 Education: Foundation for Administrative Authority and Social Behavior 121

		3.10.4 Career Advancement and Decent Paths	124
		3.10.5 Preferences, Incentives, and Responsibilities	125
		3.10.6 Elite Failures	126
		3.10.7 The Remuneration of Elites under Flexicurity: A Baseline Proposal	127
		3.10.8 Summing Up	128
	3.11	Price Formation: Time Dependent Mark-up Pricing around Long-Period Prices of Production	130
		3.11.1 Profit Maximization Not a Guide to Action	130
		3.11.2 Success Based on Satisfying Rules	131
		3.11.3 Success in Competition with Other Firms Selects the Rules with Satisfactory Results	131
		3.11.4 Business Cycle Dependent Choice of Technique and Mark-up Pricing	131
		3.11.5 Existence and Limit Propositions	132
		3.11.6 Equalizing Positive Profit Rates and Inflation Dynamics	133
		3.11.7 Demand and Supply Side Driven Output Levels	134
		3.11.8 Concluding Remarks	136
	3.12	Conclusions and Outlook	137
	Appendix 1: Stability of Balanced Reproduction		140
	Appendix 2: Sustainability of Balanced Reproduction		141
4	Unleashed Capitalism: The Starting Point for Societal Reform		143
	4.1	Introduction	143
	4.2	Real Disequilibria, Balanced Portfolios, and the Real-Financial Markets Interaction	144
	4.3	A Portfolio Approach to KMG Growth Dynamics	147
		4.3.1 Households	147
		4.3.2 Firms	150
		4.3.3 Fiscal and Monetary Authorities	153
		4.3.4 The Wage-Price Spiral	154
		4.3.5 Capital Markets: Gross Substitutes and Stability	158
		4.3.6 Cumulative Processes in Capital Gains Expectations: Chartists' Behavior	159
	4.4	A Baseline-Stability Scenario	162
	4.5	Likely Outcomes of Unleashed Capitalism: Local Instability and Regime-Switch-Induced Viability	168
	4.6	A Further Risk-Bearing Asset: Long-Term Bonds	174
		4.6.1 Households, Government, and Financial Markets	174
		4.6.2 Intensive form	177
		4.6.3 Steady State	179
		4.6.4 Comparative Statics	181
		4.6.5 Stability	186
		4.6.6 Summary	191

4.7 Interest-rate Policy in the KMG Portfolio Approach	191
4.8 Conclusion	195
5 Conclusions	197
Mathematical Appendix: Stability Theorems	199
Notes	206
References	211
Index	217

NOTATION

Steady-state values are indicated by a sub- or superscript o, depending on the particular notations used in the chapters where they appear. When no confusion arises, the letters F, G, H may also define certain functional expressions in a specific context. A dot over a variable $x = x(t)$ denotes the time derivative, a caret its growth rate: $\dot{x} = dx/dt$, $\hat{x} = \dot{x}/x$. As far as possible, we try in the notation to follow the logic of using capital letters for level variables and lowercase letters for variables in intensive form, or for constant (steady-state) ratios. Greek letters are most often constant coefficients in behavioral equations (with, however, the notable exceptions of π's and ω). We use local notation in some chapters (only used in them), and define such notation in those chapters.

B	outstanding government fixed-price bonds (priced at $p_b = 1$)
B^l	outstanding government flex-price bonds (consols, priced at $p_b = 1/i$)
C	real private consumption (demand is generally realized)
E	number of equities
G	real government expenditure (demand is always realized)
I	real net investment of fixed capital (demand is always realized)
$\mathcal{I}$	desired real inventory investment
J	Jacobian matrix in the mathematical analysis
K	stock of fixed capital
L^d	employment, i.e., total working hours per year (labor demand is always realized)
L^w	employed workforce, i.e., number of employed people
L	labor supply, i.e., supply of total working hours per year
M	stock of money supply
N	inventories of finished goods
N^d	desired stock of inventories
S_f	real saving of firms
S_g	real government saving
S_p	real saving of private households
S	total real saving; $S = S_f + S_g + S_h$
T	total real tax collections
$T_w(t_w)$	real taxes of workers (per unit of capital)
$T_c(t_c)$	real taxes of asset holders (per unit of capital)
W	real wealth of private households
Y	real output
Y^p	potential real output
Y^f	full employment real output

Notation

Y^d	real aggregate demand
Y^e	expected real aggregate demand
c	marginal propensity to consume
e	employment rate
$U = 1 - e$	unemployment rate
$f_x = f_1$, etc.	partial derivative
i	nominal rate of interest on government bonds
k	capital intensity K/L (sometimes also parameter in money demand function)
l	labor intensity (in efficiency units)
m	real balances relative to the capital stock; $m = M/pK$
ν	inventory-capital ratio; $n = N/K$
p	price level
p_e	price of equities
q	return differential; $q = r - (i - \pi^c)$ or Tobin's q
r	rate of return on fixed capital, specified as $r = (pY - wL - \delta pK)/pK$
s_c	propensity to save out of capital income on the part of asset owners
$s = s_h$	households' propensity to save out of total income
u	rate of capacity utilization; $u = Y/Y^n = y/y^n$
v	wage share (in gross product); $v = wL/pY$
w	nominal wage rate per hour
y	output-capital ratio; $y = Y/K$
y^d	ratio of aggregate demand to capital stock; $y^d = Y^d/K$
y^e	ratio of expected demand to capital stock; $y^e = Y^e/K$
z or x	labor productivity, i.e., output per worker; $z = Y/L^d$
α	symbol for policy parameters in the Taylor rule
α_i	coefficient measuring interest rate smoothing in the Taylor rule
α_p	coefficient on inflation gap in the Taylor rule
α_u	coefficient on output gap in the Taylor rule
β_x	generically, reaction coefficient in an equation determining x, $\dot{x}$, or $\hat{x}$
β_y	adjustment speed in adaptive sales expectations
β_{π^c}	general adjustment speed in revisions of the inflation climate
β_{xy}	generically, reaction coefficient related to the determination of variable x, $\dot{x}$, or $\hat{x}$ with respect to changes in the exogenous variable y
α_q	responsiveness of investment (capital growth rate) to changes in q
α_u	responsiveness of investment to changes in u
β_{nn}	inventory stock adjustment speed
α_{n^d}	desired ratio of inventories over expected sales
β_{pu}	reaction coefficient of u in price Phillips curve

β_{pv}	reaction coefficient of $(1+\mu)v - 1$ in price Phillips curve
β_{we}	reaction coefficient of e in wage Phillips curve
β_{wv}	reaction coefficient of $(v - v^o)/v^o$ in wage Phillips curve
γ	government expenditures per unit of fixed capital; $\gamma = G/K$ (a constant)
τ	lump sum taxes per unit of fixed capital; $\tau = T/K$ (a constant)
δ	rate of depreciation of fixed capital (a constant)
$\eta_{m,i}$	interest elasticity of money demand (expressed as a positive number)
κ	coefficient in reduced-form wage-price equations; $\kappa = 1/(1 - \kappa_p \kappa_w)$
κ_p	parameter weighting $\hat{w}$ vs. π^c in price Phillips curve
κ_w	parameter weighting $\hat{p}$ vs. π^c in wage Phillips curve
κ_{wp}	same as κ_w
κ_π	parameter weighting adaptive expectations vs. regressive expectations in revisions of the inflation climate
π^c	general inflation climate
$\tau_c = T_c/K$	tax parameter for T^c (net of interest and per unit of capital); $T^c - iB/p$
τ_w	tax rate on wages
ω	real wage rate w/p

∎ INTRODUCTION

This book rests on three pillars from the history of economic thought, the work of Marx, Kalecki-Keynes, and Schumpeter, or the MKS system, as Richard Goodwin has called his attempt to form an integrated overview of this work.[1] We focus specifically on Kalecki's seminal essay on the political business cycle (1943), particularly in regard to the K component, and assume the theory of effective demand by Kalecki and Keynes as the necessary background from which his article starts its study. Thus, the letter K in the MKS approach represents the work of both Kalecki and Keynes, with the other letters specifically referring to the supply side theories of Marx (1867), in particular his analysis of the "General Law of Capitalist Accumulation", and Schumpeter's (1942) views on innovations under capitalism, which lead from processes of "creative destruction", or entrepreneurship, to large enterprises and from there to some form of Western-type competitive socialism.

This seminal work of Marx, Kalecki-Keynes, and Schumpeter essentially constitutes the focus of this book. Starting from Marx's (1867) analysis of the role of the reserve army mechanism (mass unemployment) in a capitalist economy in *Capital*, volume I, we examine, in chapter 1, from a very basic perspective, the necessity of such mass unemployment for capitalism to work effectively. We focus on Goodwin's (1967) modeling of the interaction between (un-)employment and income distribution. His model of a distributive growth cycle is, however, only one aspect of the conflict between capital and labor, dealing with the distribution of income between these two types of economic factors.

Marx also investigates in depth the conflict between these two aspects of the production process, as well as the norms that shape the state of labor productivity in a certain period. Kalecki (1943) reexamines this conflict under conditions of a political system with both rising welfare state activity and efforts to combat the business cycle by means of countercyclical fiscal policies. His conclusion is that these state activities disrupt mass unemployment as a disciplining device in the process of capitalist commodity production and that, sooner or later, proponents of capitalism will convince the government of a country to return to orthodox fiscal policies, deregulation of the labor market, and other actions and thus to no longer intervene in the goods and labor markets in order to establish full employment.

The reserve army mechanism, therefore, has two different roles to play: one affecting the extraction of sufficient labor for the production process from the employed workforce and one affecting the distribution of income as wages and profits on the level of commodity circulation in the goods and labor markets. Starting from the conflict between capital and labor in the latter process, we analyze, in chapter 1, the effects of having basic income for the employed as well as the unemployed and the (positive) implications of those effects for the shape of the distributive cycle. Then, in chapter 2, we show that modern capitalist societies may be able under certain conditions to attenuate the conflict between capital and labor and turn it into a consensus-based scenario where mass unemployment may no longer be needed as a disciplining device for firms' workforces.

Thus, chapters 1 and 2 demonstrate that at least the cruder forms of capitalism that exploit labor power and in which atypically employed or unemployed worker families live in poverty—and experience social degradation as such situations persist—may be avoided, not only through more improved government intervention but also through an understanding of capital and labor of the disadvantages of a conflict-driven interaction between them (such as the generation of long-phased distributive cycles exhibiting prosperity and depression, real and nominal processes of cumulative instability, and even economic breakdown). Such an approach questions the effectiveness of certain processes of deregulation, of reducing worker participation in firms and dismantling the welfare state, and quite generally of the laissez-faire policies that have predominated since the 1970s.

Chapter 1 focuses on the external relationship between capital and labor, their interaction in the external labor market, and the conflict over income distribution. This conflict underlies the formation of the wage-price spiral of a given country in a specific period. The resulting distributive cycle is a long-phased one—as the case of the US economy, for example, shows (see chapter 3)—where prosperity phases gradually give way to recessions or depressions that are sometimes long lasting. The wage-price spiral may be very active in the prosperity phase of the distributive cycle (leading eventually to stagflationary periods), and it may be fairly inactive in its stagnant period, because of downward nominal wage rigidity, in particular.

During a boom we have a build up of a profit squeeze, whereas during a bust, by contrast, a wage squeeze mechanism is at work. Chapter 1 shows that these two phases of the distributive cycle and the pronounced reserve army mechanism underlying it can be significantly moderated in amplitude—at least in theory—if both labor and capital can reach consensus on maximum real wages in the boom phase and minimum real wages in the bust phase. We cannot show conclusively, however, whether this moderation can be sustained in actual capitalist economies in the long run, because the conflict between capital and labor over income distribution may be an integral part of capitalism if it is to work properly, as suggested by Marx's analysis of the General Law of Capitalist Accumulation in *Capital*, volume 1, in 1867.[2]

We believe, however, that at least some of today's capitalist economies have been characterized by a partial consensus reached by capital and labor in the past, and still are, at least in carrying out some sort of concerted action in the management of wage income. Germany in the early 1970s was not, however, an example of this happening successfully.

Chapter 2, by contrast, examines the internal relationship between capital and labor, their interaction in the production process within firms, and their internal labor markets. Here we make use of Kalecki's analysis of the Political Aspects of Full Employment, which asserts that capitalist economies will enter a stagnant phase after a prosperity phase, because industrial leaders do not like full employment policies and can indeed enforce a return from Keynesian policy to orthodox policies. Phases of high employment lead—in their view—to declines in work discipline and labor productivity, through various ways of cheating by the employed workforce. In addition, technical change may be slowed through increased workforce participation, and there may be more negative effects. This motivates industrial leaders to influence and indeed persuade not only politicians but also economists to stop supporting Keynesian full-employment strategies and opt for a return to tight fiscal and monetary policies, even during the stagnant phase of the distributive cycle.

One may conclude from Kalecki's 1943 analysis that this conflict—within firms as well as generally—is inevitable under capitalism, causing the welfare state to rise but subsequently to fall, and with the intrafirm conflict exacerbated by the external conflict described earlier. We hope in this book, however, to show that both types of conflict, external and internal, can be managed in an educated and democratic society, and that they are, thus, not as ineluctable as the original work on these topics suggests.

In chapter 3 we focus on more complicated aspects of turning the conflict between capital and labor into a consensus-based interaction between them, which does not exploit the weakness of one party during the employment cycle of a capitalist economy. We start from Schumpeter's (1942) consideration of the possibility of a Western type of competitive socialism that solves not only the coordination problem in such an economy but also the incentive problem in the principal-agent scenario of a socialist economy.

Schumpeter answered the question as to whether his model of socialism was workable positively, but viewed from today's perspective, we would at least question his solution to the coordination problem under socialism (which, by and large, was of a static Walrasian type). Capitalism and a competitive form of socialism as well are, however, very dynamic types of economies, leading to radically transformed wavelike "social structures of accumulation", as we will call them, within a range of fifty to sixty years, as, for example, the period after World War II clearly shows. The modeling of such structures must, therefore, be done in a strictly dynamic context, which is not evident in Schumpeter's (1942) discussion of (late) capitalism, socialism, and democracy.

An active income and labor market policy is, moreover, not a focal point of Schumpeter's *Capitalism, Socialism and Democracy*, but it may be the solution to the problems we identify in chapters 1, 2, and 3. The actual evolution of modern capitalist economies may, however, not incorporate the principles we formulate in chapter 3.

A recent and intense debate within the European Union and its institutions concerns how to implement a so-called flexicurity system, that is, a labor-market reform that combines flexibility, in particular in the hiring and firing processes of firms, with security in employment (not jobs) and income for the workforce. Such a flexicurity reform of the labor market—if it is feasible and also competitive compared to other forms of capitalism—would not only integrate the concepts discussed in chapters 1 and 2 but would—in the shape we propose in discussing the flexicurity debate in chapter 3—also make Schumpeter's (1942) type of socialism unnecessary for the economy to work properly in the type of democratic societies he was envisaging. Moreover, many aspects of capitalism—its microeconomic institutional experience of running small, medium-sized, or large enterprises in particular—would simply remain intact under a new social structure of accumulation. A solution to the coordination problem of modern market economies thus needs not to be invented anew, but simply improved from mechanisms already in existence. Of course, the incentive problem in the envisaged new type of principal-agent relationship that would exist in such a framework must be carefully considered and solved.

We view the debate over a flexicurity society as a very stimulating and ongoing one. Its concepts and their stepwise realization in actual capitalist economies may indeed change the world significantly, at least in those countries in which a sufficient degree of maturity of the given capitalist system has been reached. In our view, there are aspects of an MKS system involved in the further theoretical development of the problems and prospects of flexicurity societies, but a design for such societies must be based on three quite different pillars. These pillars relate to the proper shaping and interrelation of flexicurity-type labor-market institutions, the underlying educational system, and the process of forming decision (not power) elites in a democratic society. These three pillars introduce quite different perspectives into any discussion of further social evolution, because they encompass, among other things, equal opportunities on the level of primary and secondary education (and, also, on the level of preschool education), citizenship awareness on the part of the adult population, and the cultivation of responsible and well-conducted behavior, in particular by those elected into elite decision-making positions.

Researchers with a background in the Marxian theory of capitalism may find these views fairly, if not totally, idealistic and illusionary. Nonetheless, the debate on flexicurity is taking place in the European Union with increasing popular participation, and we consider the possible outcomes as fairly open, from a theoretical perspective, as we will discuss in chapter 3, but also from an empirical-institutional perspective, because the actual paths of progress of the various countries in the EU may be very different. Thus, chapter 3 should be regarded as an abstract, theoretical contribution on the level of formal model building, rather than a contribution that considers transitional processes and the institutional changes they may involve.

In chapter 4, finally, we contrast an ideal flexicurity economy with what we would call a model of "unleashed capitalism." We consider labor-market and goods-market disequilibria (characterizing prosperity phases as well as deep depression, but also the normal working of the business cycle) in combination with the rate of return and capital gain oriented portfolio choice of the asset holders in this economy. We discuss balanced growth paths for this type of economy, as well as their limited stability, on the one hand, and the cumulative forces that affect them, on the other hand, which create large swings in the economic activity of business cycles and also of long-wave frequency. We also briefly study the effectiveness of countercyclical fiscal- and monetary-policy rules in such a framework, which, in principle, could turn the persistent fluctuations of the private sector of the economy into damped ones.

We do not here propose a reform of this type of (un-)leashed capitalism toward a flexicurity system, but leave integration of the ideas of chapters 3 and 4 for future research. In chapter 4 we share another three-pillar view of the working of the economy, discussed in Hanusch and Pyka (2007b), namely, that we now have a model at hand that is detailed in its description of the adjustment processes in the real markets, as well as detailed in its description of the financial sector of the economy—along lines proposed by Tobin (1982)—and which gives the public sector a role to play in the dynamics generated by the model. There is, however, one aspect of this kind of economic analysis, the Neo-Schumpeterian Corridor, that we do not consider. Hanusch and Pyka (2007b) do discuss this subject from a perspective they call Comprehensive Neo-Schumpeterian Economics or, briefly, a CNSE system. This aspect concerns, among other things, the analysis of technical change and innovation, in particular Schumpeter's process of creative destruction, which we do not treat here; we assume fixed proportions in production throughout (possibly subject to exogenous and disembodied Harrod-neutral technical change as well). Integrating the Neo-Schumpeterian Corridor—and, quite generally, aspects of the theory of endogenous growth—into our Keynesian portfolio approach to macrodynamics is a topic also for future research.[3]

Though a flexicurity system can be considered as a possible next step in the evolution of capitalism and thus preserves the problem-solving techniques successfully developed under unleashed capitalism as well as in its welfare state modifications, it must be considered—if successful—as a huge step forward, particularly, away from human degradation through mass unemployment, away from selective schooling systems with their neglect of equal opportunity principles, away from property rights that are based on ownership without qualified business-decision-making expertise, away from financial markets that are occupied only with themselves instead of channeling savings properly into real investment, and away from innovations that are problematic from the perspective of human rights or moral sentiments.

The central question we approach, though it is too difficult and far reaching to allow a satisfying answer in one book, is whether the reserve army mechanism of unleashed capitalism is inevitable if profit-oriented production processes are to function properly or whether rational wage-management processes, innovation-management processes, and credit management can be designed and conducted by appropriately qualified elites such that the dynamic efficiency of capitalism can be preserved without unemployment as a disciplining device. We hope that institutional change within the European Union will show that this is a possibility that should be pursued further in the twenty-first century.

A number of professional colleagues deserve special thanks, in particular Robert Boyer, Carl Chiarella, Richard Day, Duncan Foley, Gangolf Groh, Horst Hanusch, Camille Logeay, Sigrid Luchtenberg, Reinhard Neck, Christian Proaño, John Roemer, Willi Semmler, Peter Skott, Lance Taylor, Vela Velupillai, and many others, who offered valuable comments as discussants at presentations of aspects of the material of this book at various international conferences and on other occasions. Of course, none of the aforementioned is responsible for the remaining errors in this work, with respect to either form or substance.

Moreover, we thank four anonymous referees of this book for a variety of valuable suggestions that have helped to improve considerably its contents. We are also very grateful to Joe Jackson from Oxford University Press for his comprehensive editorial assistance. Last but not least, we want to thank Terry Vaughn from Oxford University Press for his encouragement to keep the book focused on a stream of thoughts from various stages of economic theorizing that—though modeled in abstract terms—if successfully implemented in actual capitalist economies, may be of decisive importance for the happiness of future generations. Of course, much more research, as well as political work, is needed here for such an outcome.

ACKNOWLEDGMENT

Peter Flaschel acknowledges support through an Opus Magnum Research Grant from the Fritz Thyssen/Volkswagen Stiftungen, which allowed him to focus exclusively on this and other research projects during the winter term 2007 to 2008.

1 Marx: Socially Acceptable Capitalism?

1.1 ■ INTRODUCTION

In 1817, **David Ricardo** (1970, p. 105), drew the following far-reaching conclusion from his theoretical (corn) model of the dynamics of capital accumulation (see Sraffa [1970], p. 105):

> These then are the laws by which wages are regulated, and by which the happiness of far the greatest part of every community is governed. Like all other contracts, wages should be left to the fair and free competition of the market, and should never be controlled by the interference of the legislature. The clear and direct tendency of the poor laws is in direct opposition to these obvious principles: it is not, as the legislature benevolently intended, to amend the condition of the poor, but to deteriorate the conditions of both poor and rich; ...

In 1867, **Karl Marx**'s (1954, p. 597) ironic comment on the working of this Malthusian iron law of natural wages was this: "A beautiful mode of motion this [is] for developed capitalist production!" He instead analyzed the interaction between capital and labor in the following way:

> ... a rise in the price of labor resulting from accumulation of capital implies the following alternative: ... accumulation slackens in consequence of the rise in the price of labor, because the stimulus of gain is blunted. The rate of accumulation lessens; but with its lessening, the primary cause of that lessening vanishes, i.e., the disproportion between capital and exploitable labor-power. The mechanism of the process of capitalist production removes the very obstacles that it temporarily creates. The price of labor falls again to a level corresponding with the needs of the self-expansion of capital, whether the level be below, the same as, or above the one which was normal before the rise of wages took place. We see thus: In the first case, it is not the diminished rate either of the absolute, or of the proportional, increase in labor-power, or laboring population, which causes capital to be in excess, but conversely, the excess of capital that makes exploitable labor-power insufficient. In the second case, it is not the increased rate either of the absolute, or of the proportional, increase in labor-power, or laboring population, that makes capital insufficient, but, conversely, the relative diminution of capital that causes the exploitable labor-power, or rather its price, to be an excess. It is these absolute movements of the accumulation of capital which are reflected as relative movements of

the mass of exploitable labor-power, and therefore seem produced by the latter's own independent movement.

Marx (1954, pp. 580/1)

Instead of the basically monotonic law of natural wages, Marx develops here a picture of an industrial cycle as the consequence of the growth of capital for "the lot of the laboring class." Growth will—according to this passage—consequently be accompanied by fluctuations in economic activity that originate from changing labor market conditions and their effect on the distribution of income between capital and labor. Furthermore, Marx does not see this cyclical process as something involving forces that are active near a steady state. Instead, this cycle represents a global mechanism by which the viability of the capitalistic system in the long term is guaranteed. In Marx's own words this reads as follows:

> The rise of wages therefore is confined within limits that not only leave intact the foundations of the capitalist system, but also secure its reproduction on a progressive scale. The law of capitalistic accumulation, metamorphosed by economists into pretended law of Nature, in reality merely states that the very nature of accumulation excludes every diminution in the degree of exploitation of labour, and every rise in the price of labour, which could seriously imperil the continual reproduction, on an ever-enlarging scale, of the capitalistic relation. It cannot be otherwise in a mode of production in which the labourer exists to satisfy the needs of self-expansion of existing values, instead of, on the contrary, material wealth existing to satisfy the needs of development on the part of the labourer. As, in religion, man is governed by the products of his own brain, so in capitalistic production, he is governed by the products of his own hand.
>
> Marx (1954, p. 582)

From the viewpoint of developed Western capitalism, Malthusian population dynamics is of course no longer relevant to the working of such an economy. The question we pursue in this chapter, however, is whether the Marxian reserve-army mechanism is a compelling (iron) law for the proper working of capitalism or whether one can redesign this reserve-army mechanism such that at least the worst outcomes of it can be avoided in a modern capitalist society.

We will consider this question in this chapter[1] assuming a homogenous labor market; see Flaschel, Greiner, Logeay, and Proaño (2009) for additional treatment of a low-income wage sector in such an economy. This kind of market is embedded in the supply-driven macrodynamic framework of Goodwin's (1967) reserve-army growth cycle type, with respect to which we will show that minimum wages, as well as basic income guarantees, do indeed improve the working of such an economy from a longer-term perspective, whereas markets in other frameworks may or may not show some adjustment problems as far as unemployment is concerned. This suggests that income protection is best implemented in the prosperity phases of this classical growth-cycle mechanism and accompanied by reducing maximum-wage regulations to reduce employment fluctuations, which should make negotiations between capital and labor in regard to income protection easier. Such negotiations are more easily conducted the more insight there is into the accumulation dynamics that we study in this chapter, which is of quite a different type than the microeconomic reasonings that dominate the discussion on minimum wages in the literature.

The rest of the chapter is organized as follows. Section 1.3 provides a brief discussion of what we call the reserve-army mechanism of capitalist economies. In Section 1.4 we introduce an extended version of the Goodwin (1967) model of cyclical growth, to be used in this chapter as a point of reference. The primary Section 1.5, considers how general regulations concerning basic income needs, minimum wages but also maximum wages modify (and improve) the growth dynamics generated by the model. We will also briefly discuss a modern approach to wage negotiations that will improve the restricted growth cycles obtained in the model even further.

1.2 ■ THE MINIMUM WAGE DEBATE

A current controversy in Germany in parliament, in the media, and also among economists, concerns whether minimum wages should be introduced in certain sectors or even throughout the economy. This debate was triggered by the rise of jobs with low salaries at or even below the subsistence level from the 1990s. It was also caused by the observation that the income of top managers has been rising drastically more than the average income of employees over the last decades. For example, according to Klesse and Voss (2007), the annual income of top managers of the largest 100 companies in Germany, with total revenues exceeding 5 billion euros, has increased by a factor of 8 over the last 30 years, while the GDP has risen by a factor of 4.5. In order to raise the income of the lowest wage earners and reduce the gap between the highest and lowest incomes, proponents call for a minimum wage and some of them even for an upper limit on wage revenues.

Opponents of such policies by and large argue with the employment costs of such regulation of capitalism (see, e.g., Sinn, 2007). Because opponents assume perfect competition (price-taking behavior)[2] in which employers hire labor up to the point where real wages are equal to marginal products, a lower limit on the *real* wage rate reduces employment and, thus, raises unemployment, with all its negative effects for the economy (assuming that the marginal product at the current point of employment is below the minimum real-wage rate). This assumption lacks justification, particularly because it is obvious that the real world is not at all well represented by a Walrasian economy with price-taking firms throughout. In this chapter, we, therefore, consider wage w and price p setting behavior,[3] and in addition a fixed proportions technology for simplicity.

We do not initially consider low-skilled labor in this framework, because we believe that the macro consequences of a general minimum real wage should be considered first. A minimum wage for low-income labor should, however, not alter the overall macrobehavior of the economy too strongly, so that we may conclude that the demonstrated gains in economic performance (less severe fluctuations in income distribution and in the employment rate) will also apply to the low-skilled segment, particularly because part of this segment is complementary to the sector of normal work in a one-good model.

Another and different aspect is that social progress implies an evolution of societies that comprises more than just economic goals in a narrow sense. In particular, the question of whether societies succeed in achieving human rights for their citizens, and to what extent, should be a major concern for policymakers. This point is often neglected by economists who look only at the economic subsystem of societies when enunciating policy recommendations.

In this chapter we will show in a supply-side framework that minimum—and maximum—real wages will be beneficial to the working of a capitalist economy, at least in the long term. We would stress, in first addressing this topic, that it can be pursued only in a dynamic framework that includes the forces of growth and income distribution, and, thus, not by means of static arguments or even static and partial ones, as are used in the standard debate on minimum wages. Second, minimum-wage levels must be chosen with some care; our analysis will show that at most they delay the rise in employment to a certain degree but thereafter lead to economic and social outcomes that are clearly preferable to those when there are no minimum wages. Finally, upper limits as real wages evolve may help in this model, showing that the solution to the problem of mass unemployment involves the active participation (and cooperation) of both capital and labor in the process of cyclical growth as considered in this chapter. We emphasize that the term *maximum wages* refers here to the general wage level and is not intended only to limit the wages of the highest wage earners. Thus, wage-price spirals, such as those in Germany during the 1970s, which had detrimental effects on the whole economy, would be avoided in this model.

1.3 ■ SUSTAINABLE SOCIAL EVOLUTION THROUGH AN UNRESTRICTED RESERVE-ARMY MECHANISM?

We start with the hypothesis that Goodwin's (1967) classical employment cycle does not represent a process of social reproduction that can be considered adequate and sustainable in a democratic society in the long term, because of the degradation of a part of the workforce during periods of mass unemployment. To ameliorate the effects of this cycle, this chapter formulates an unemployment-benefit system for the unemployed and a minimum-wage rule for the employed, which would disrupt this form of cyclical growth and economic reproduction of capitalism and its accompanying workforce degradation. A society would achieve

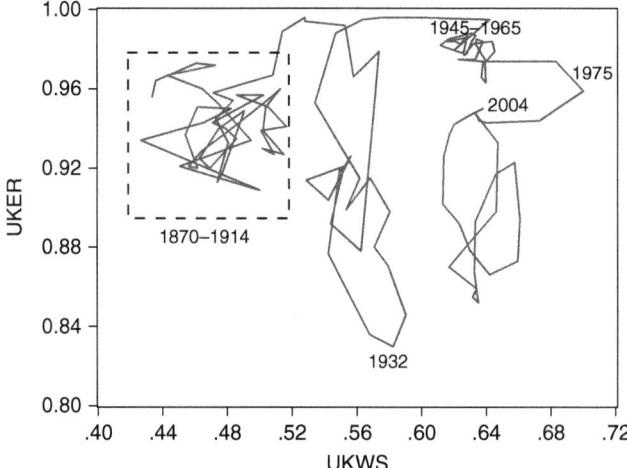

Figure 1.1 UK distributive cycles 1870–2004: WS = wage share, ER = employment rate.

such an outcome by protecting workforce skills and family structures through general base-income payments, coupled with an obligation of lifelong learning. This system provides particularly high labor mobility (particularly in regard to hiring and firing), where fluctuations of employment in the labor market of the economy (the private sector) are made socially acceptable through the security aspect of this revised form of Goodwinian growth cycle dynamics. We can show, in this framework, that minimum (and maximum) real wages provide extra stability to such dynamics by decreasing the amount of overshooting of income distribution and of employment they are otherwise subject to. See figure 1.1 for a historical illustration of the distributive cycle in the case of the UK economy.[4] Note that the model we will use focuses on the long-term aspects of the cycles, that is, on the long-phased distributive cycles after World War II (and not on the Keynesian business cycle features figure 1.1 also contains).[5]

One insight that can be obtained for the United Kingdom in the period 1855–1965 from figure 1.1 is that the Goodwin cycle must have been significantly shorter before 1914, and that there was a major change in it after 1945. This may be explained by significant changes in the adjustment processes of market economies for these two periods: primarily price adjustment before 1914 and primarily quantity adjustments after 1945. Based on data up to 1965, one could have claimed that the growth cycle had become obsolete (and maybe even the business cycle, as was claimed in the late 1960s). Yet the data shown in figure 1.1, taken from Groth and Madsen (2007), make clear that nothing of this sort took place in the UK economy. In fact, we see in figure 1.1 two periods of excessive overemployment (in the language of the theory of the nonaccelerating rate of inflation [NAIRU]), followed by periods of dramatic underemployment; both began with periods of more or less pronounced occurrence of stagflation. Generating economic viability through large swings in the unemployment rate is one way to make capitalism work, but it must be questioned with respect to its social consequences, since such a reproduction mechanism may not be compatible in the long run with the social foundations of a democratic society.

Therefore, we contrast this situation with an alternative social structure of accumulation and its labor market institutions, which allow a combination of a competitive market economy (including freedom to hire and fire) with a human rights bill that includes the right (and the obligation) to do (social) work (including the preservation of workforce skills), and to get income from this work that, at the least, supports basic needs for happiness. By contrast, a laissez-faire capitalistic society that harms family structures to a considerable degree (through alienated work and degrading unemployment) cannot be made compatible with a democratic society in the long term, because it produces effects ranging from social segmentation to class conflicts.

1.4 ■ CLASSICAL GROWTH DYNAMICS

In this section we briefly reconsider an extended version of the Goodwin (1967) growth cycle model of the interaction of income distribution and (un)employment, considered in detail in Flaschel (2008, chapter 4). This model serves as a baseline framework for our subsequent discussion of the role of base-income payments to all unemployed members of the workforce and minimum wages for the employed part of the workforce. This classical model of fluctuating growth, based on labor market and accumulation dynamics, was originally formulated in real terms. Goodwin (1972), however, also suggested a nominal version of this model, which separates wage from price inflation. We use the corresponding reformulation in Flaschel (2008, chapter 4) for our subsequent discussion of supply-side unemployment cycles and their modification through unemployment benefits and minimum-wage payments.[6]

Let us start with the formulation of the model. The growth rate of the money wage, $\hat{w}$, is assumed to be given by ($e = L/L^s$ the employment rate):

$$\hat{w} = \beta_w(e - \bar{e}) + \eta\hat{p}, \quad \hat{w} = \dot{w}/w, \quad \hat{p} = \dot{p}/p \qquad (1.1)$$

This represents a conventional nominal-wage Phillips curve, augmented by price inflation $\hat{p}$ in the conventional way (through an accelerator term if $\eta \geq 1$ holds).[7] We assume $\bar{e} \in (0, 1)$ where $1 - \bar{e}$ denotes the NAIRU unemployment rate. For price dynamics, we posit a dynamic markup pricing rule ($v = wL/(pY)$ the wage share, that is, unit costs divided by the price level):[8]

$$\dot{p} = \beta_p\left[A\frac{wL}{Y} - p\right] \Rightarrow \hat{p} = \beta_p[Av - 1] \qquad (1.2)$$

For reasons of consistency, we assume for the markup factor A with $Av^* = 1$ for v^*, the steady-state value of the share of wages. Thus, there is no inflation in the steady state.

Assuming a linear technology with no technical change, that is, on the basis of given input–output proportions $\bar{y} = Y/K = \text{const.}$, $\bar{z} = Y/L = \text{const.}$, and assuming Say's law in the form $I \equiv S = (1 - v)Y$, Goodwin's accumulation equation is given by

$$\hat{K} = \bar{y}(1 - v), \quad \hat{K} = \dot{K}/K$$

Concerning savings propensities, we assume that $s_c = 1$; $s_w = 0$ holds for the savings rates out of profits and out of wages. Using $\bar{y} = Y/K = \text{const.}$ and $\bar{z} = Y/L = \text{const.}$, we get from the definitional equation $e = L/L^s$,

$$\hat{e} = \hat{K} - n, \quad \hat{e} = \dot{e}/e$$

with n the exogenous growth rate of labor supply L^s. From the foregoing equation we get:

$$\hat{v} = \hat{w} - \hat{p} - \hat{\bar{y}} = \beta_w(e - \bar{e}) + (\eta - 1)\beta_p[Av - 1] \qquad (1.3)$$

$$\hat{e} = \bar{y}(1 - v) - n \qquad (1.4)$$

Thus, two autonomous differential equations in the variables v, e are obtained.

The interior steady-state solution is

$$v^o = 1 - n/\bar{y}, \quad e^o = \bar{e} \quad \hat{p}^o = 0 \; (Av^o = 1)$$

It is easy to check that $\eta = 1$ is a bifurcation value for the behavior of the dynamics that separates nonexplosive ($\eta < 1$) from explosive cyclical behavior ($\eta > 1$) by center type stability at $\eta = 1$. We would call the first case a consensus-based economy and the second case an economy that is driven by dissent, because here capital and labor interact in a destabilizing manner by way of inconsistent income claims.

It is not difficult to prove these assertions from a local perspective. Yet a more general proof, since it is global, is one that employs a Liapunov function for the dynamics (1)–(2) around its steady state $e^o = \bar{e}$, $v^o = 1 - n/\bar{y}$. The function

$$H(v, e) = \int_{e^o}^{e} \beta_w(\tilde{e} - e^o)/\tilde{e} \, d\tilde{e} - \int_{v^o}^{v} (\bar{y}(1 - \tilde{v}) - n)/\tilde{v} \, d\tilde{v}$$

defines such a Liapunov function. It has the following shape over the phase space $(v, e) \in \mathfrak{R}_+^2$:

14 ■ FLEXICURITY CAPITALISM

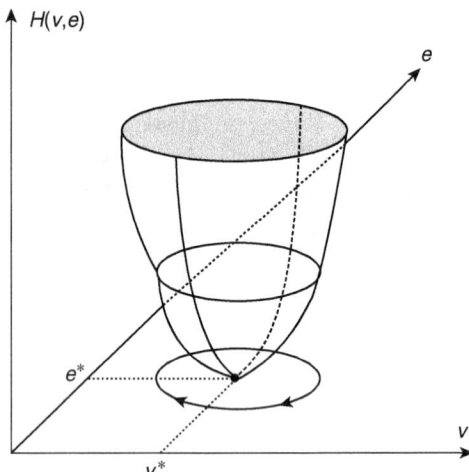

Figure 1.2 A Liapunov function for the extended Goodwin dynamics.

Its level surfaces[9] correspond to the Goodwin (1967) growth cycles, the case $\eta = 1$; see the closed curve in figure 1.2 in the v, e phase space. The function is zero at the steady state and it is well defined and strictly positive[10] elsewhere in the positive orthant $\Re_+^2$. Moreover, its time derivative along the solution curves of the above dynamical system reads

$$\dot{H} = H_v \dot{v} + H_e \dot{e}$$
$$= -(\bar{y}(1-v) - n)\hat{v} + \beta_w(e - \bar{e})\hat{e}$$
$$= +(\bar{y}(1-v) - n)(1 - \eta)\beta_p[Av - 1]$$

which gives zero for $v = v^o$. For $v \neq v^o$ we get on the other hand:

$$\dot{H} < 0 \quad \text{if } \eta < 1$$
$$= 0 \quad \text{if } \eta = 1$$
$$> 0 \quad \text{if } \eta > 1$$

since $\bar{y}(1-v) - n$ and $Av - 1$ are of different signs to the left and to the right of $v = v^o$.

Theorem 2 of Hirsch and Smale (1974, pp. 195) is applicable, because $\dot{H} = 0 \Leftrightarrow v = v^o$ (for $\eta \neq 1$). We thereby get

$\eta < 1$: a globally asymptotically stable dynamics in the invariant domain $\{(u, v) \in \Re^2, u, v > 0\} = \Re_+^2$

$\eta > 1$: a totally unstable dynamics in this same invariant domain.

$\eta = 1$: all trajectories in $\Re_+^2$ are closed orbits, representing the original Goodwin growth cycles.

These results are intuitively plausible because the sign of the derivative $\dot{H}$ simply expresses whether the trajectories of the dynamics in v, e-space are accompanied by declining, rising, or constant magnitudes of their corresponding value $H(v, e)$ (see figure 1.2). Trajectories accompanied by a rising $H(v, e)$ for example must, therefore, be explosive.

The preceding model provides a neat and simple generalization of Goodwin's (1967) classical growth cycle of the dynamic interaction of the employment rate and income shares in the conflict over income distribution. With respect to the closed orbit shown in figure 1.2, as well as any other such orbit, this conflict over income distribution points inside and thus produces convergence to the steady state for parameter values $\eta < 1$ and outside, implying divergence, for $\eta > 1$.

Two problems might arise in the latter situation. First, $(e, v) > (0, 0)$ holds automatically along the orbits of the model, but we also have to ensure that $(e, v) \leq (1, 1)$ holds true. Second, the case $\eta > 1$ is not yet viable, that is, the dynamics are still incomplete in this case. What, however, guarantees outer limits if economically implausible values are approached and, thus, instability results? An answer to this question is provided in Flaschel (2008, chapter 4) but need not concern us here, because we will find other delimiters in such problematic cases in this chapter.

The situation $\eta > 1$ provides an example of what we would call a dissent-driven economy. There is instability due to too excessive wage claims, totaling an amount higher than that due to actual inflation.[11] Because of the explosive nature of the dynamics, the full employment ceiling $e = 1$ will be approached sooner or later, and it will give rise to significant increases in the wage share, which continues and generates increasing price inflation, even when the employment rate falls again (though it would still be higher than the NAIRU rate of employment). This period of stagflation may be followed (if the wage share stays below 1) by a long period of stagnation during which there is rising mass unemployment; degradation of skills, particularly for the long-term unemployed; decay in family structures due to the lack of basic income provisions; and other effects. In the following sections, we discuss basic ingredients that help avoid such occurrences in a modified social model. Therefore, we will not consider the conflict-driven case of the Goodwin model here any further.

1.5 ■ HIRING AND FIRING, SOCIAL SECURITY, AND RESTRICTED RESERVE-ARMY FLUCTUATIONS

We assume for the time being the prevalence of a balance between a consensus- and a dissent-driven economy, that is, the limit case $\eta = 1$, which implies the closed-orbit structure of the original Goodwin (1967) growth-cycle model.

The question, then, is whether such an economy (where there is significant overshooting in unemployment and income distribution) can be improved by allowing for both unemployment compensation and minimum wages (and later on also maximum wages), an improvement implying certain compromises in the interaction between capital and labor.

1.5.1 Human Rights: Basic Income and Minimum Wages

1. Everyone has the right to work, to free choice of employment, to just and favorable conditions of work and to protection against unemployment.
2. Everyone, without any discrimination, has the right to equal pay for equal work.
3. Everyone who works has the right to just and favorable remuneration ensuring for himself and his family an existence worthy of human dignity, and supplemented, if necessary, by other means of social protection.
4. Everyone has the right to form and to join trade unions for the protection of his interests.

> United Nations (1998, Article 23): Universal Declaration of Human Rights, 1948 (http://www.un.org/Overview/rights.html)

In this section we show that the quoted Article 23 from the United Nations' Declaration of Human Rights not only represents a normative statement but can also be justified from the economic point of view in the context of our supply-side analysis of the process of capital accumulation. We believe that capitalism is a very robust system of resource allocation and income distribution that can adjust to many social restrictions if these restrictions are justified. For more detailed discussion of this view, see Bowles, Gordon, and Weisskopf's (1983) work, *Beyond the Waste Land*, and in particular the chapter on an economic bill of rights.

We augment our analysis of the working of the reserve-army mechanism in a capitalist economy of the preceding section with two fundamental human rights: the right for basic (real) income when unemployed and the right when employed for wages not to fall below a certain real minimum level. Of course, there are also obligations connected with the formulation of these rights, which concern the need to preserve skills when unemployed and contributing to the provision of adequate social services. In this chapter our focus is, however, on the macroeconomic sustainability of such minimal restrictions on the working of a capitalist economy and not on detailed analysis of how such a system works on the microlevel. We argue that the social costs of reproduction mechanisms as shown in figure 1.2 are much higher than the costs that result under the changes, already mentioned, in a capitalist economy, and that it is the duty of capital, as well as labor, to facilitate the realization of these restrictions in practice.

1.5.2 Capital's and Labor's Responsibility: Minimum Wages and Basic Income Needs

The dynamical system underlying this section can be described as:

$$\hat{v} = \beta_w(e - \bar{e}) \tag{1.5}$$

$$\hat{e} = \bar{y}(1 - v) - n \tag{1.6}$$

We now modify this system by assuming that a certain fraction τ of the real-wage income of the employed must support unemployment insurance, and by assuming the restriction that the real wage $\omega = w/p$ of the employed can at most fall to the level ω_{min}. We then derive the basic income of the unemployed by positing that their real wage is a certain fraction of this minimum real wage given by $\bar{\omega}$. The supply of labor of the unemployed is $(1 - e)L$, which we assume will be used for activities that relate to skill preservation or for social services. Because labor productivity z is given, the aforementioned assumptions can be equally represented by constraints $v_{min}, \bar{v}$.

Thus, we assume for the aforementioned dynamics (in terms of wage shares now) that $\bar{v} < v_{min} < v^o$, and that $v_{min} \leq v$ holds true at all points in time (because minimum wages must of course lie below the steady-state value). The only modification that this implies for the aforementioned dynamics is that they are now augmented by $\hat{v} = 0$ in the cases where $v = v_{min}$ applies in the original Goodwin growth-cycle dynamics.

To consider the viability of the structure for the assumed transfer payments, we represent reserves for unemployment benefits (a physical inventory[12] of durable consumption goods in this model type[13]) with the symbol R. Their rate of change is on the basis of the previously described assumptions given by

$$\dot{R} = \tau\omega eL - \bar{\omega}(1 - e)L$$

where L is the total labor supply. Transferred to intensive form magnitudes, this gives

$$\dot{R}/K = \tau\omega\bar{y}/\bar{y} - \bar{\omega}(1 - \bar{y}/\bar{z}) = \tau v\bar{y} - \bar{v}(\bar{z}l - \bar{y})$$

For the dynamic of the intensive form variable $r = R/K$ we get from these equations:

$$\hat{r} = \hat{R} - \hat{K} = \frac{\dot{R}}{K}/r - \hat{K}, \quad \text{i.e.} \tag{1.7}$$

$$\dot{r} = \tau v\bar{y} - \bar{v}(\bar{z}l - \bar{y}) - (\bar{y}(1 - v))r \tag{1.8}$$

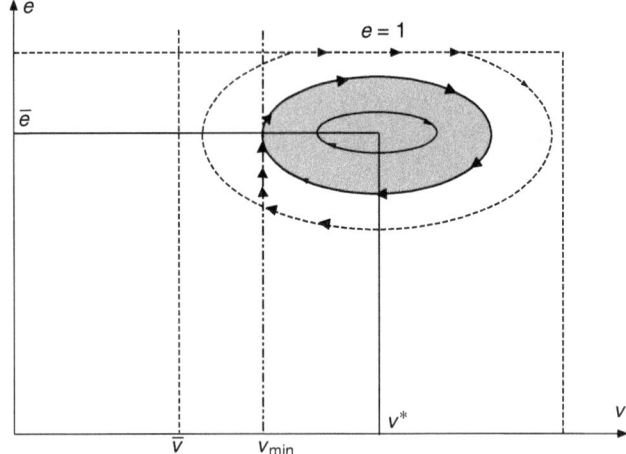

Figure 1.3 The distributive cycle with a minimum-wage restriction.

For the steady-state value of r this gives

$$r^o = \frac{\tau v^o \bar{y} - \bar{v}(\bar{z}l^o - \bar{y})}{n} = \frac{\bar{y}[\tau v^o - \bar{v}(1/\bar{e} - 1))]}{n}$$

that is,

$$\left(\frac{R}{L}\right)^o = \frac{r^o}{l^o} = \frac{(\tau\omega^o + \bar{\omega})e - \bar{\omega}}{n}$$

Assuming, for example, the parameter values $n = 0.02$, $\tau = 0.15$, $\bar{\omega} = 0.5\omega^o$ and as a minimum for the actual employment rate $e = 0.8$ gives for $(R/L)^o$ the value $\bar{\omega}$, which means that the steady-state reserves for unemployment benefits per worker—at an unemployment rate of 20 percent—are just equal to the basic income wage, whereas steady-state employment is $\bar{e}$ and steady-state real wages are given by $\omega^o = (1 - \frac{n}{\bar{y}})\bar{z}$. At least in steady state, therefore, the economy is reproducible at base income wages $0.5\omega^o$, the minimum wage $\omega_{min} \in (\bar{\omega}, \omega^o)$ having no role to play in this case.

The question now, however, is how the dynamics of the original Goodwin model are modified on a large scale through the assumption of a minimum wage rate for the employed workers. Figure 1.3 shows what happens in the growth-cycle dynamics if a minimum wage restriction is added to the model. With respect to this figure, we stress that the base-income real wage does not matter for it, because it only concerns the redistribution of income between employed and unemployed workers (who both have a propensity to spend equal to 1).

The smallest cycle[14] in figure 1.3, first of all, shows that nothing changes if the minimum real wage is less than the lowest real wage along this cycle.

The minimum-wage restriction then simply is not binding. If, however, as shown by the largest cycle, the minimum wage limit is hit, the economy will move along this boundary upward (since profitability is above the steady-state profit rate) until it reaches the NAIRU rate of employment. From that point, real wages rise again along the cycle, which is just tangent to the minimum-wage restriction. The result, therefore, is that all larger cycles will be dampened toward this boundary case (around the gray area in figure 1.3). Minimum real wages, therefore, make the fluctuations in the economy less severe, reduce periods of stagflation, and diminish the volatility in the employment rate in the long run.

This is clearly a more desirable situation from an economic point of view, since it avoids excessive fluctuations of the employment rate. It is also more desirable socially, because the social consequences of unemployment are now avoided through the transfer payments underlying this tamed operation of the classical reserve-army mechanism. Moreover, moderately increasing minimum real wages will improve this situation further. A return to a cold-turkey strategy of no minimum wages at all may end the depression faster, but it reintroduces severe fluctuations in the employment rate and in income distribution, with all their social consequences. We note that this latter case also characterizes the case of combined wages (see the digression that follows).

Let us next consider the asymptotically stable case $\eta < 1$. In this case, the Liapunov approach implies that all trajectories point inward with respect to the closed orbits of the original Goodwin model. The situation shown in figure 1.3 implies that the generated trajectories must enter the gray area sooner or later after real wages have started to rise again. They will then converge to the steady state by an inwardly directed crossing of the closed orbits of the Goodwin case inside (see the one shown in figure 1.3). Note, however, that the law of motion

$$\hat{v} = \beta_w(e - \bar{e}) + (\eta - 1)\beta_p[Av - 1]$$

now implies an upward sloping $\dot{v} = 0$-isocline in place of a horizontal one (with an unchanged steady state), which means that real wages start rising earlier than in the case $\eta = 1$, moving the economy into the gray area in figure 1.3 sooner.

In the unstable case $\eta > 1$ we have a declining $\dot{v} = 0$-isocline, which means that real wages start rising later than in the case $\eta = 1$. In this case, the trajectory generated hits the minimum wage barrier outside the Goodwin closed orbit shown in figure 1.3, and it also moves along the real wage barrier farther until real wages start rising again as before. This generates a single closed orbit—with a recurrent minimum wage regime now—but it removes the explosiveness of the unrestricted case. The economy is, thus, made a viable one in the long run through a minimum real-wage restriction, as shown in figure 1.4. It may, however, also need a maximum wage restriction in case the wage share approaches its maximum value 1 after the prosperity phase (where the employment rate and the wage share increase simultaneously). We note here that similar conclusions apply in the case of a stable limit cycle, as described in Flaschel (2008, chapter 4), because minimum (and maximum) real wages, if appropriately chosen, then again restrict the explosive (but now convergent) trajectories inside the limit cycle such that a situation as shown in figure 1.4—now within the limit cycle—is again obtained. The initially considered Goodwin (1967) closed-orbit structure, therefore, only provides the starting point for our analysis of the stabilizing role of minimum and maximum wages, which in principle can be applied, also, to models of the distributive and demand cycles as they are considered in Barbosa-Filho and Taylor (2006), at least in cases in which convergence to the steady state is not given.

We conclude that minimum real wages can contribute significantly to an improvement of the classical growth-cycle of section 1.3 in cases where convergence to the steady state is not given originally. Such an additional restriction to falling real wages—when enforced by law and not based on an agreement between capital and labor—also, however, may modify the behavior of agents in the case of unrestricted wage-price dynamics, for example, through increased bargaining power of the workers, once minimum-wage legislation has been implemented. This may, of course, happen and it is not easy to include in the global analysis here. The advantages of minimum-wage rules may, therefore, be undone if the unrestricted lower part of the cycles shown in figures 1.3 and 1.4 are moving down toward lower rates of employment through increased aggressiveness on the part of workers' unions.

Here, however, we would, recommend introduction of minimum as well as maximum wages as follows. First, they should come about through a consensus between capital and labor in the prosperity phase of the cycle, when such agreement would be easier, in order to limit overshooting wage claims, as they occurred, for example, in Germany around 1970. We thus need to be aware of the evils of stagflation, which may end the prosperity phase more or less rapidly. Second, a compromise on upper real-wage limits is easier to reach if combined with an agreement on a lower limit for real wages, because this balances advantages and disadvantages for both capital and labor. Third, such cooperation may also make the wage bargaining process less prone to conflict if the economy is between the upper and the lower real-wage limit.

Partial cooperation between capital and labor may make the low employment part of the cycles shown in figures 1.3 and 1.4 less pronounced. If convergence to the steady state thereby occurs, this adds to the stability of the economy. If this convergence does not occur, we can only conjecture here that a decrease in the steepness of the wage Phillips curve will improve the situation further. Such a result is not easily established by means of the Liapunov function we use in our study of stability. We conjecture, however, that this decrease makes the unrestricted cycle longer and less severe, but we leave this conjecture for future research. Our view is that an increase in cooperation between capital and labor will improve the working of the distributive cycle we are considering. The unemployment benefit system needs to be a prerequesite for such improved

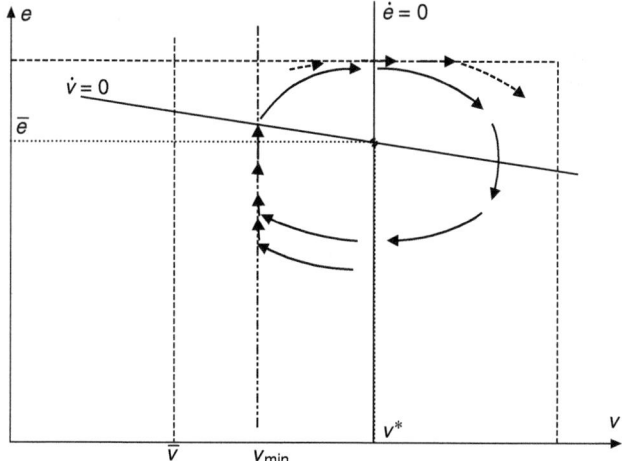

Figure 1.4 The unstable distributive cycle with a minimum-wage restriction.

cooperation between the two opponents in the cyclical process of capital accumulation and resulting mitigation of the conflict over income distribution.

Combined Wages in Place of Minimum Wages

For the case in which combined wage payments replace the minimum-wage barrier as a type of government subsidy of minimum-wage payments to workers (which frees firms from this social obligation), we get the following law of motion for the evolution of the funds out of which unemployment benefits and the excesses of the minimum wage over the actual wage (in depressions) are paid:

$$\dot{R} = \tau \omega e L - \bar{\omega}(1-e)L - \phi(1-\tau)(\omega_{min} - \omega)eL$$

where ϕ is 0 for $\omega_{min} \leq \omega$ and 1 otherwise. Whereas minimum wages represent a change in collective-bargaining policies, this requirement for accumulation of workers'-funds does not intervene in the labor market but leaves wage negotiations to the social partners in the labor market. From this law of motion, we now get for the evolution of $r = R/K$:

$$\hat{r} = \hat{R} - \hat{K} = \frac{\dot{R}}{K}/r - \hat{K} \quad \text{i.e.}$$

$$\dot{r} = \tau v \bar{y} - \bar{v}\bar{y}\frac{1-e}{e} - (\bar{y}(1-v))r - \phi(1-\tau)\bar{y}(v_{min} - v), \quad v = \omega/\bar{z}$$

$$= \bar{y}(\tau v - \bar{v}\frac{1-e}{e} - (1-v)r - \phi(1-\tau)(v_{min} - v))$$

The steady-state value of the state variable r is the same as before, since v_{min} is assumed to lie to the left of its steady-state value. And for the dynamics of r, we must restrict our analysis to growth-cycle magnitudes that do not lead to values of the state variables v, e that imply $\dot{r} < 0$. To do so involves choosing the right parameter sizes or choosing an appropriate modification of the model such that $r > 0$ is ensured endogenously.

There is, however, one central implication of the combined wage approach that makes it clearly inferior to the approach we considered previously. This implication arises from the fact that the original Goodwin growth cycle is reestablished through the combined wage scenario, because profits of firms are not modified through this institutional regulation. The Goodwin overshooting mechanism here remains fully effective and leads us back to the large recurrent distributive cycle we considered in section 1.3. By contrast, in the minimum-wage regime, we have at most only one traverse to the left of the cycle, which takes us to a smaller cycle and which does not reoccur any more ($\eta \leq 1$). We conclude that combined wages represent an inferior policy compared to an economy-wide minimum-wage regulation.

1.5.3 Capital's and Labor's Responsibility: Upper Bounds for Real Wage Increases

One may ask how the lower limit of real-wage payments is in fact monitored in a society in which wage negotiations are about money wages and not about real wages and are subject to collective bargaining (tariff autonomy). The answer to this question is theoretically not a difficult one because it only requires that wages increase exactly with price inflation when minimum real wages are reached (as long as employment is below the NAIRU). The problem may be for capital and labor to reach agreement on the management of wage inflation in this phase of the distributive cycle, which would primarily mean agreement by capital, since labor is in a weak position.

A compensation that can be offered by labor is that a similar rule is applied when labor is in a strong position, that is, when the maximum real wage shown in figure 1.5 has been reached. Wage inflation is then higher than price inflation (since the real wage is increasing) and reaching agreement requires compromise primarily from the unions, specifically agreement that there will be only inflationary compensation until the NAIRU level $\bar{e}$ has been reached again. If such agreement is reached between capital and labor, the result is shown in figure 1.5, and, thus, further improvement occurs in cyclical behavior, generated by the wage-price Phillips-curve mechanisms and by the pace of capital accumulation this implies.

The choice of the correct levels of minimum (and maximum) wages may, however, run into problems when they are set too close to the unobserved steady-state level. Though doing so may dampen the fluctuations in the rate

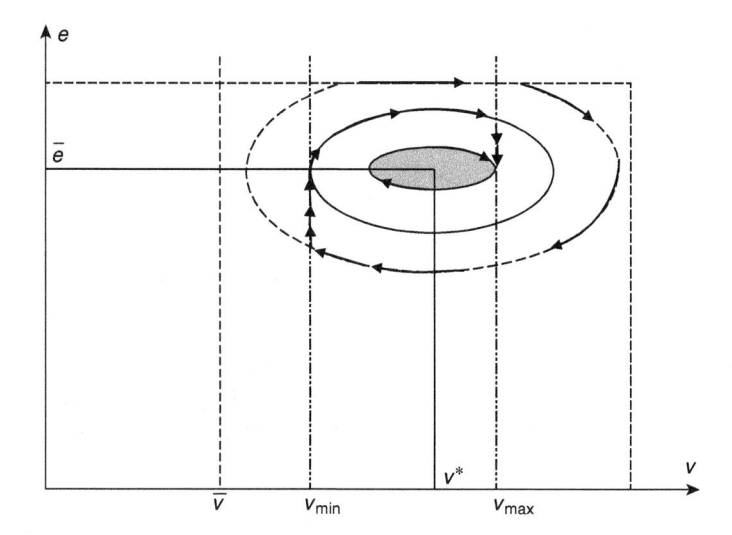

Figure 1.5 The distributive cycle with a maximum-wage restriction.

of employment further if it really stays below ω^o it will lead to disastrous consequences if set above the steady-state level. This is true because profits then are not sufficient to maintain even the current level of employment, which will fall unchecked if this choice of the minimum-wage level is not revised. It may, therefore, be wise to use a sense of proportion in establishing the minimum and expect the maximum real-wage level to help tailor fluctuations in growth and employment most effectively.

1.5.4 Automatic Stabilizers: Blanchard and Katz Error-Correction Terms

In the appendix to this chapter we provide a sketch of Blanchard and Katz's (1999) microfoundation of the wage Phillips curve, which we mentioned earlier but have not used. This microfounded type of Phillips curve extends the Phillips curve shown in eq. (1.1) in the following way (in the case $\eta = 1$ [see the appendix for details]):[15]

$$\hat{w} = \beta_{we}(e - \bar{e}) - \beta_{wv}(v - v^o) + \hat{p} \qquad (1.9)$$

Making use of the Liapunov function in section 1.3:

$$H(v, e) = \int_{e^o}^{e} \beta_w(\tilde{e} - e^o)/\tilde{e} \, d\tilde{e} - \int_{v^o}^{v} (\bar{y}(1 - \tilde{v}) - n)/\tilde{v} \, d\tilde{v}$$

we get, with respect to the extended Phillips curve (which implies $\hat{v} = \beta_{we}(e - \bar{e}) - \beta_{wv}(v - v^o)$) the following result:

$$\dot{H} = H_v \dot{v} + H_e \dot{e}$$
$$= -(\bar{y}(1-v) - n)\hat{v} + \beta_w(e - \bar{e})\hat{e}$$
$$= -(\bar{y}(1-v) - n)(-\beta_{wv}(v - v^o))$$
$$= \bar{y}(v^o - v)\beta_{wv}(v - v^o) = -\bar{y}\beta_{wv}(v - v^o)^2 \leq 0$$

The unrestricted Goodwin growth cycle is, therefore, now globally convergent to the steady state of the economy in the case $\eta = 1$ by the arguments we used in section 1.3 for the case $\eta < 1$. Because the cycles that so far have resulted from either minimum or maximum real wages are tangent to these restrictions, we conclude from the previous considerations that they are only needed once to restrict the unrestricted excessive cycle. Thereafter, such limits are no longer necessary, since the next cycle remains inside these limits and converges to the steady state eventually. We thus see from the microfounded and estimated wage Phillips curve of Blanchard and Katz (1999) type, at least for Europe as far as their study is concerned, that minimum and maximum wages will dampen the fluctuations of the unrestricted reserve-army mechanism significantly and make it thereafter convergent to its long-term equilibrium position.

1.6 CONCLUSIONS

In this chapter we have departed from the conventional discussion of the impact of minimum wage legislation, which is only partial in nature, by considering the macroeconomic effects of such legislation. We think that sector-specific rules concerning minimum wages can be discussed only against the background of macrofoundations in which the medium- and long-term consequences of minimum wages are the focus, rather than the short-term adjustment problems such legislation may cause.

We have made use of the supply-driven macroeconomic framework of Goodwin (1967) reserve-army type and shown that minimum wages as well as basic income guarantees do indeed improve the working of such an economy from a longer-run perspective, while the traverse to this model may or may not show adjustment problems as far as unemployment is concerned. This suggests that income protection is best implemented in the prosperity phases of this classical growth cycle mechanism, accompanied by maximum-wage regulations to reduce employment fluctuations, which should make negotiations between capital and labor on income distribution easier. These negotiations are more easily conducted the more insight there is into the accumulation dynamics we have formulated and discussed in this chapter.

We thus conclude that the introduction of a general level of minimum (or maximum) real wages into a supply-side macromodel of fluctuating growth does not do much harm to capital accumulation and employment as described through this model. In addition, it definitely and significantly improves the performance of the implied cyclical growth path over time (if the wage negotiation process remains unchanged within the assumed real wage limits). Such an economy not only experiences less severe fluctuations in income distribution and employment compared to the unrestricted case (where there is unlimited working of the wage-price spiral and the reserve-army mechanism) but it also avoids the social consequences of mass unemployment through basic income payments.

An educated society, in which the principle of equal opportunities is reflected in its educational system, may also be a very important ingredient in the success of a social structure in which partial workforce degradation is avoided by continuing skill training for the unemployed and lifelong learning for the employed (see Flaschel et al. [2008] and chapter 3 of this book for details on a hypothetical flexicurity economy and its educational institutions). We believe that the considered ratios of capital productivity, labor productivity, and, also, capital depreciation are improved and much more robust in such a society than in one in which mass unemployment, workforce degradation, social segmentation, and so forth dominate the social structure of accumulation of its economy.

The advantage of using the Goodwin approach to cyclical growth, employed as a reference case here, is that it is not biased against capitalist interest, since it entails that unions bear responsibility for overshooting wage shares in the prosperity phase of the cycle.[16] They therefore might have avoided the subsequent stagnant phase to some degree by prudent upper real-wage restrictions. By contrast, minimum wages come to the help of unions in stagnant phases by helping the economy avoid the severe consequences of mass unemployment. We note that both minimum and maximum real wages are easier to implement in the prosperity phase of the cycle than in its stagnant or depressed phase. Compared to combined wages—also assumed to work in an otherwise unchanged Goodwin-type model—we can, in any case, show that upper- and lower-wage restrictions are the better choice for moderating the effects of the Marxian reserve-army mechanism.

Of course, there may be obstacles to such a social structure of accumulation, due to the sclerosis of existing social structures (e.g., degraded skills of long-term unemployed persons, segmented labor markets, for underemployment, job offers, and such). Globalization may also represent a big challenge for our reformulated Goodwin growth-cycle dynamics, if we consider international competition for traded commodities and services, workforce migration, outsourcing, and other factors. Addressing this issue essentially requires that the basic flexi(bility sec)curity system discussed in this chapter be further refined along the lines proposed in Flaschel et al. (2008).

APPENDIX: WAGE DYNAMICS: A SPECIFIC THEORETICAL FOUNDATION

This appendix builds on the article by Blanchard and Katz (1999) and briefly summarizes their theoretical motivation of a money-wage Phillips curve, which is closely related to our dynamic eq. (1.1) and its extension at the end of section 1.4.[17] Blanchard and Katz assume—following standard models of wage setting—that expected real wages of workers, $\omega^e = w_t - p_t^e$, are basically determined by the reservation wage, $\bar{\omega}_t$, current labor productivity, $y_t - l_t$, and the rate of unemployment, U_t:

$$\omega_t^e = \theta\bar{\omega}_t + (1-\theta)(y_t - l_t) - \beta_w U_t$$

Expected real wages are thus a Cobb-Douglas average of the reservation wage and output per worker, but they depart from this expected normal level by the demand pressure on the labor market. The reservation wage in turn is determined as a Cobb-Douglas average of past real wages, $\omega_{t-1} = w_{t-1} - p_{t-1}$, and current labor productivity, augmented by a factor a < 0:

$$\bar{\omega}_t = a + \lambda\omega_{t-1} + (1-\lambda)(y_t - l_t)$$

Inserting the second into the first equation results in

$$\omega_t^e = \theta a + \theta\lambda\omega_{t-1} + (1-\theta\lambda)(y_t - l_t) - \beta_w U_t,$$

which gives, after some rearrangement,

$$\Delta w_t = p_t^e - p_{t-1} + \theta a - (1-\theta\lambda)[(w_{t-1} - p_{t-1}) - (y_t - l_t)] - \beta_w U_t$$
$$= \Delta p_t^e + \theta a - (1-\theta\lambda)u_{t-1} + (1-\theta\lambda)(\Delta y_t - \Delta l_t) - \beta_w U_t$$

where Δp_t^e denotes the expected rate of inflation, u_{t-1} the past (log) wage share, and $\Delta y_t - \Delta l_t$ the current growth rate of labor productivity. This is the growth law for nominal wages that flows from the theoretical model referred to in Blanchard and Katz (1999).

In this chapter, we operationalized this theoretical approach to money-wage inflation by defining the short-term cost push Δp_t^e with myopic perfect foresight. Furthermore, we proposed $\Delta y_t - \Delta l_t = n_x = 0$ because of the assumed fixed proportions technology. We end up with an equation for wage inflation of the type employed at the end of section 1.4, but with a specific interpretation of the model's parameters from the perspective of efficiency wage or bargaining models.[18]

2 Kalecki: Full Employment Welfare Capitalism?

2.1 ■ INTRODUCTION

In 1968, **Milton Friedman** introduced the concept of the "natural rate of unemployment" into economic theory in order to characterize as unsound the Keynesian attempt to reach full employment in a capitalist economy:

> At any moment of time there is some level of unemployment which has the property that it is consistent with equilibrium in the structure of *real* wage rates.... The 'natural rate of unemployment', in other words, is the level that would be ground out by the Walrasian system of general equilibrium equations, provided there is imbedded in them the actual structural characteristics of the labor and commodity markets, including market imperfections, stochastic variability in demands and supplies, the cost of gathering information about job vacancies and labor availabilities, the cost of mobility, and so on.
>
> Friedman (1968, p. 8)

From quite a different perspective, published in 1943 in the *Political Quarterly* this was also the topic of **Michal Kalecki**'s essay on the *Political Aspects of Full Employment*, where we find the following passage:

> But even if this opposition were overcome—as it may well be under the pressure of the masses—the *maintenance* of full employment would cause social and political changes which would give a new impetus to the opposition of the business leaders. Indeed, under a regime of permanent full employment, the 'sack' would cease to play its role as a disciplinary measure. The social position of the boss would be undermined and the self assurance and class consciousness of the working class would grow. Strikes for wage increases and improvements in conditions of work would create political tension. It is true that profits would be higher under a regime of full employment than they are on the average under *laisser-faire*; and even the rise in wage rates resulting from the stronger bargaining power of the workers is less likely to reduce profits than to increase prices and thus affects adversely only the rentier interest. But 'discipline in the factories' and 'political stability' are more appreciated by the business leaders than profits. Their class instinct tells them that lasting full employment is unsound from their point of view and that unemployment is an integral part of the normal capitalist system. (Kalecki, 1971, pp. 140–1)... In this situation a powerful block is likely to be formed between business

and the rentier interest and they would probably find more than one economist to declare that the situation was manifestly unsound.

Kalecki (1971, 1943, p. 144)

Our approach in this chapter[1] is to model a capitalist Kalecki-Goodwin-type economy in which industrial leaders react to a growing employment rate in a negative way—in addition to a tight monetary policy (to be considered later in this chapter)—a reaction that is intended to remove inflationary pressure from the labor market by lowering workers' bargaining position and decreasing their influence on decision making within firms. Increasing unemployment is, therefore, actively pursued as a disciplinary device by economic means and, from Kalecki's perspective, by influencing political opinion and policymakers. This latter aspect and the implied return to an orthodox type of monetary and fiscal policy was the focus of interest of Kalecki's (1943, 1971) seminal article, originally published long before the orthodox critique of Keynesianism by Milton Friedman and subsequent macroeconomic approaches.

In our Kalecki-Goodwin-type model, however, situations are conceivable in which the interaction between capital and labor is consensus based. Such situations, therefore, question Kalecki's views on the necessity of the reserve-army mechanism for the viability of a capitalist market economy. Full-employment capitalism may thus become a possibility for an advanced capitalist welfare state if both capital and labor understand the process they are subject to and cooperate. This was already discussed with respect to establishing a minimum and maximum regime within a Goodwin (1967) supply-side model (and its basic income guarantees) in the preceding chapter. Still, however, in the long term, particularly in economic crises, that cooperation can break down, leading to less acceptance of welfare-state principles. Welfare-state configurations that tend to be biased toward workers, therefore, may be vulnerable and may need to be supplemented by active labor market policies. We discuss these policies in chapter 3. Our analysis in this chapter addresses the basic issue, from a historical perspective, of the necessity of further evolution (via workfare configurations) in welfare states. For further discussion, see chapter 3, under the heading of Flexicurity in the European Union.

Welfare reforms that involve how income distribution between capital and labor is regulated (and similarly employee participation within firms) may be too one-sided a process to create a viable social structure of capital accumulation—a view that extends the ideas of Kalecki to take into account postwar capitalist prosperity phases and other developments. The stage we reach in this chapter may not be one that produces a capitalist society without recurrent mass unemployment.

Section 2.2 discusses the approach we use in this chapter from the general perspective for this type of model building. Section 2.3 then presents the structural model. In section 2.4 we derive the laws of motion that characterize its economy.

Section 2.5 examines their steady state and basic stability properties. In section 2.6 we consider the essential feedback structures of this model type and compare them with other ones.[2] We then use these feedback structures to construct a case in which local stability of the steady state arises. We call this case a consensus-based economy, and consider its properties at the end of this section.

Section 2.7 then considers the case of local instability in the steady-state solution, which characterizes a conflict-driven economy. This provides various scenarios of disequilibrium growth that may nevertheless allow for upper, as well as lower, turning points from a global point of view, that is, that make the considered dynamics economically viable from the global point of view. In the case of a conflict-driven economy, order is established only through large fluctuations in economic activity or enforced through economic policy. Section 2.8 provides some numerical illustrations of the model. Section 2.9 points to some problems on the nominal side of the considered economy that, though they do not feed back into the real dynamics, call for an extension of the model to include interest-rate effects on aggregate demand and an active Taylor interest-rate-policy rule as monetary policy, in order to tame the explosive dynamics that exist in the nominal part of the model. Besides such monetary policy we also consider Keynesian fiscal policy, which augments and stabilizes the causal structure of the private sector of our Keynes/Kalecki-Goodwin/Rose economy.

2.2 ECONOMIC AND POLITICAL ASPECTS OF FULL EMPLOYMENT

Whether the welfare state promotes or retards economic growth has become a major issue in recent macroeconomic studies. In this chapter, we examine some of the aspects of a welfare state in a macroeconomic model[3] with a labor-market adjustment process, a wage-price spiral, and a Keynesian dynamic multiplier setup.

The aggregate demand schedule underlying this dynamic multiplier is derived from classical views of saving habits and an investment function that assumes that investment reacts not only to changing profitability in capitalist economies but also to the conditions characterizing the capital-labor relationship, where persistently high employment rates may give rise to extensive welfare-state measures. Those are usually labor-market institutions that favor labor, generous unemployment benefits, labor-force participation in firms' decision making (i.e., in the hiring and firing practices of firms), and a considerable reduction of the work day, which are not all favored by "industrial leaders" as Kalecki (1943, chapter 12) has observed regarding those practices.

Our model has Kaleckian features with regard to investment behavior, savings behavior, and its multiplier approach to the market for goods. It is Goodwinian with respect to labor-market dynamics and capital stock growth, though we find at least four possible regimes for real-wage adjustment (see Rose [1967] on this issue, instead of the single one in the Goodwin [1967] growth cycle approach). Goodwin's approach considered only a situation that was profit-led coupled with one that was labor-market-led, because of the supply side orientation of the Goodwin model (see table 2.1 for details).

Furthermore in our model, we employ, in place of Goodwin's (1967) real-wage Phillips curve, a money-wage and a price-level Phillips curve, both of which are fairly advanced types, in which wage dynamics allows for insider-outsider considerations and Blanchard and Katz (1999) error correction. The price dynamics can be considered a generalization of Kalecki's theory of markup pricing, with a markup that depends on the state of the business cycle and again a term that represents the Blanchard and Katz (1999) type error correction (a second positive, i.e., level, effect) of the real wage on the rate of price inflation.

Because of the separate consideration of labor force and workforce utilization rates (the employment rate of the external labor market and the utilization ratio of the workforce within firms), we need a two-stage Okun-type link between the goods and labor markets. The first stage leads from the utilization of the capital stock (as measured by the output-capital ratio) to the utilization ratio of the employed workforce (as a more or less technological relationship), and the second stage leads from there to the employment rate of the labor force by way of the employment policy of firms. Here, we view firms' employment policies as dependent on the utilization ratio of their workforce in comparison to a utilization ratio they desire in view of the state of the external labor market.

We thus distinguish, with respect to the labor market, the rate of employment characterizing this market from the utilization ratio of the workforce of firms, and thus we pursue an insider-outsider approach as far as wage negotiations and the employment policies of firms are concerned. The utilization ratio of the workforce is always immediately adjusted to the utilization ratio of the capital stock and thus fluctuates as does that ratio depending on the state of aggregate demand in the market for goods, though with a different amplitude (depending on the technology of the firm sector).

The change in the external employment rate (in the labor market), by contrast, is determined by the employment policies of firms, which may be subject to many influences (economic and political ones) and thus represents the volatile element in this two-stage formulation of Okun's (1970) law, leading from capacity utilization of firms to their labor force utilization and from there to the recruitment (or dismissal) of laborers into (or from) the existing workforce of firms. As we have already observed, firms also pay attention to the state of the labor market when deciding on the size of their investment projects. We view the interaction of inside workforce utilization with outside employment rates as a capillary system in which pressure, as measured by the rate of money wage growth, is shifted from the inside component to the outside component and back in order to achieve—from the viewpoint of firms—as little combined pressure as possible.

TABLE 2.1. *Four types of real-wage adjustment processes.*

	Wage-Led Goods Demand	Profit-Led Goods Demand
Labor-market-led Real-wage adjustment	adverse = divergent	normal = convergent
Goods-market-led Real-wage adjustment	normal = convergent	adverse = divergent

As the model is formulated, we can distinguish between wage-led and profit-led situations in the market for goods, depending on whether aggregate demand increases or decreases with increases in the real wage. In addition, in regard to increases in economic activity, we can differentiate labor-market-dominated influences from goods-market-dominated influences on the growth rate of real wages. The former occurs when the growth rate of real wages essentially depends positively on factor utilization rates. The latter happens in the opposite case, in which the dynamics of the price level dominates in the formation of real wages (and not the dynamics of the money wage). Table 2.1 summarizes the scenarios possible in such an environment; it implies that empirical analysis is needed in order to draw definite conclusions with respect to which entry in the table is relevant in a particular country at a particular time.

If aggregate demand and real-wage dynamics are wage led and labor-market led, respectively, the economy experiences increasing real wages and a procyclical real-wage dynamic (with a quarter phase displacement). Thus, we get instability from this two-fold positive feedback mechanism. The other cases included in table 2.1 reflect similar results, thus giving rise to two types of adverse and two types of stabilizing real-wage reaction patterns.

In this chapter we concentrate on situations in which the real-wage dynamics are labor market led (for which there is some evidence in the US economy [see Chen et al. (2006)] and also the ongoing debate on procyclical real wages in this regard). Chen et al. (2006) analyze profit-led-goods market activities, but the literature is not extensive on this topic, since post-Keynesian authors normally assume wage-led situations in their analysis. We show that wage-led situations are always coupled with dynamic multiplier stability, but are—as we argued earlier—plagued by real-wage instability if money wages respond strongly to labor-market pressure (in particular inside pressure). Profit-led situations by contrast are plagued by dynamic multiplier instability, but imply a stable or convergent partial real-wage-adjustment mechanism.

We, therefore, have, in both cases, unstable scenarios: in the first case via the real-wage feedback structure and in the second case via a quantity adjustment process in the goods-market that works too fast. In the first scenario, downward money wage rigidity may help control the explosive dynamics of real wages;

in the second case, a weakening of the multiplier process far off the steady state may allow for bounded dynamics, though not convergent ones. Our model, therefore, allows for interesting alternative stability scenarios, depending on the working of the wage-price spiral. This allows Blanchard and Katz type error correction terms, which Chen et al. (2006) found to be relevant in the case of the US economy, and employment policies pursued by firms in a Keynesian aggregate demand situation in which income distribution and the state of the labor market matter.

Moreover, this model type includes interesting steady-state relationships, underlying its dynamics. On the one hand, we find in the steady state that owners of capital get what they spend, because their profit rate is solely determined by their trend-investment behavior. On the other hand, as the model is formulated, we find that the steady-state rate of employment in the labor market is determined solely by the target rate in the investment function. Finally, the steady-state ratio of capacity utilization is generally only equal to the utilization ratio of the capital stock desired by firms. This condition holds if workers adjust their behavior to the steady-state rate of employment set by capitalist firms and if their reaction with respect to the insider utilization ratio of the workforce is the same as the firms' reaction pattern. This steady-state ratio of capacity utilization is a fairly complicated function of the parameters of the model and thus depends on a variety of exogenous factors in the interaction of goods and labor market dynamics.

There are, however, processes on the nominal side of the model that may modify such situations significantly. If there is accelerating inflation, the interest rate policy pursued by the central bank may not only enforce upper turning points in economic activity but also modify the economy's steady-state position back to natural rates of employment and capacity utilization, if these rates are known to the central bank. Such monetary policy thus exercises a strong influence on the working of the economy, which may not really function without it. In deflationary episodes, however, the role of the central bank may be much more limited, because there is a floor to the setting of the nominal rate of interest. In a deflationary episode, downward money wage rigidity and, thus, the behavior of workers may be of decisive importance for the viability of the economy.

2.3 ■ THE MODEL

We consider in this section the private sector of the macroeconomy in isolation from the government sector (and fiscal and monetary policies). We consider the role and implications of macroeconomic policy for the modeled investment and employment dynamics in a later section. We start from wage-price dynamics, or the aggregate supply side of the model, as it is often called in the literature. For the description of aggregate supply we employ the following general formulation of a wage-price spiral mechanism (related to the work of Rose [1967, 1990] and Blanchard and Katz [1999]):

$$\hat{w} = \beta_{we}(e - \bar{e}) + \beta_{wu}(u_w - \tilde{u}_w(e)) - \beta_{w\omega}\ln(\frac{\omega}{\omega_0}) + \kappa_w\hat{p} + (1 - \kappa_w)\pi^c \quad (2.1)$$

$$\hat{p} = \beta_{py}(y - \bar{y}) + \beta_{p\omega}\ln(\frac{\omega}{\omega_0}) + \kappa_p\hat{w} + (1 - \kappa_p)\pi^c \quad (2.2)$$

In these equations, $\hat{w}$, $\hat{p}$ denote the growth rates of nominal wages w and the price level p (their inflation rates) and π^c, a medium-term inflation-climate expression, which, however, is of no relevance in the following discussion because we neglect real interest-rate effects on the demand side of the model. We denote by e the rate of employment in the external labor market and by u_w the ratio of utilization of the workforce within firms. Workers compare this latter ratio of employment in their negotiations with firms with their desired normal ratio of utilization $\tilde{u}_w(e)$, $\tilde{u}'_w < 0$, which can depend, as we assume here, negatively on the external rate of employment e, since higher employment in the labor market implies demands for less work time within firms. We thus have two employment gaps: an external one—$e - \bar{e}$—and an internal one—$u_w - \tilde{u}_w$—that determine wage inflation rate $\hat{w}$ from the side of demand pressure within or outside of the production process. In the wage Phillips curve (PC) we employ, in addition, a real-wage error-correction term $\ln(\omega/\omega_0)$, as in Blanchard and Katz (1999) (see Asada, Chen, Chiarella, and Flaschel [2006] for details), and as the cost pressure term a weighted average of short-term (perfectly anticipated) price inflation $\hat{p}$ and the medium-term inflation climate π^c in which the economy is operating.

As the wage PC is constructed, it is subject to an interaction between the external labor market and the utilization of the workforce within firms. Higher demand pressure in the external labor market translates itself into higher workforce wage-demand pressure within firms (and demand for reduced length of the normal working day, etc.), an interaction between two utilization rates of the labor force that must be and is taken note of in firms' employment policies. Demand pressure in the labor market thus exhibits two interacting components, which employed workers may use to adjust their behavior.

We use the output-capital ratio $y = Y/K$ to measure the output gap in price inflation PC and the deviation of the real wage $\omega = w/p$ from the steady-state real wage ω_0 as the error correction expression in the price PC. Cost pressure in this price PC is formulated as a weighted average of short-term (perfectly anticipated) wage inflation, and our concept of an inflationary climate π^c. In this price PC we have three elements of cost pressure interacting with each other: a medium-term one (the inflationary climate) and two short-terms ones, basically the level of real unit-wage labor costs (a Blanchard and Katz [1999] error correction term) and the current rate of wage inflation, which, taken by itself, would represent a constant markup pricing rule. This basic rule is, however, modified by other cost-pressure terms, and, in particular, it is made dependent on the state of the business cycle by way of the demand pressure term $y - \bar{y}$ in the market for goods.

On the demand side of the model we use, for reasons of simplicity, the conventional dynamic multiplier process (in place of a full-fledged Metzlerian inventory adjustment mechanism) as in Asada, Flaschel, and Skott (2006), that is,

$$\hat{Y} = \dot{Y}/Y = \beta_y(Y^d/Y - 1) + \bar{a} \qquad (2.3)$$

where Y^d, Y denote aggregate demand and supply and $\bar{a}$ denotes a trend term in the behavior of capitalist firms to be explained later. Assuming a fixed proportions technology with given output-employment ratio $x = Y/L^d$ and potential output-capital ratio $y^p = Y^p/K$ allows us to determine from the output-capital ratio y the employment u_w of the workforce within firms that corresponds to this activity measure y:

$$u_w = y/(xle), \quad u_w = L^d/L^w, l = L/K, e = L^w/L \qquad (2.4)$$

(with L^d hours worked, L^w the number of workers employed within firms, and L denoting labor supply). This relationship represents, by and large, a technical relationship (to be calculated by engineers) and relates hours worked to goods market activity as measured by y in the way shown earlier.

This technical relationship must be carefully distinguished from an employment (recruitment) policy of firms that reads in intensive form:

$$\hat{e} = \dot{e}/e = \beta_{eu}(u_w - \tilde{u}_f(e)) - \beta_{e\omega}(\omega - \omega_o) + \bar{a} - \hat{L} \qquad (2.5)$$

that is,

$$\dot{e} = \beta_{eu}(y/(xl) - \tilde{u}_f(e)e) - \beta_{e\omega}(\omega - \omega_o)e + (\bar{a} - \hat{L})e, \quad \tilde{u}'_f > 0 \qquad (2.6)$$

The basis of this formulation of an employment policy of firms in terms of the employment rate is—by assumption—the following level form representation of this relationship:

$$\dot{L}^w = \beta_{eu}(L^d - \tilde{u}_f(e)L^w) - \beta_{e\omega}(\omega - \omega_o)L^w + \bar{a}L^w \qquad (2.7)$$

that is,

$$\hat{L}^w = \beta_{eu}(L^d/L^w - \tilde{u}_f(e)) - \beta_{e\omega}(\omega - \omega_o) + \bar{a} \qquad (2.8)$$

where $\bar{a}$ integrates the trend term assumed by firms into their employment policy and where $\tilde{u}_f(e)$ represents firms' desired utilization ratio of the workforce. This ratio is made dependent on the rate of employment in the external labor market in a positive way, since firms will accept higher demand pressure within their workforce employment relationship (instead of recruiting new workers) if the external labor market has become tighter. Firms, therefore, react to both measures of demand pressure (in the labor market and within the production process) by attempting to obtain some balance in these two types of wage pressure, just as in a physical capillary system. The growth rate of the workforce of firms is thus a positive function of the utilization gap $u_w - \tilde{u}_f$ of the workforce within firms, where the benchmark utilization ratio $\tilde{u}_f$ desired by firms depends positively on the outside employment ratio, since firms are inclined to allow, on average, for larger utilization rates within firms when the outside labor market situation is becoming more tense. In order to obtain eq. (2.6) as the resulting law of motion for the rate of employment, one simply has to take note of the definitional relationship $\hat{e} = \hat{L}^w - \hat{L}$, where L denotes the labor supply in each moment. We have also included in the aforementioned recruitment policy a term in which intended recruitment will be lowered in case of increasing real-wage costs of firms.

In order to close the model, we assume extremely classical saving habits ($s_w = 0$, $s_c = 1$), that is, the consumption-output ratio is given simply by ω/x. For investment behavior we, moreover, assume

$$I/K = i(\cdot) + \bar{a} = i_\rho(\rho - \rho_o) - i_e(e - \bar{e}_f) + \bar{a} \quad (2.9)$$

with $\rho = y(1 - \omega/x)$ the current rate of profit.[4] In this equation, the magnitude $\bar{a}$ denotes a given trend investment rate, representing investors' "animal spirits", from which firms depart in a natural way if there is excess profitability (and vice versa). Moreover, firms have a view on what the rate of employment should be in the external labor market (see Kalecki's [1943, chapter 12] analysis of why employers dislike full employment) and thus reduce their (domestic) investment plans (driven by excess profitability) in a tense labor market. Thus, they take pressure from the labor market in the future evolution of the economy by their implicit collective understanding that high pressure in the capillary system we have considered earlier will lead to conditions in the capital-labor relationship firms do not want, because persistently high employment rates may significantly change workforce participation in firms' decision making about hiring and firing decisions, reductions of the work day, and so forth, in ways disliked by "industrial leaders." Note here that the same would happen in principle if a Keynesian countercyclical fiscal policy rule were implemented, but that a reduction of the welfare state may demand more than that, namely, a return to an orthodox fiscal policy that allows for persistent mass unemployment in order to tame the aspirations of workers and their unions on a broader scale, rather than an increase in government spending in the bust.

We view the rate $\bar{a}$, the trend investment decision of capitalist firms, as the (mathematically seen) independent variable of the model, whereas any changes in the growth rate n of the labor force, the so-called natural rate of growth, follow the growth rate of the capital stock more or less passively, and have, in any case, little to do with the biological reproduction rate of a given society. There are, of course, many possible ways in which the growth rate of the labor force $\hat{L}$ (not the growth rate of the working population) is governed by the accumulation path of the economy. In this chapter we make two specific (simplifying) assumptions in this regard: First $\hat{L} = \bar{a}$ and, later, $\hat{L} = \hat{K}$, in order to concentrate on the interaction of income distribution with the dynamics of the goods market and the demand pressures on the labor market these dynamics give rise to.

On the quantity side, the model neglects unintended inventory changes, and, on the value side, the model neglects windfall profits or losses caused by the assumed possibility of a discrepancy between savings and investment. It describes, through its equations, a closed economy in which we abstract from all government activities and in which we ignore the behavior of central banks because of our neglect of real-interest effects on the demand side of the model (consisting solely of workers' consumption and firms' investment demands). We also abstract here from the role of financial markets in the financing of investment decisions by assuming that all profits are paid out as dividends and that investment is purely equity-financed with no feedback on assumed consumption behavior (see Chiarella and Flaschel [2000a], chapter 6) for the budget equations that allow for such flow consistency.

As in earlier work (see Asada, Chen, Chiarella and Flaschel [2006] in particular), we can derive as reduced forms from the described wage-price spiral a real wage dynamic $\hat{\omega} = \hat{w} - \hat{p}$, which does not depend on the inflationary climate term π^c, and an augmented reduced-form price PC where π^c has a coefficient of unity. However, since the real rate of interest is no issue in our model, this latter reduced-form equation does not yet play a role in the implied dynamical system to be considered later. In this system, we need to consider only the dynamics of real wages ω, of the output-capital ratio y and of the rate of employment e (plus full employment labor intensity $l = L/K$ if the natural rate of growth is given exogenously).

2.4 ■ THE IMPLIED LAWS OF MOTION

We now reduce the considered macrodynamic model to a system of four differential equations in the pairs of state variables y, e and ω, l. The first pair can be considered to describe the Keynes-Kalecki goods market and employment dynamics, and the second one can be considered to describe the Goodwin-Rose growth-cycle dynamics, though Kalecki and Rose also included income distribution effects and goods-market effects respectively, in their analysis of the capital accumulation process. Later we assume, by way of a special assumption on labor supply L, that the state variable l stays at its steady-state level, and thus we will reduce the dynamics to dimension 3 in that discussion.

As the model is formulated it, therefore, includes two laws of motion on its supply side, a law describing the dynamics of real wages, and one growth law, describing the capital accumulation induced by the assumed investment behavior. The inflationary tension resulting on the nominal side of the dynamics we consider does not yet play a role in their core activities, because we do not have any real-interest-rate effects or wealth effects included in its formulation. On the demand side, the model includes the law of motion for capacity utilization of firms, measured by $y = Y/K$, and the law of motion of the employment rate e in the external labor market implied by the employment policy of firms.

Note that we assume in this section that $\hat{L}$ is given by $\bar{a}$, that is, this latter trend term also applies to the conditions of labor supply and not only to investment and the dynamic multiplier story that is based on it (and the employment policy of firms). Note, furthermore, that aggregate demand per unit of capital, the Keynesian heart of our accumulation dynamics, is always given by the expression

$$y^d = (\omega/x)y + i(\cdot) + \bar{a}, \quad i(\cdot) = i_\rho(\rho - \rho_o) - i_e(e - \bar{e}_f), \quad \rho = (1 - \omega/x)y$$

2.4.1 The DAD Module: Multiplier and Employment Dynamics

The disequilibrium aggregate demand (DAD) part of the model is given by:

$$\dot{y} = -\beta_y \left(1 - \frac{\omega}{x}\right) y + (\beta_y - y)i(\cdot) + \beta_y \bar{a}, \quad y = Y/K \quad (2.10)$$

with

$$\dot{y}_y = -\beta_y \left(1 - \frac{\omega}{x}\right) + (\beta_y - y)\left(1 - \frac{\omega}{x}\right)i_\rho = -\beta_y(1 - i_\rho)\left(1 - \frac{\omega}{x}\right) - y\left(1 - \frac{\omega}{x}\right)i_\rho$$

We assume that $\beta_y > y_o$ holds in all of the following and thus we have the sign of $1 - i_\rho$ decisive for the sign of $\dot{y}_y$, which is negative if the propensity to invest in capital-stock growth from the obtained profit rate is <1 at the steady state.

This law of motion is obtained from

$$\frac{\dot{Y}}{Y} = \beta_y \left(\frac{Y^d}{Y} - 1\right) + \bar{a}, \quad C = \omega L^d = \frac{\omega}{x} Y \quad (s_w = 0, s_c = 1)$$

and

$$\frac{I}{K} = i(\cdot) + \bar{a} = i_\rho \left(y\left(1 - \frac{\omega}{x}\right) - \rho_o\right) - i_e(e - \bar{e}_f) + \bar{a}$$

We furthermore have

$$u_w = \frac{1}{xl} \frac{y}{e}$$

via fixed proportions in production, which represents a static (technical) relationship between the ratio of capital-stock utilization y = Y/K and the ratio of workforce utilization u_w within firms. Finally

$$\dot{e} = \beta_{eu}(y/(xl) - \tilde{u}_f(e)e) - \beta_{e\omega}(\omega - \omega_o)e - i(\cdot)e, \quad \tilde{u}_f' > 0 \qquad (2.11)$$

gives the law of motion for the employment policy of firms.

The reduced-form dynamic IS relationship depends on income distribution (due to the assumed savings behavior) and on the investment decisions of firms in a specific way, translated into the time rate of change of the output-capital ratio by means of the adjustment speed in the dynamic multiplier process that is driving the goods market. The utilization ratio of the employed labor force is a linear function of the ratio between the utilization ratio of the capital stock y and the utilization rate of the labor force e in the external labor market, with a multiplier that is given by the product of the reciprocal values of both labor productivity and the full-employment labor-capital ratio (this expression has to be inserted into the laws of motion in various places in order to get an autonomous system of four differential equations describing the evolution of the model's macroeconomy). The expression u_w can be altered by firms through changes in labor productivity (technical change), by manipulating labor supply or the external employment rate, or—politically—by enforced changes in income distribution that lead to appropriate changes of Keynesian aggregate demand.

2.4.2 The DAS Module: Real-Wage Dynamic and Capital Accumulation

The disequilibrium aggregate supply (DAS) part of the model is given by[5]

$$\frac{\dot{\omega}}{\omega} = \kappa[(1 - \kappa_p)(\beta_{we}(e - \bar{e}) + \beta_{wu}(u_w - \tilde{u}_w(e))) - (1 - \kappa_w)\beta_{py}(y - \bar{y})]$$

$$- \kappa\left[(1 - \kappa_p)\beta_{w\omega}\ln\left(\frac{\omega}{\omega_o}\right) + (1 - \kappa_w)\beta_{p\omega}\ln\left(\frac{\omega}{\omega_o}\right)\right], \quad u_w = \frac{1}{xl}\frac{y}{e} \qquad (2.12)$$

$$\hat{I} = \hat{L} - \hat{K} = -i_\rho(\rho - \rho_o) + i_e(e - \bar{e}_f) = -i(\cdot) \qquad (2.13)$$

if it is assumed that labor-force growth is governed by $n = \hat{L} = \bar{a}$, which is an assumption of at least the same ideal type as the assumption of constant-labor-force growth.

The law of motion for the real wage depends on a variety of demand-pressure items, because all cost-pressure terms (relating to the κ-coefficients) can be reduced to their underlying demand-pressure terms when the two linear equations of nominal wage and price dynamics are solved for the two unknowns

$\hat{w} - \pi^c, \hat{w} - \pi^c$, from which $\hat{\omega} = \hat{w} - \hat{p}$, and $\omega = w/p$ can be obtained. Of course, demand-pressure terms in the labor market influence real wages in a positive fashion, and those in the goods market influence real wages in a negative way. The Blanchard and Katz real-wage error-correction terms in the wage PC and price PC both act on real wages in a negative way, as suggested by the label for their operation.

We assume, in a later stability analysis for the law of motion of real wages, that the insider term $\beta_{wu}(u_w - \tilde{u}_w(e))$ is of a size that does not alter the positive dependence of real-wage growth on the rate of employment e or its negative dependence on the ratio of capacity utilization y. Depending on the choice of parameter values, however, the term $u_w = \frac{1}{xl}\frac{Y}{e}$ may easily overthrow the negative influence of y on the growth rate of real wages, in which case the dynamics of real wages is completely dominated by the labor market both inside and outside firms and thus is completely led by the labor market. Because u_w depends negatively on the rate of employment e, an overall negative dependence of $\hat{\omega}$ on the rate of employment may also be established. The movement of real wages is thus subject to a variety of influences, which may imply that it is not moving in a clear or even in a strictly procyclical manner.

2.5 ■ STEADY-STATE CONFIGURATIONS AND REDUCED-FORM THREE-DIMENSIONAL DYNAMICS

In this section we calculate the steady state of the dynamics of eqs. (2.10)–(2.13). This system is an autonomous one, once the definitions of u_w and ρ have been inserted into it. As steady-state solutions we then get balanced growth in the four-dimensional dynamics.

2.5.1 Balanced Growth in the Four-Dimensional Dynamics

From the conditions $\dot{y} = 0, \hat{l} = -i(\cdot) = 0$ our first steady-state result dictates that there must hold for the rate of profit ρ

$$\rho_o = y_o(1 - \omega_o/x) = \bar{a} \qquad (2.14)$$

that is, capitalists get what they spend in the steady state. Note that the values of y_o, ω_o are restricted by this steady-state condition, but remain to be determined.

Next we find, by way of $i_\rho(\cdot) = i(\cdot) = 0$, that there holds for the steady-state rate of employment in the external labor market

$$e_o = \bar{e}_f \neq \bar{e} \qquad (2.15)$$

in general. This equation asserts that the steady-state rate of employment (not to be interpreted as an inflation-oriented NAIRU rate of employment)[6] is solely determined by the investment behavior of firms, that is, by the benchmark level they set for this rate, beyond which firms believe that the social structure of accumulation (workforce participation in firms' decision making and the like) will change significantly to their disadvantage.

As an intermediate step, we furthermore get for the value of $(y/l)_o$ by way of the condition

$$\tilde{u}_f(e_o) = (y/l)_o/(xe_o)$$

the steady-state value

$$(y/l)_o = \tilde{u}_f(e_o)xe_o$$

and from this for the utilization ratio of the workforce of firms in the steady state

$$u_{wo} = \tilde{u}_f(e_o)$$

The steady-state utilization rate of the labor force is determined by the benchmark rate in the employment policy of firms that, in turn, depends on the external rate of employment that firms desire in order to keep workforce relationships within firms under sufficient control.

Making use of the condition $\hat{\omega}(\cdot) = 0$ in the reduced form expression for real wage dynamics then gives ($\kappa_w < 1$)

$$y_o = \bar{y} + \frac{(1 - \kappa_p)(\beta_{we}(e_o - \bar{e}) + \beta_{wu}(\tilde{u}_f(e_o) - \tilde{u}_w(e_o)))}{(1 - \kappa_w)\beta_{py}} \neq \bar{y} \qquad (2.16)$$

because the Blanchard / Katz error correction terms are zero in the steady state (by assumption). We assume that the adjustment parameters in the numerator of this expression are sufficiently small that—where $e_o - \bar{e}$ or $u_{wo} - \tilde{u}_w(e_o)$ become negative—the steady-state output-capital ratio y_o stays positive. We note also that increasing labor-market flexibility, in whatever form, may in this approach have positive or negative effects on steady-state capacity utilization $y_o = (Y/K)_o$, depending on the benchmark choices of both workers and firms. We note, however, that the model is ill-defined (i.e., indeterminate) when price inflation does not depend on demand pressure in the market for goods.

Common inside and outside employment benchmark levels of firms and workers give rise to $y_o = \bar{y}$ (also to $\beta_{py} = 0$) and to specific deviations from this simple benchmark case. We note, however, that there need not exist any pressure around the balanced-growth path (and even less far away from it) that tends to harmonize the various benchmarks in the labor and the goods markets with each other. Instead, the departure of steady-state values from their corresponding benchmark values, in the wage and price PC in particular, simply means that the steady state inherits some of the problems that govern the course of the economy in general, such as upward or downward pressure on wage and price inflation that is neutralized through opposing deviations from the benchmark levels.

On the basis of the steady-state value for the output capital ratio y_o we finally get

$$\omega_o = (1 - \bar{a}/y_o)x \qquad (2.17)$$

$$l_o = y_o/(y/l)_o \qquad (2.18)$$

where ω_o is the value used in the dynamic error correction mechanism (and the corresponding ρ_o in the investment equation of firms) as the relevant benchmark values.

All steady-state values are positive as long as this holds for the parameter $\bar{a}$. Here it must also be assumed that $\bar{a} < y_o$ holds true. If this parameter is increased, the steady rate of profit increases while the steady-state value of the real wage declines (since output per unit of capital remains constant in such a case). There are no further changes implied by such an increase in trend investment, besides the fact that capitalist firms always exactly get what they spend. Note, furthermore, that the steady-state value of y depends on various adjustment speeds in the wage-price module and is, in particular, not defined if β_{py} becomes zero (unless equal to $\bar{y}$). This problem on the real side of the model's dynamics will disappear when we take nominal adjustment problems and a Taylor interest rate policy rule into account in a later section.

If—by contrast—the employment rate target of firms is decreased (because they want to exercise further pressure on the behavior of their workforce) the steady-state rate of employment in the external labor market fully adjusts to this new target of firms, implying a fall in the steady-state values of y_o, ω_o, while the steady rate of profit does not change. Such a situation thus leads to a lower steady-state employment rate, a lower steady rate of capacity utilization, and a lower-steady state share of wages in national income.

2.5.2 Reduced-Form Three-Dimensional Dynamics

We now assume for the following stability analysis that $n := \hat{K}$ holds (for analytical simplicity) and has the same steady-state solution as before (with l now frozen—by assumption—at its predetermined steady-state value l_o at all times). The implication of this assumption is a modified law of motion for the employment rate, which now integrates the capital accumulation relationship (as represented by the law of motion for full employment labor intensity ratio $l = L/K$) into the law of motion for e. The implied DAS-DAD dynamics now are

$$\dot{y} = f(y, e, \omega) = -\beta_y \left(1 - \frac{\omega}{x}\right) y + (\beta_y - y)i(\cdot) + \beta_y \bar{a} \qquad (2.19)$$

$$\dot{e} = g(y, e, \omega) = \beta_{eu}\left(\frac{y}{xl_o} - \tilde{u}_f(e)e\right) - \beta_{e\omega}(\omega - \omega_o)e - i(\cdot)e \qquad (2.20)$$

$$\hat{\omega} = h(y, e, \omega), \quad h_y < 0, \; h_e > 0, \; h_\omega < 0 \quad \text{[see eq. (2.12)]} \qquad (2.21)$$

with $i(\cdot) = i_\rho(\rho - \rho_o) - i_e(e - \bar{e}_f)$, $\rho = (1 - \omega/x)y$. Note again that we have assumed in the third law of motion (see eq. [2.12]) that real-wage growth depends positively on the rate of employment e; that is, we take a Goodwin (1967) perspective in this matter. However, the influences of changing capacity utilization y are separated from employment rate changes and act negatively on real-wage growth, dominating the positive effect on this growth rate caused by the accompanying parallel effect on workforce utilization ratios. Note also that the first equation allows for two cases (and a borderline case), namely,

$$\text{Case 1:} \quad f_y < 0, \; f_e < 0, \; f_\omega > 0$$

or

$$\text{Case 2:} \quad f_y > 0, \; f_e < 0, \; f_\omega < 0$$

respectively. This is implied by the following partial derivatives:

$$\dot{y}_y = c\left(1 - \frac{\omega}{x}\right), \quad \dot{y}_\omega = -c\frac{y}{x}, \quad c = -\beta_y(1 - i_\rho) - yi_\rho = (\beta_y - y)i_\rho - \beta_y$$

Thus, a partially stable integrated multiplier process (i_ρ sufficiently small) is necessarily coupled with a wage-led regime in the aggregate demand function and an unstable multiplier process with a profit-led regime in the aggregate demand function. These two cases give rise to two typical stability scenarios in our model of Kalecki-Goodwin-Rose (KGR) accumulation and employment dynamics. The critical condition that separates these two cases from each other is given by $i_\rho^c = \beta_y/(\beta_y - y_o) > 1$ or $\beta_y^c = y_o i_\rho/(i_\rho - 1)$ as far as analysis of steady-state stability is concerned. Note that the steady state of the reduced three-dimensional dynamics is the same as the one calculated for the originally four-dimensional dynamics (if their steady-state value l_o is inserted into the three-dimensional case).

On the basis of the assumed dominance of the labor and goods markets in the third law of motion, we indeed get for the sign structure in the Jacobian of the dynamics at the steady state (under the not very restrictive assumption $\beta_y - y_o > 0$ sufficiently large)

$$J = \begin{pmatrix} + & - & - \\ \pm & \pm & \pm \\ - & + & - \end{pmatrix} \quad \text{or} \quad \begin{pmatrix} - & - & + \\ \pm & \pm & \pm \\ - & + & - \end{pmatrix}$$

We assume for the time being that the entry J_{23} is positive, that is, that $\beta_{e\omega}$ is chosen sufficiently small.

The first case results in instability, particularly if the dynamic multiplier process works with sufficient speed (β_y sufficiently large in the entry J_{11}), and thus there is a Kaldor (1940) situation with respect to the search for bounding mechanisms (in a profit-led environment). In the other case, a wage-led situation in the goods market ($\hat{y}_\omega > 0$) results, and thus there is instability in the assumed case of labor-market led real-wage dynamics if this feedback structure becomes sufficiently dominant (in the destabilizing interaction resulting from the entries J_{13}, J_{31} in the Jacobian J). Between these two situations there are, also, parameter domains with local stability characteristics. The overall conclusion, however, is that, generally, certain bounding mechanisms (like downward money wage rigidity) have to be added in order to keep the dynamics economically viable.

Summing up, on this level of generality a model type is one in which trend investment and target employment of firms basically determine the long-term outcome and where the dynamics around the implied steady-state positions is driven in an unstable or stable fashion by a Keynesian dynamic-multiplier process that depends on income distribution and by an advanced type of wage-price spiral and the resulting real wage dynamics, with insider and outsider effects and a recruitment policy of firms that links inside employment rates with outside employment rates.

2.6 ■ FEEDBACK STRUCTURES

In this section we briefly compare the model of this chapter with the related Keynes Metzler Goodwin Steindl (KMGS) model introduced and discussed in Asada, Flaschel, and Skott (2006). Our purpose is to show how these two related models compare in their feedback channels and which feedback channels of a Kaleckian approach to accumulation dynamics are still missing in the Keynes Goodwin Rose (KGR) model in this chapter.

2.6.1 Feedback Channels in KMGS Growth

The original KMG model (see Chiarella and Flaschel [2000] and Chiarella, Flaschel, and Franke [2005] for its derivation and detailed investigation), contains four important feedback chains: the interest rate channel (Keynes vs. Mundell effects), the real wage channel (normal vs. adverse Rose effects), the Metzlerian inventory dynamics (of a multiplier-accelerator type) and the Harrod-type investment accelerator mechanism. The KMGS model of Asada, Flaschel, and Skott (2006)—like this model—excludes two of these feedback chains (Keynes and Mundell effects), but introduces two new feedback chains: a dynamic Harrodian accelerator mechanism in fixed capital formation and a Kalecki-Steindl reserve-army mechanism. These feedback chains interact with each other in the full five-dimensional dynamics of the KMGS model, and different feedback mechanisms can become dominant, depending on the parameters of the model.

1. The Keynes and Mundell effects: Neither the stabilizing Keynes effect nor the destabilizing Mundell effect is present in the KMGS model. The reason is simple: We have excluded any influence of the real rate of interest on investment and consumption (and also ignored wealth effects on consumption). Thus, although price inflation appears in the real wage dynamics, it does not affect aggregate demand.
2. A Metzler-type inventory accelerator mechanism: The Metzlerian inventory adjustment process defines two laws of motion, one for sales expectations and one for inventory changes. The crucial parameters in these adjustment equations are the adjustment speeds of sales expectations and of intended inventory changes, respectively, where the first one tends to be stabilizing and the second one destabilizing.
3. A Harrod-type investment accelerator mechanism: This mechanism works in Asada, Flaschel, and Skott (2006) through parameters in the investment equations. Increased capacity utilization leads to higher investment (both directly and via the gradual changes in the trend of capital accumulation), thereby leading to an increase in aggregate demand. As a result, sales expectations increase and produce a further rise in output and capacity utilization. Hence, a dynamic Harrodian multiplier-accelerator process interacts with distribution effects and the Metzlerian inventory adjustment process. Trend investment can be seen as representing an investment climate—like the inflation climate—or as slowly evolving "animal spirits," and it may be reasonable to assume that the direct effect on current investment is stronger than the indirect effect on trend investment.
4. A Goodwin-Rose type reserve-army mechanism: There are additional feedback channels of the Goodwin-Rose type. The specification of aggregate demand in KMGS implied that the short-term effect of real wages on goods demand is positive (via workers' consumption). Hence, real wages will further stabilize if price flexibility with respect to demand pressure in the market for goods is sufficiently high and wage flexibility with respect to demand pressure in the market for labor is sufficiently low (the delayed negative effect of real wages on investment behavior will, of course, lead to the opposite results).
5. A Kalecki/Steindl type of reserve-army mechanism (the conflict about full employment and its consequences): This conflict is represented in this chapter by the parameter i_e. We here assume, as in Flaschel and Skott (2006) and Asada, Flaschel, and Skott (2006), that "bosses dislike full employment." Increases in the employment rate e thus exert a downward pressure in the investment demand function, leading to reduced economic activity and providing a check to further increases in the rate of employment.

TABLE 2.2. *The feedback structure of the KMGS model (u: capacity utilization).*

1. Metzlerian Accelerator Mechanism:	$y^e \xmapsto{+} y \xmapsto{+} y^d \xmapsto{+} y^e$
2. Harrodian Accelerator Mechanism:	$u \xmapsto{+} \dot{a} \xmapsto{+} \dot{u}$
3. Goodwin/Rose Reserve-Army Mechanism:	$\omega \xmapsto{+:C(-:I)} u, e \xmapsto{+/-} \hat{\omega}$
4. Kalecki/Steindl Reserve-Army Mechanism:	$e \xmapsto{-} \dot{a} \xmapsto{+} \dot{u} \xmapsto{+} \dot{e}$

The feedback channels 2–5 are summarized in table 2.2.

The full interaction of these feedback chains determines the stability of the interior steady-state position of the considered model. Based on our partial analysis of the feedback channels, we confirmed in Asada, Flaschel, and Skott (2006) that wage flexibility, fast inventory adjustment, and fast investment-trend adjustment are destabilizing, whereas price flexibility is stabilizing (if the corresponding Rose effect is tamed by assuming appropriate investment behavior). Manipulating the stabilizing parameters appropriately may thus help to create local stability or at least ensure the boundedness and economic viability of the trajectories in the case of local instability.

2.6.2 The Feedback Structure of the KGR Model of Capital Accumulation and Employment Dynamics

Comparing the feedback chains of the KGR model of this chapter to the feedback channels just discussed shows that the Keynes and Mundell effects are ignored here, too. There is not yet a real rate of interest effect in aggregate-goods demand (monetary policy, whether money-supply oriented or interest-rate oriented, is not yet an issue here).

Furthermore, in KGR growth we use only a dynamic multiplier story (to describe the Keynesian process of quantity adjustment in the goods market) in place of a (possibly accelerating) Metzlerian-inventory and sales-expectations adjustment process. Nevertheless the multiplier process, too, can include unstable adjustment aspects if we assume that the propensity to spend in aggregate demand is >1. Besides not using a Metzlerian accelerator mechanism, we also exclude Harrodian fixed-capital-investment accelerator processes.

As in the KMGS approach, we have two reserve-army mechanisms present in our KGR variant of this approach that are related to the work of Goodwin (1967) and Kalecki (1943) and that interact with Rose (1967) type real wage feedbacks:

$$\omega \xmapsto{\pm} y^d \xmapsto{+} y \xmapsto{+} u_w = \frac{1}{xl_o} \frac{y}{e} \xmapsto{+} e \xmapsto{\pm} \hat{\omega}$$

In this feedback channel, we also have (via our formulation of Okun's Law) a direct effect of real wages on the rate of employment, a negative effect of the rate of employment on its rate of change (via the workforce utilization target of firms), and, finally, the influence of the assumed labor supply reaction to capital stock growth. Furthermore, there are opposing influences of economic activity y on the growth rate of real wages, via the goods market and price inflation dynamics and via the utilization ratio of the workforce within firms and the dynamics of money-wage inflation. Finally, there is also the ambiguous effect of changes of the rate of employment on the real wage, directly and positively through the external labor market and indirectly and partially negatively through changes in workforce utilization within firms.

The Goodwin reserve-army mechanism is working in this environment of Keynesian aggregate demand if increases in real wages and decreases in profitability decrease aggregate demand (if this demand is profit led) and if this in turn decreases the rate of employment via decreases in capital-stock utilization, thereby providing a check on further real-wage increases. Yet the Goodwin reserve-army mechanism was initially a purely supply side phenomenon and is not easily identified in a Keynesian goods-demand environment, as we will see later. Furthermore, the alternative reserve-army mechanism, the one of Kalecki (1943), works independently of the shown real-wage feedback channel, because it postulates that increases in the rate of employment directly decrease the growth rate of the capital stock, which decreases aggregate demand and output, and thereby provides a check on further increases in the rate of employment. Although the real wage channel may give rise to a variety of (un)stable feedback situations, the Kaleckian mechanism should, by and large, contribute to the stability of the considered steady state (though it may undermine this stability to a certain degree if labor supply is driven by capital-stock growth).

In closing this discussion, we stress again the importance of the assumed Okun-type two-stage links from the goods market to the labor market, which translate capital-utilization ratio into labor-force-utilization ratios and changes in the rate of employment in the external labor market. Taking all these feedback mechanisms into account, we intend to make use of them in the numerical section such that an assumed locally explosive adjustment process around the balanced growth path is turned into economically viable (bounded) dynamics through appropriate nonlinearities in the adjustment functions of the model. But, first of all, we consider a situation in which, under strong assumptions, a locally asymptotically stable and thus attracting steady state can indeed be shown to exist.

In the preceding section we considered minor further destabilizing feedback chains based on our assumptions about labor-force growth. However, these assumptions are not of central importance in this chapter, since they are easily modified by way of other assumptions about this rate of growth. Nevertheless, these feedback chains suggest that recruitment policies of firms (acting on the participation rate of the domestic labor force or in foreign labor markets) may indeed contribute to economic instability when coupled with certain further reaction patterns of the model.

2.6.3 A Feedback-Suggested Local-Stability Scenario

We now examine the interaction of the feedback structures considered in the preceding subsection on the basis of the following additional assumptions (besides the ones already made for real-wage dynamics: $\hat{\omega}_y < 0$, $\hat{\omega}_e > 0$ and for the dynamic-multiplier process $\dot{y}_y < 0$ ($\beta_y > y_o$), which implied $\dot{y}_\omega > 0$).

Assumptions:

1. We first assume that β_{eu}, $\beta_{e\omega}$ are large enough to dominate the signs of the partial derivatives in the law of motion for the employment rate e.
2. Furthermore, we assume the parameter β_y to be large enough (and $i_\rho < 1$) that the sign of $b = a_1(\beta_y)a_2(\beta_y) - a_3(\beta_y)$ in the Routh-Hurwitz conditions is determined by $a_1(\beta_y)a_2(\beta_y)$, which is a quadratic function of β_y, whereas the determinant is only linear in β_y. The economy is wage led in such a situation and the dynamic multiplier is stable from the perspective of the involved partial derivatives.
3. Finally, we assume that the parameters β_{we}, β_{wu} are small enough to thus be not decisive for the sign of the determinant of the system at the steady state (the Rose feedback channel $J_{13}J_{21}J_{32}$ for this wage-led economy is assumed as being sufficiently weak).

This means that the influence of the $-i(\cdot)$ term in the equation for the adjustment of the employment rate, describing the effect of the recruitment policy of firms in their search for additional labor-force supply, is not strong enough to overcome the direct effects of increased capacity utilization, increased external employment, and an increasing real wage.

For the considered Jacobian, this gives:

$$J = \begin{pmatrix} J_{11} & J_{12} & J_{13} \\ J_{21} & J_{22} & J_{23} \\ J_{31} & J_{32} & J_{33} \end{pmatrix} = \begin{pmatrix} - & - & + \\ + & - & - \\ - & \pm & - \end{pmatrix}$$

In this Jacobian, the first row contains the negative multiplier effect $J_{11} < 0$, the Kaleckian reserve-army effect $J_{12} < 0$, and the positive effect of a wage-led economy $J_{13} > 0$. The second row contains the assumed dominance of the β'_es and a negative effect of real wages on (recruited) labor-force growth, represented by J_{23}.

Under the assumed conditions, we can easily derive the validity of the Routh-Hurwitz conditions ($a_1, a_2, a_3, b > 0$). We obviously have $a_1 > 0$ for the diagonal terms in J. With respect to a_2 only the term $J_{23}J_{32}$ can create instability problems. We have, however, assumed this term to be negligible. This same assumption (on J_{23}) also allows us to ignore a destabilizing effect in the determinant of J.

Thus the parameters β_y, $\beta'_e s$ and $\beta_{w's}$, i_ρ can be crucial for macroeconomic stability (with the former chosen sufficiently large and the latter sufficiently small). Yet the opposite situation may be only one among many others, where no local stability result may hold. Therefore, it is not unlikely that the steady state may be locally repelling, and the forces that can make such an economy a viable one must be found in certain behavioral nonlinearities that limit the dynamics to economically meaningful domains when the model departs too much from its steady-state position.

Remark:

The stability result just achieved will disappear in situations in which insiders dominate the evolution of the real wage (both with respect to the rate of employment e and the rate of capacity utilization y), particularly if Blanchard and Katz error correction is weak, because an increasing parameter β_{wu} will imply a negative value for the a_2 Routh-Hurwitz polynomial parameter (if chosen sufficiently large). Insiders may, therefore, destabilize situations of economic prosperity if they last sufficiently long.

2.6.4 Consensus-Based Economies: Attraction Toward Accepted Steady-State Positions

The Kaleckian reserve-army mechanism (like the Goodwinian one) may not be optimal for the stable evolution of modern market economies, both from the economic and social points of view. Both mechanisms correct results that are not wanted by firms and their owners through mass unemployment (and supporting economic policy), with all its consequences for the economic and social evolution of the society. We thus introduce some additional assumptions on the parameters of the model that characterize our economy, which imply its stable evolution around a steady-state path that is satisfactory both from the workers' and the firms' points of view.

Specifically, we assume that demand pressure in the labor market (both inside and outside the firm) does not influence the rate of wage inflation very much, that is, the wage level is a fairly stable magnitude. Furthermore, the Kaleckian reserve-army mechanism is absent from the model ($i_e = 0$). Moreover, the benchmark values for demand pressures and the employment policy of firms are all given magnitudes, consistent with each other, and all are sufficiently high to not imply labor-market segmentation and significant disqualification of unemployed workers (this can be coupled with flexible hiring and firing policies; i.e., the parameter β_{eu} may be chosen large). Finally, though not really necessarily, we may assume $\kappa_w, \kappa_p = 0$, that is, cost pressure in the market for labor as well as for goods is relevant only if it becomes permanent.

These conditions imply a Jacobian matrix around such a "satisfactory" steady state:

$$J = \begin{pmatrix} J_{11} & J_{12} & J_{13} \\ J_{21} & J_{22} & J_{23} \\ J_{31} & J_{32} & J_{33} \end{pmatrix} = \begin{pmatrix} - & 0 & + \\ + & - & \pm \\ - & 0 & - \end{pmatrix}$$

It is easy to show for this wage-led economy that all Routh-Hurwitz conditions are valid in this situation; that is, the steady state of the economy is not only sufficiently good in nature but also attracting. Thus, a flexible labor market, a balanced workforce participation within firms, and a balanced choice of working hours per week may be in harmony with one another and may work satisfactorily well in an environment that is close to balanced growth. Such consensus-based economies can be usefully compared with economies that are equally flexible in their adjustment mechanisms, but that are, in addition, subject to significant reserve-army fluctuations, as well as economies in which a variety of rigidities are in effect.[7]

2.7 ■ LOCAL INSTABILITY AND GLOBAL BOUNDEDNESS

We continue to examine the three-dimensional dynamics in the state variables y, e, ω:

$$\dot{y} = f(y, e, \omega) = -\beta_y(1 - \frac{\omega}{x})y + (\beta_y - y)i(\cdot) + \beta_y \bar{a} \tag{2.22}$$

$$\dot{e} = g(y, e, \omega) = \beta_{eu}\left(\frac{y}{xl_o} - \tilde{u}_f(e)e\right) - \beta_{e\omega}(\omega - \omega_o)e - i(\cdot)e \tag{2.23}$$

$$\hat{\omega} = h(y, e, \omega), \quad h_y < 0, \ h_e > 0, \ h_\omega < 0 \tag{2.24}$$

where $i(\cdot) = i_\rho(\rho - \rho_o) - i_e(e - \bar{e}_f)$, $\rho = (1 - \omega/x)y$, in order to analyze partial situations (in phases of prosperity or stagnation, respectively) in which local steady-state instability will, sooner or later, be tamed by certain turning points during the evolution of such booms or busts. First, we consider reasons that lead to the instability of the balanced growth path of such an economy; then, we study factors that may lead to turning points in these phases when the economy departs too much from the balanced-growth-path scenario.

2.7.1 Conflict-Driven Economies: Repelling Steady-State Configurations

Here again, we consider the regime of a stable-multiplier process, that is, the process of a wage-led economy, which is the empirically more relevant one.

We consider such a regime close to the steady state of the model's dynamics. We assume that the Kaleckian reserve-army mechanism is not working close to the steady state ($i_e = 0$), that the parameter $\beta_{e\omega}$ in Okun's law is small, close to balanced growth, and that Blanchard and Katz error correction is weak around the steady state ($\beta_{w\omega} = 0, \beta_{p\omega} = 0$). Furthermore, we assume insider effects to represent the dominant factor (dominating the y effect) in real-wage dynamics, and outsider effects dominate with respect to e in money wage dynamics. The matrix of partial derivatives J of system (2.22)–(2.24) is, therefore, characterized by

$$J = \begin{pmatrix} J_{11} & J_{12} & J_{13} \\ J_{21} & J_{22} & J_{23} \\ J_{31} & J_{32} & J_{33} \end{pmatrix} = \begin{pmatrix} - & 0 & + \\ + & - & + \\ + & + & 0 \end{pmatrix}$$

By and large, the Rose real-wage channel is thus the destabilizing force in this situation, augmented by a secondary destabilizing effect caused by the recruitment of labor supply according to the growth rate of the capital stock. These effects make the determinant of J unambiguously positive and thus imply local instability around the steady state by means of the Routh-Hurwitz conditions.

By contrast, a profit-led economy would have a negative determinant in the considered situation, but would in turn be unstable if the parameter β_y is chosen sufficiently large (giving rise to a positive trace thereby) or if the $\hat{\omega}_y$ effect is sufficiently weak or even negative (due to a larger parameter β_{py}), because the minors of order 2 of the Jacobian J then all become negative. This latter effect is again a destabilizing Rose or real-wage effect, now situated in a profit-led environment.

If we consider the assumptions just made from a broader perspective, the objective to establish divergent dynamics around the steady state is likely met for the KGR economy, that is, that there generally will be repelling forces around its balance growth path (due to a variety of reasons like dominant insider behavior).

2.7.2 Kalecki-Type Upper Turning Points

In a situation with initially strong, but subsequently weakening economic growth (as occurred in the 1950s, 1960s and early 1970s), we expect the following sign structure in the considered Jacobian J to be the relevant one (and assume $i_\rho \leq 1$ in particular).

$$J = \begin{pmatrix} J_{11} & J_{12} & J_{13} \\ J_{21} & J_{22} & J_{23} \\ J_{31} & J_{32} & J_{33} \end{pmatrix} = \begin{pmatrix} - & - & + \\ + & - & - \\ - & + & - \end{pmatrix}$$

We consider the stabilizing role of the Kaleckian reserve-army mechanism (via $J_{12}J_{21}$ in particular), a stabilizing interaction between real wages and the rate of employment (via $J_{23}J_{32}$ in particular), a stabilizing feedback established via the dynamics of capacity utilization and wage-led goods demand (via $J_{13}J_{31}$ in particular), and only stabilizing eigen-feedbacks along the diagonal of the matrix J.

This scenario includes a wage-led goods market dynamics, dominance of the β_e terms in employment dynamics, and dominance of the goods market with respect to utilization ratios and of the labor market with respect to employment rates as far as real wage dynamics are concerned. Thus, there are a negative trace and only positive minors of order 2 for the matrix J. The only problematic term in the determinant of J is then given by the term $J_{13}J_{21}J_{32}$, representing again a destabilizing real-wage channel within these dynamics. The other five products composing the determinant of J are all negative, which suggests that the determinant is negative if this real-wage channel does not work with extraordinary strength. A value of the parameter β_{ey} chosen sufficiently low (i.e., a recruitment policy of firms that is sufficiently sluggish in this situation) may, for example, generate such a situation. For the Routh-Hurwitz condition

$$a_1 a_2 - a_3 = (-\text{tr} J)(J_1 + J_2 + J_3) + \det J$$

the only problematic term in this expression is given by $J_{12}J_{23}J_{31}$, because $J_{13}J_{21}J_{32}$ is positive and because all other terms in the determinant are contained in the expressions that form $a_1 a_2$. Again, it is very likely that this problematic term is dominated by the many expressions that form the remainder of $a_1 a_2$. This is, for example, the case when the Kaleckian reserve-army mechanism works sluggishly (i_e is small, i.e., the mechanism only works when high employment rates are becoming persistent). One may assume here that this is coupled with a weak real-wage effect on the recruitment policy of firms and also a weak entry J_{31} in the dynamics of real wages.

If these conditions are established, the Routh-Hurwitz conditions would imply local stability of the steady state. Yet we assume these conditions to prevail in a boom phase far off the steady state, in which case we can only speculate (and test this speculation numerically) that this contributes to global stability by implying an upper turning point for the considered phase of the long cycle in income-distribution and factor-utilization ratios.

Of course, there may be supply-side bottlenecks in this situation, because of the conditions $e \leq 1$, $y \leq y^p$, which may help to enforce upper turning points if these limits to the employment rate and the ratios of capacity utilization are reached. Furthermore, $\tilde{u}_f(e)$ may become steep at or close to the ceiling of absolute full employment $e = 1$.

2.7.3 Goodwin-Type Upper Turning Points?

The original Goodwin (1967) growth-cycle model considered a classical profit-led economy in which aggregate Keynesian goods demand does not yet play a role and in which, therefore, the term *profit-led* simply means that reduced profit slows down capital stock growth and the growth rate of the economy (and vice versa). This leads to increasing unemployment, which, sooner or later, corrects income distribution in favor of higher profitability. The turning points in the classical growth-cycle model are, therefore, solely a consequence of changing income distribution, whereas production is always at full capacity.

This situation is different in the model type considered in this chapter, because *profit-led* here means that the investment parameter i_ρ is so large (measured relative to the adjustment speed β_y) that, at the same time, real-wage increases act negatively on (Keynesian) aggregate goods demand, and the dynamic multiplier process—considered in isolation—is unstable, because of the strong influence of income y on aggregate goods demand. Profit-led economies are, therefore, plagued by partial multiplier instability, which may be so strong that the trace of the Jacobian becomes positive and then this partial instability leads to the overall outcome.

In a profit-led economy, the following sign distribution occurs in the Jacobian J in the case of a booming economy (for which we assume that insider-outsider effects are such that real wage growth depends both positively on the utilization ratio of the workforce within firms and on the employment rate characterizing the external labor market).[8]

$$J = \begin{pmatrix} J_{11} & J_{12} & J_{13} \\ J_{21} & J_{22} & J_{23} \\ J_{31} & J_{32} & J_{33} \end{pmatrix} = \begin{pmatrix} + & - & - \\ + & - & - \\ + & + & - \end{pmatrix}$$

Manipulating (reducing appropriately) the speed of adjustment β_y characterizing the dynamic multiplier process (and the first row of the foregoing matrix J) we find the trace of J becomes negative. In the same way we can also ensure that the principal minors of order 2 are all positive. Concerning the determinant of J we also find (since J_{11}, J_{13} are thereby reduced simultaneously) that the expression $-J_{12}(J_{21}J_{33} - J_{23}J_{31})$ becomes the dominant term in det J. Yet this remaining term has contradicting signs in its two product expressions (the first one is negative and thus supportive, whereas the second one is positive and thus dangerous for economic stability). Manipulating the speed term β_y is thus not sufficient for stability and the creation of eigenvalues with only negative real parts.

Finally, we consider the Routh-Hurwitz condition $-\text{trace}J(J_1 + J_2 + J_3) + \det J$. Here, only the terms $J_{12}J_{23}J_{31} + J_{13}J_{21}J_{32}$ in det J can create problems, because all others cancel against some of the all-positive terms in the $-\text{trace } J(J_1 + J_2 + J_3)$ expression. With respect to these remaining terms, only the second one is negative and thus problematic for stability. The two terms $J_{12}J_{23}J_{31}, J_{13}J_{21}J_{32}$ must, therefore, be made small relative to their respective counterparts in order to ensure the stability of these dynamics, in addition to what can be achieved by lowering the adjustment speed of the dynamic multiplier in the range of a profit-led regime.

Closer study, however, reveals that the size of J_{13} can again be manipulated via an appropriate reduction of the speed parameter β_y such that the remaining terms in $-\text{trace } J(J_1 + J_2 + J_3)$ will dominate the second of the foregoing problematic terms. Moreover, choosing the parameter $\beta_{e\omega}$ in an appropriate range may eliminate the final problem for stability and thus turn all real parts of eigenvalues of the Jacobian J into negative magnitudes.

We stress, however, once again that the Jacobian has only been evaluated properly at the steady state and that this, therefore, only proves the local asymptotic stability of this steady-state position. Yet numerical experience with growth models of this type suggests that such results apply also far off the steady-state position and thus at least give rise to the hope that one can enforce turning points in economic activity (in a period of accelerating growth) by assuming the foregoing parameter restrictions to hold sufficiently far above the steady-state position.

Overall, we find that Keynesian profit-led regimes may be plagued by multiplier instability to such an extent that there are no trajectories that are bounded from above. Policy action—of the type described in Kalecki (1943), but also monetary policy—may, therefore, be needed to enforce upper turning points in such periods of strong economic growth and bring about the significant changes in the capital-labor relationship that are implied thereby.

2.7.4 Rose-Type Lower Turning Points

By contrast, in situations of a depressed economy, we may find that the following sign structure in the Jacobian J can apply.

$$J = \begin{pmatrix} J_{11} & J_{12} & J_{13} \\ J_{21} & J_{22} & J_{23} \\ J_{31} & J_{32} & J_{33} \end{pmatrix} = \begin{pmatrix} - & 0 & + \\ + & - & + \\ - & 0 & 0 \end{pmatrix}$$

The Kaleckian reserve-army mechanism is surely absent in such a situation ($i_e = 0$), and the Blanchard and Katz error-correction terms may be as well. Furthermore, the dependence of real wages on the rate of employment e may be weak, since the β'_ws are sufficiently small. In such a situation, the coefficients $a_1, a_2, a_3, a_1a_2 - a_3$ in the Routh-Hurwitz conditions are all positive. The basic stabilizing mechanism is thus a normal real wage or Rose effect, which stimulates the economy if real wages begin to increase due to falling prices.

This situation would again imply local asymptotic stability around the steady state, but we once more take it as an indication that there are tendencies for a recovery in the depressed state of the economy that give rise to a lower turning point in economic activity. This tentative result must be tested with numerical simulations of the model that establish the considered situations for lower (and upper) turning points far off the steady state.

2.7.5 Goodwin-Type Lower Turning Points?

In the profit-led economy, in its depressed phase, we assume the following sign distribution in the Jacobian J.[9]

$$J = \begin{pmatrix} J_{11} & J_{12} & J_{13} \\ J_{21} & J_{22} & J_{23} \\ J_{31} & J_{32} & J_{33} \end{pmatrix} = \begin{pmatrix} + & 0 & - \\ + & - & + \\ + & 0 & 0 \end{pmatrix}$$

We have assumed in this matrix that the Kaleckian reserve-army mechanism does not work in the downward direction (because it characterizes only the economic and political aspects of full employment) and that the influence of the rate of employment on the dynamics of the real wage can be neglected in this type of economy. We also assume Blanchard and Katz error correction to be sufficiently weak in the depression.

Dynamic multiplier instability can thus be tamed by assuming that β_y is chosen such that the trace of J is negative and such that the term $J_{13}J_{31}$ dominates the principal minors of order 2. Moreover, in this situation we the determinant of J is always negative and is part of the $a_1 a_2$ expressions, implying that the Routh-Hurwitz conditions can be fulfilled in this case by an appropriately low choice of the size of the parameter β_y within the profit-led goods-demand regime. The case of lower turning points is thus easier to handle in this regime than the case of upper turning points, though, here too much depends on the speed with which firms adjust their output decisions toward their observation of aggregate goods demand.

2.8 ■ NUMERICAL EXAMPLES

We have shown in the preceding section that the steady state of the considered KGR dynamics may likely be an unstable one and that there are a variety of possibilities that may nevertheless keep the resulting dynamics limited during prosperity or depression and thus economically viable. The actual occurrence of such limitation mechanisms may change over time, and thus they may be confined to certain episodes in the evolution of capitalistic market economies. Moreover, monetary or fiscal policy may also be important in factually explaining the occurrence of such regime changes in the postwar evolution of industrialized economies (for example, from the welfare state to Reaganomics and economic and social deregulation). See the next section in this regard. The relevance of the model of this chapter is, therefore, not so much in its implication of a unique cyclical pattern of capital accumulation and employment dynamics around its steady-state position, but in its flexibility in explaining a variety of partial scenarios in the evolution of capitalism after World War II. Clearly, though this is welcome from an economic point of view, the mathematical and numerical analysis of the dynamics is thereby made more complicated and unattractive compared to other cycle models, like Goodwin (1967) growth-cycle dynamics, and thus less appealing from the mathematical point of view.

In this section we briefly consider, in addition to our analytical results, some numerical simulations of the model of this chapter on its three-dimensional reduced-form level. We simplify the model somewhat by assuming fixed ratios $\bar{e}, \bar{u}_w, \bar{y}, \bar{e}_f, \bar{u}_f$ for the various benchmark comparisons in the wage and price PC, in the investment function, and in Okun's law, and we assume in addition a situation in which the steady-state value of y is equal to $\bar{y}$. We thus make use in this section of the following parameter set:[10] $\beta_{we} = 0.5, \beta_{wu} = 0.6, \kappa_w = .5, \bar{e} = 0.9, \bar{u}_w = 0.9, \beta_{py} = 0.385, \kappa_p = 0.5, \bar{y} = 0.9, \beta_y = 1.2, \beta_{ey} = 0.3, \bar{u}_f = 0.9, \beta_{ew} = 1.5, x = 2, y^p = 1, i_\rho = 1.5, i_e = 0.1, \bar{a} = 0.3, \bar{e}_f = 0.9$.

In figure 2.1 we show for wage adjustment speeds $\beta_{we} = 0.5, \beta_{we} = 1$ the damped oscillations that result from these two adjustment speeds. The unexpected result of this simulation run is that there are indeed multiple steady-state solutions as the model is formulated, one economically meaningful solution for the lower adjustment speed and one that runs into supply bottlenecks in the labor market and thus cannot remain in the form shown in the fluctuation around the higher steady-state value for e in figure 2.1. We thus see that increasing wage flexibility with respect to demand pressure in the external labor market may destabilize the steady state in the model and lead to cyclical convergence to another interior steady state with a higher NAIRU level $\bar{e}$ in the labor market and a lower NAIRU level $\bar{y}$ in the market for goods. Such results hold for a large range of adjustment speeds β_y in the market for goods and can also occur when the parameter β_{we} is decreased instead of increased as earlier. Note, finally, that the movements

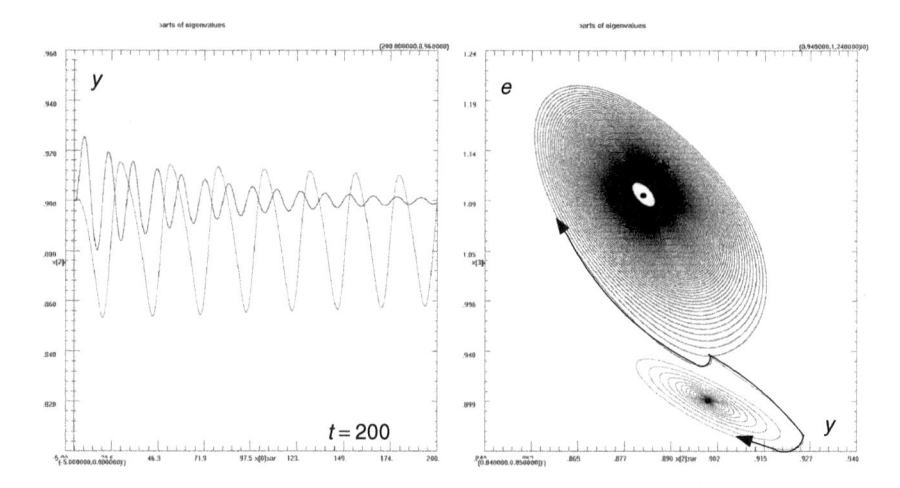

Figure 2.1 Damped fluctuations in Kaleckian investment and employment dynamics.

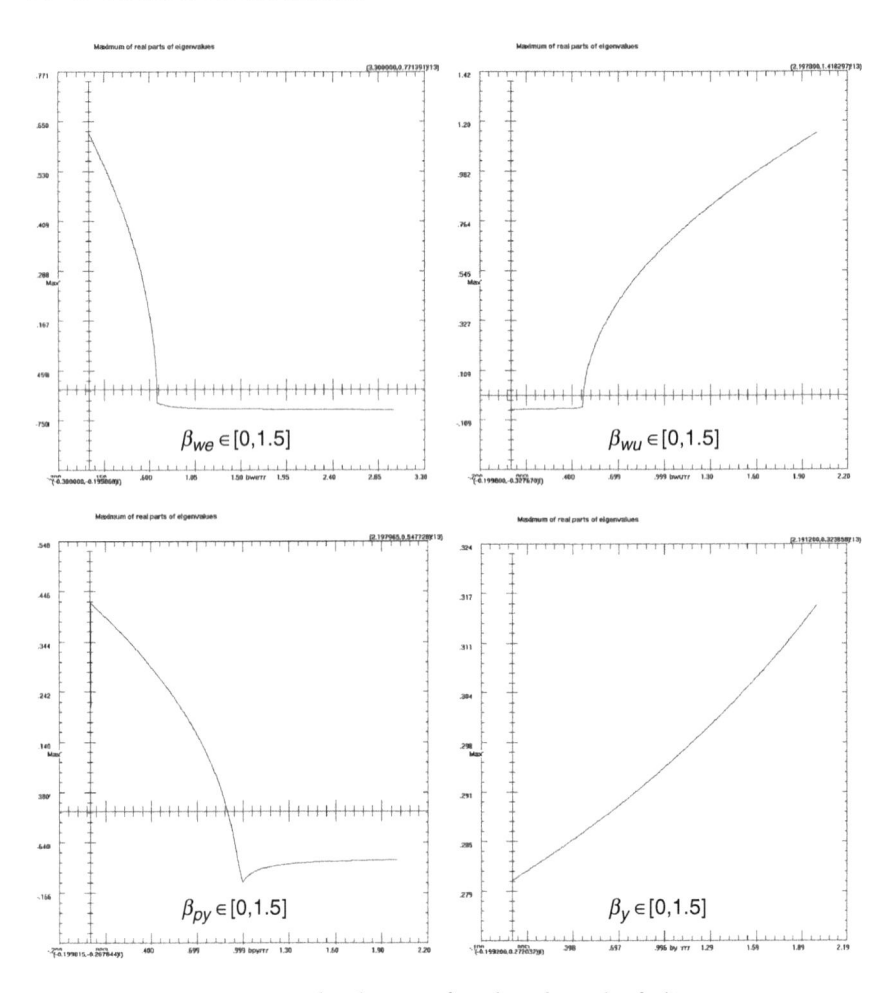

Figure 2.2 Eigenvalue diagrams for selected speeds of adjustment.

in capacity utilization and the rate of employment are far from being positively correlated, because of our extended formulation of Okun's law.

In figure 2.2 we consider eigenvalue diagrams—showing the maximum real part of eigenvalues as a function of selected adjustment speeds—in order to show where the steady state becomes locally unstable (when the real part being discussed becomes positive). We can see from this figure that increasing the parameters β_{we}, β_{py} stabilizes the economy, but we must decrease the parameter β_{wu} in order to achieve this. The parameter β_y, when increased, does not stabilize the economy, in contrast to what one would expect from the partial derivative of $\dot{y}$ with respect to y, which is negative. Our base parameter set is chosen such that our steady-state solution is unstable—as is indicated by the eigenvalue diagram for β_y—but leads

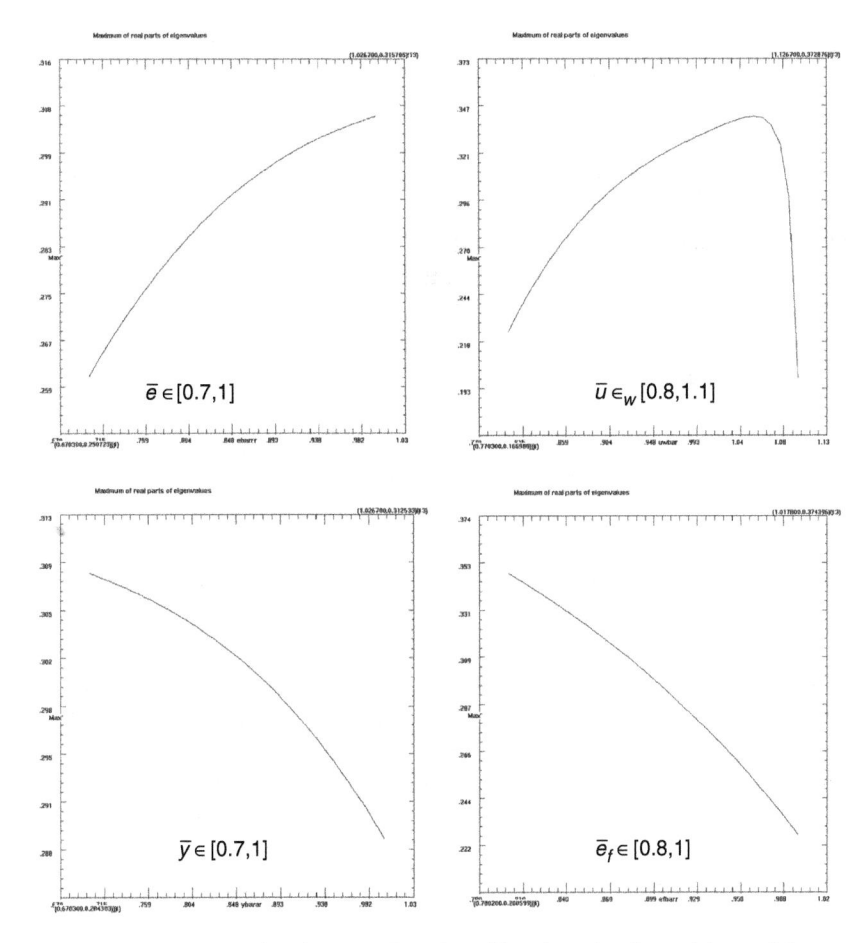

Figure 2.3 Eigenvalue diagrams for selected benchmark values of the model.

nevertheless to convergent fluctuations, as figure 2.1 shows, yet convergence to a steady state for which the eigenvalues have not been calculated here.

Figure 2.3 shows further eigenvalue diagrams, for the benchmark levels that define NAIRU-type utilization rates in the labor and goods markets as well as the benchmark value for the employment rate in firms' investment behavior. From the diagrams we see that higher NAIRU levels in the labor market destabilize the economy further, whereas a higher NAIRU level in the goods market reduces the explosiveness of the steady state we consider, because of the choice of our base parameter set. Moreover, the result for increases in the benchmark level $\bar{e}_f$, by which firms judge whether there is pressure on them due to changing work conditions, in fact stabilizes the economy (whereas increases in the reaction coefficient i_e—not shown—do not). We conclude that the implications of the dynamics in this model can be numerous and need not confirm what is suggested

58 ■ FLEXICURITY CAPITALISM

through partial reasoning (concerning isolated entries of the Jacobian matrix of the dynamics at the steady state).

2.9 ■ POLITICAL ASPECTS OF THE KALECKIAN INVESTMENT AND EMPLOYMENT CYCLE

In this chapter we have shown that the private sector of a capitalist economy may generate long cycles in investment and employment with specific upper and lower turning points, possibly depending on the specific historical episodes that this model type can study in detail. Missing so far—in the model's laws of motion—has been any influence from monetary policy or fiscal policy, the first because of our neglect of interest rates and financial markets, and the second, because neither government expenditure nor taxes, nor other means of financing such expenditure were taken into account. Besides the purely economic implications of full employment and the resulting investment and employment cycles, the political aspects of this situation—as they were briefly and brilliantly described in Kalecki (1943) (see the quotation in the introduction of this chapter)—must also be taken into account in discussion of such employment-cycle mechanisms.

Our analysis of the dynamics of the private sector is, in one important respect, still partial, even on this level, because it does not consider what happens on the nominal side of the model. We derive, in section 2.3, the reduced-form real-wage dynamics that results from our wage-price spiral mechanism, but we have not yet considered explicitly the underlying reduced form equations for money wage and price level inflation rates (from which the real-wage dynamics has been derived). With respect to nominal price inflation, particularly, the reduced-form expression explaining the forces behind price inflation reads:[11]

$$\hat{p} = \frac{\dot{p}}{p} = \pi^c + \kappa[\beta_{py}(y - \bar{y}) + \beta_{p\omega}\ln(\omega/\omega_o)$$
$$+ \kappa_p(\beta_{we}(e - \bar{e}) + \beta_{wu}(u_w - \tilde{u}_w(e)) - \beta_{w\omega}\ln(\omega/\omega_o))]$$

In order to allow for steady inflation rates, the term following π^c in the preceding equation must be zero in the steady state, which gives, for the output-capital ratio in such a situation:

$$y_{oo} - \bar{y} = \frac{\kappa_p(\beta_{we}(e_o - \bar{e}) + \beta_{wu}(\tilde{u}_f(e_o) - \tilde{u}_w(e_o)))}{\beta_{py}} = \frac{(1 - \kappa_w)\kappa_p}{1 - \kappa_p}(y_o - \bar{y})$$

A comparison with the steady-state value of y_o, however, immediately reveals that this output-capital ratio is equal to the steady-state ratio only in very special cases (concerning the weights in the cost-pressure terms of both wage and price inflation), whereas there will be smaller or larger values of this y compared to y_o, in general (for example, $y_{oo} = \bar{y} + 0.5(y_o - \bar{y})$ in the balanced case where

$\kappa_w = \kappa_p = 0.5$). If the real part of the economy is in the steady state, the economy thus may have persistently falling inflation rates ($\hat{p} < \pi^c$) or rising inflation rates ($\hat{p} > \pi^c$) in its nominal part, a process that surely cannot go on forever. Political pressure may, therefore, occur that may (or may not) induce an adjustment of $\bar{e}$, $\bar{e}_f$ and of $\tilde{u}_{wo}$, $\tilde{u}_{fo}$ toward each other, respectively. In this case,

$$y_o = \bar{y}, \quad \bar{e} = \bar{e}_f, \quad u_{wo} = u_{fo}$$

will be established, that is, there is only one NAIRU in the external and internal labor markets of firms and in the capital stock utilization ratio, and these common benchmark levels are—as the model is presently formulated and applied—completely determined by the benchmark utilization and employment ratios as they are set by firms, if firms cannot be forced to alter their target levels in this respect.

2.9.1 Monetary Policy

We next assume that the monetary authority can influence economic activity, via its interest-rate policy, by making investment dependent on the actual real rate of interest in the following way:

$$I/K = i(\cdot) + \bar{a} = i_\rho(\rho - \rho_o) - i_e(e - \bar{e}_f) - i_r((r - \hat{p} - \rho_o) + \bar{a} \quad (2.25)$$

As interest-rate policy of the central bank, we assume, in addition, the following classical type of the Taylor rule:

$$r^* = \rho_o + \hat{p} + \alpha_p(\hat{p} - \bar{\pi}) \quad (2.26)$$

$$\dot{r} = \alpha_r(r^* - r) \quad (2.27)$$

The target interest rate of the central bank r* is made dependent on the steady-state real rate of interest (the real rate of profit) augmented by actual inflation back to a nominal rate, and is, as usually, dependent on the inflation gap. With respect to this target, we assume an interest rate smoothing of strength α_r. Here we consider only an extreme case of such a Taylor interest-rate-policy rule, namely, the limit case $\alpha_r = \infty$ of no interest rate smoothing (the other limit case being an interest rate peg):

$$r = \rho_o + \hat{p} + \alpha_p(\hat{p} - \bar{\pi})$$

$$I/K = i_\rho(\rho - \rho_o) - i_e(e - \bar{e}_f) - i_r\alpha_p(\hat{p} - \bar{\pi}) + \bar{a}$$

$$\hat{p} = \pi^c + \kappa[\beta_{py}(y - \bar{y}) + \beta_{p\omega}\ln(\omega/\omega_o)$$

$$+ \kappa_p(\beta_{we}(e - \bar{e}) + \beta_{wu}(u_w - \tilde{u}_w(e)) - \beta_{w\omega}\ln(\omega/\omega_o))]$$

The result of such an extension of the model toward a treatment of monetary policy in its context is that the function i(·) is now extended by a third term in which the negative influence of the employment rate on the rate of investment is enhanced and augmented by similar effects of u_w and y on it (with the same negative sign), so that the inflation climate π^c and its adaptive revision under the law of motion

$$\dot{\pi}^c = \beta_{\pi^c p}(\hat{p} - \pi^c)$$

now feeds back into the real part of the economy.

We see that the negative influence of economic activity (measured by the employment rate and now also the utilization ratios of both labor and capital) on the rate of investment is, thereby, strengthened, which possibly adds further stability to the dynamics, as implied by our discussion of the economy's turning points (as a substitute for the traditional Keynes effect in models of exogenous money supply). Furthermore, the indirect inclusion of the inflation climate among the determinants of the rate of investment now adds a Mundell effect to the dynamics, but a stabilizing one, since—because of our formulation of monetary policy—increasing inflation and thus an increasing inflationary climate effect a negative influence on investment and thus on economic activity, and provide a check on further inflation. Monetary policy may thus add further stability to the model's dynamics, particularly on its nominal side, which is now fully integrated.

More important, however, is the impact of the added monetary policy on the steady-state behavior of our economy.[12] In order to provide a simple illustration of this assertion we disregard the Blanchard and Katz error-correction terms in the wage and price Phillips curves. The aforementioned law of motion for the inflation climate and the law of motion for real wages (2.21) provide two independent equations for the determination of the steady-state values of e, y. Assuming for the influence of insider effects on the wage inflation rate

$$\tilde{u}_w(\bar{e}) = \bar{y}/(xl_o\bar{e}),$$

that is, a consistency requirement for the benchmark value of the utilization ratio of the workforce in the steady state, gives the values $\bar{e}$, $\bar{y}$, for the steady-state values of both e, y (since $\rho_o = \bar{a}$ continues to hold true). From the $\dot{e} = 0$ equation, the steady-state value for labor intensity is l_o. Finally, the determination of e_o through the level $\bar{e}_f$ now disappears from the set of steady-state conditions, which imply by means of i(·) = 0

$$i_e(e_o - \bar{e}_f) + i_r(\hat{p}_o - \bar{\pi}) = 0$$

This gives an equation for determining the steady-state rate of inflation in its deviation from the target rate of the central bank (and it also provides the steady-state value of the nominal rate of interest i_o by $\rho_o + \hat{p}_o$).

The addition of interest-rate effects on investment behavior and a specific interest-rate-policy rule thus imply that steady-state levels of the employment rate and the utilization ratios of both workers and capital are now given by their NAIRU levels and no longer by the target rate of firms, intended to control the social structure of accumulation. Furthermore, this latter target $\bar{e}_f$ now determines the steady-state rate of inflation (together with the NAIRU $\bar{e}$ and the target rate $\bar{\pi}$ of the central bank) and it makes this rate higher the less rigid the employment target of firms in their investment function becomes. Lowering the NAIRU $\bar{e}$ itself implies the steady-state rate of inflation due to the relationship

$$\hat{p}_o = i_e(\bar{e}_f - \bar{e})/i_r + \bar{\pi}$$

that is, the model exhibits a long-term PC that is negatively sloped (and which allows for zero steady-state inflation, if $\bar{e}_o = \bar{e}_f + i_r\bar{\pi}/i_e$ holds true).

The case of an interest-rate policy becomes considerably more complex if we add to the model a Tobinian portfolio sector whose return characteristic influences investment behavior. Monetary policy must then work its way through the portfolio substitution process, and the process depends on how the long-term interest, Tobin's q, and other important variables, determined by portfolio choice and asset accumulation, feed back into the investment decisions of firms. We leave such complications for the conduct of monetary policy for future research (see Chiarella, Flaschel, Hung, and Semmler [2006] on these matters). The direct control of investment behavior in this model type as well as in models of the New Keynesian variety represents only a first step into an analysis of the implications of monetary policy for economic activity and capital accumulation.

2.9.2 Fiscal Policy

Concerning fiscal policy, Kalecki (1943, chapter 12) gives a variety of reasons why industrial leaders may be opposed to full employment. In view of our model, and its formulation of this opposition on the level of private investment formation, it is somewhat astonishing to note that a government expenditure function of roughly Keynesian type—like monetary policy—may provide further strength to the negative impact of the rate of employment on the rate of capital accumulation. Therefore, the outcome may be in line with what industrial leaders may have instinctively or consciously (through their common insight) established as a necessary reaction to an increase in the rate of employment toward (absolute) full employment.

In order to substantiate this assertion, we assume, as fiscal policy rule, the following expenditure function:

$$G/Y = (G/Y)_o - \alpha_g(e - \bar{e}_g), \quad \text{i.e.,} \quad g = G/K = (G/Y)_o y - \alpha_g(e - \bar{e}_g)y$$

where we posit that the component of $(G/Y)_o = (T/Y)_o$ in national income is purely tax-financed (and the remainder is financed through changes in government debt and open-market operations of the central bank, which affect the portfolio choice of asset holders, which we have not yet considered in this chapter). Part of the aforementioned expenditures may be infrastructure expenditures, which expand the capital stock like private investment and can thus be added to the i(·) term again (as in our formulation of monetary policy), and the remainder may represent unproductive government expenditures to be added to the aggregate demand expression y^d directly. In both cases, however, we introduce a term into the goods-market dynamics, which enhances the working of the term $i_e(e - \bar{e})$, if $\bar{e}_g = \bar{e}_f$ is assumed. A proper Keynesian fiscal policy rule (whereby government spending increases during periods of stagnation and decreases in periods of prosperity) thus works in principle as industrial leaders would prefer it to work in situations of an increasing employment rate.

The real difference between such policies and the intentions of industrial leaders, therefore, may be found in the fixing of the benchmark level $\bar{e}_g$, from which future government expenditure will be more than the tax-financed portion. Considering fiscal policy in Germany under Chancellor Willy Brandt, for example, provides evidence for a target rate $\bar{e}_g$ equal to 1 and, considering the behavior of other governments in that period, surely a rate much above the level that industrial leaders see as consistent with their view on the evolution of the social structure of accumulation (which favors not increasing—but in fact reducing—workforce participation, not decreasing labor market flexibilities, and the like). The opposition of firms and their managers may be more directed against the level of $\bar{e}_g$ than against the fact that a government pursues a Keynesian policy in the ups and downs of the business cycle, which may help to stabilize the firms' goods demand around a level compatible with managers' views of a convenient level of unemployment in the external labor market and the implications for the labor market within firms.

Note that the simplest way to introduce this fiscal policy into the model is to assume that $(G/Y)_o = (T/Y)_o$ represents government consumption and is financed by taxing wages, and the rest of government expenditure is debt financed and used for investment purposes, since this leaves total goods consumption unchanged and adds the cyclical component of government expenditures again to investment behavior without changing its determinants significantly (if $\bar{e}_g = \bar{e}_f$ is assumed). This latter assumption may be justified in steps, by way of a long phase of significant unemployment in the labor market, which removes considerations of workforce participation, workforce firing, and workday reductions established during the prosperity phase of the Kaleckian investment and employment cycle. If fiscal policy is, moreover, conducted symmetrically over the considered cycle, the evolution of government debt may only become a problem if downturns are long and upswings are short. In such a case a more conservative (asymmetric) expenditure rule may also be established, which does not give depressions less weight than upswings as far as countercyclical expenditure management is concerned. In this way, the social structure of accumulation may be adjusted toward a growth path that again reaches a prosperity period sooner or later. Note, however, that we have so far bypassed all problems that may be implied by the working of the financial markets and the portfolio choice of asset holders—nationally or even more in periods of rapid globalization—for real macroeconomic activity in the goods and labor markets.

2.10 ■ CONCLUSIONS

This chapter's model of the Keynes/Kalecki-Goodwin/Rose variety has an advanced type of wage-price spiral, a simple dynamic multiplier story that is based on a theory of aggregate demand that includes Kaleckian (1943, chapter 12) opposition of industrial leaders to the establishment of long phases of full employment on the labor market—and an advanced type of Okun's law linking goods and labor markets. In studying extensively the reduced form three-dimensional real dynamics implied by the model, their local and global stability features, and the partial feedback structures that underlie these stability considerations, we find of particular interest local instability of the steady-state solution and the derivation of various scenarios that may allow for upper as well as lower turning points from a global point of view, in order to make the model's dynamics economically viable. Section 2.7 provided numerical illustrations of the model. Since there are no feedbacks into the real dynamics problems on the nominal side of the economy noted in Section 2.9, we had to extend the model to take into account interest effects on aggregate demand and a Taylor interest-rate-policy rule in order to tame the explosive aspects of the nominal part of the dynamics. Besides monetary policy, we also considered the role of fiscal policy of a Keynesian type, which augmented the private sector of our Keynes/Kalecki-Goodwin/Rose economy in a simple and straightforward way.

Although Kalecki's (1943) essay on the political aspects of full employment was thus one of the focal points of this chapter, we treated it here in a very basic format, because the chapter concentrated primarily on the economic aspects of full employment. These aspects included the role of longer-phased cycles of prosperity and stagnation, considered in Asada, Flaschel, and Skott (2006), based on a theory of aggregate demand that included Kalecki's (1943, chapter 12) discussion of the opposition of industrial leaders to long phases of full employment in the labor market; that theory includes cyclical evolution in the kind and degree of the welfare state and its various aspects, in contrast to what is normally discussed under the label "business fluctuations." By and large, we view the employed workforce, the insider, to represent the dominant element that destabilizes long-lasting situations of full employment, leading, in particular, to the reactions of industrial leaders and the government (including the central bank) that bring about upper turning points in economic activity and subsequent strong recessions or depressions in such booming economies. Yet we have seen that a variety of further reasons may be involved in explaining actual pronounced turning points in economic activity, upper as well as lower ones, particularly about whether the real-wage dynamics are led by the goods or labor market and about whether the dynamics of the goods and labor markets are led by wage or profit. Therefore, specific historical reasons may explain lasting changes in labor-market and inflation regimes, a point that makes the analysis here considerably less closed than comparable models of the ordinary business cycle.

Once it is assumed that the rate of employment in the labor market adjusts only gradually to the rate of capacity utilization of firms, an important further topic of the chapter was that one must introduce the utilization ratio of the workforce to get a meaningful chain of events that lead from the utilization of the capital stock of firms to this rate of employment. As in a capillary system, there are two labor-market pressures for firms, one outside and one inside, which may be treated and manipulated in different ways by firms during phases of prosperity or depression. Such an extension of Okun's law is a necessary step in any approach that wants to formulate the link from the goods market to the labor market on a theoretically coherent basis, thus making it essential to our framework. During phases of prosperity, however, the dominance of insiders in the wage-price spiral may lead to the partially destabilizing situation in which real-wage changes may depend negatively on the rate of employment and positively on the rate of capacity utilization, in contrast to what is expected in a framework that does not allow for insider effects in the dynamics of goods and labor markets, and where, therefore, employment is always immediately adjusted to the activity level implied by the working of the market for goods.

We treated one issue only briefly in this chapter: the distinction between conflict-driven and consensus-based economies. The first type of economy exhibits a repelling steady-state path and, thus, requires nonlinearities, far off the steady state in order to keep its trajectories bounded. Such economies generate order by more or less large-scaled cycles in employment and economic activity, which are endogenously generated and subject to supportive monetary or fiscal policy. The question here is whether this is a socially acceptable way of running the economy (disregarding efficiency issues) or whether ways have to be found to allow the economy to progress to a situation that we have called a consensus-based economy.

Consensus-based and conflict-driven economies can be further differentiated as shown in table 2.3. Besides "Scandinavian-type" consensus-based economies and strictly conflict-driven ones in table 2.3 we distinguish between developed economies that are very flexible but exhibit an unstable steady-state position and those that are fairly inflexible around a stable depressed steady-state situation. They may be even further differentiated on the basis of the details of their steady-state position.

TABLE 2.3. *Four types of market economies.*

	High Steady State	Low Steady State
Stable steady state	Nordic consensus-based economy	Kaleckian market economy type I
Unstable steady state	Kaleckian market economy type II	Southern conflict-driven economy

Such questions must remain for future research. In these and other respects, we provide an introduction to Kaleckian long-phased cycles (not business cycles, as Kalecki characterized the situation) with features more or less typical of a welfare state in their prosperity phase and an emphasis on deregulation processes in their stagnation phase. We hope that the classifications provided in this chapter will stimulate further work on the Kaleckian (1943) type of reserve-army mechanism as it has been distinguished here from a Goodwin (1967) type of reserve-army mechanism (driven by the conflict over income distribution).

In view of the four types of capitalist market economies, however, we admit that minimum- and maximum-wage regulations (as considered here) and the establishment of Keynesian fiscal and monetary policy rules may not be sufficient for a social structure of capital accumulation that is viable from the long-run perspective, even in Nordic welfare states, unless mass unemployment is used from time to time to remove the limits to capital accumulation that such a social structure entails. Activating labor market reforms may, therefore, be indispensable in order to make such a welfare system work in the long run. The next chapter introduces elements for such reform on the macrolevel in a coherent social accounting framework and its first basic—and then increasingly more complex—market interactions and law of capital accumulation.

3 Schumpeter: Capitalism, Flexicurity, and Democracy?

3.1 ■ INTRODUCTION

In 1932, Ludwig von Mises wrote in the preface to the second German edition of *Socialism: An Economic and Sociological Analysis*:

> The arguments by which I demonstrated that, in a socialist community, economic calculation would not be possible have attracted especially wide notice.... It may truly be said that the discussion is now closed; there is today hardly any opposition to my contention.
>
> von Mises (1932, 1951, p. 18)

The subsequent debate on (post-Lange) market socialism is summarized—with reference to the contributions by John Roemer and his coauthors in particular—in Yunker (1995). Astonishingly, however, the seminal contribution by Joseph A. Schumpeter, *Capitalism, Socialism and Democracy*, first published in 1942, is not mentioned there (or, indeed, in many other contributions to the topic of market socialism). Schumpeter asserted:

> CAN socialism work? Of course it can. No doubt is possible about that once we assume, first, that the requisite stage of industrial development has been reached and, second, that transitional problems can be successfully resolved. One may, of course, feel very uneasy about these assumptions themselves or about the questions whether the socialist form of society can be expected to be democratic and, democratic or not, how well it is likely to function. All that will be discussed later on. But if we accept these assumptions and discard these doubts the answer to the remaining question is clearly Yes.
>
> Schumpeter (1942, 1976, p. 167)

In subsequent sections on the socialist blueprint, Schumpeter argues how planning is performed and centralized in such an economy:

> More precisely, our question may be formulated as follows: Given a socialist system of the kind envisaged, is it possible to derive, from its data and from the rules of rational behavior, uniquely determined decisions as to what and how to produce or, to put the same thing into the slogan of exact economics, do those data and rules, under the circumstances of a socialist economy, yield equations which are independent, compatible—i.e., free from contradiction—and sufficient in number to

determine uniquely the unknowns of the problem before the central board or ministry of production? ... The answer is in the affirmative.

Schumpeter, (1942, 1976, p. 172)

We do not question here what indeed distinguishes the Schumpeterian concept of a Western type of socialism, erected on the pillars built by the Rockefellers, Vanderbilts, and others from the Lange-Lerner type of socialism, but instead begin one step further by reformulating capitalism from the viewpoint of the flexicurity concept now being intensively discussed in the European Union. In our approach to reform of capitalism, we, therefore, by and large consider—as did Schumpeter (1942, 1976)—the foundations of planning and the conduct of big (but also medium-sized and small) capitalist enterprises as they exist in actual leading capitalist market economies.

Reform or the path of progress under a flexicurity system basically addresses the working of the labor market (the abolishment of the Marx-Kaleckian reserve-army mechanism) and the financial markets, specifically their function to channel savings into investment rather than their casino-like features that are widely recognized by the public. No Schumpeterian socialist blueprint is, therefore, necessary in a flexicurity society.

However, in regard to the political superstructure, while we agree with Schumpeter's analysis of the superiority of majority voting over percentage voting in advanced democracies, we do not treat this topic in this chapter in detail, because we focus on the three pillars of flexicurity, namely, highly developed full employment, sophisticated school systems, and equitable selection of elites, which are the central features for the proper conduct of (democratic) flexicurity societies.[1] Schumpeter (1942) analyzes "democracy" in part 4 of his book, examining the essential characteristics of and functional requirements for democratic decision making in great depth. In light of the preceding quotations from von Mises and Schumpeter, we concentrate on why "socialism" (of whatever kind) is not necessary to achieve full employment, basic income needs, equal opportunities, support of talents, self-realization, political influence, and more.

Section 3.2 discusses our approach from the general perspective behind this type of model building. In section 3.3 we particularly emphasize the distinction between skilled and highly skilled workers, both in the private and the public sectors of such an economy. Section 3.4 considers the economy's stability, in which dynamics is determined by highly skilled workers according to a Blanchard and Katz type PC and in which labor intensity growth is determined by realized profits. In section 3.5 we expand the model by considering its implications for accumulation in company pension funds and possibly using such funds to supply credit to firms. Section 3.6 considers Finland's school system and its implications for our hypothetical flexicurity model. Particularly we study in this section the equal opportunity principle at schools (and preschools) and the lifelong learning hypothesis.

In section 3.7, we extend discussion of the real credit supply we introduced in section 3.5 to a treatment of nominal financial assets and the resulting Keynesian demand problems and macroeconomic business cycle fluctuations, which enhance the economic role and social importance of a system of flexicurity capitalism. Section 3.8 reconsiders the Schumpeterian dynamic entrepreneur and processes of creative destruction in the framework of flexicurity capitalism as well as other forms of firm behavior. Section 3.9 summarizes the chapter's discussion to that point. In section 3.10 we discuss in detail the role that elites play or should play in a flexicurity society, including their remuneration under favorable conditions (positive profits) as well as nonfavorable conditions (company losses). This topic introduces some microeconomic aspects into the considered macrodynamic model, particularly coordination and incentive problems. Microaspects are also the topic of section 3.11 in which we study processes of supply-side price formation in a business-cycle environment. Proofs of the stability and sustainability propositions we make are provided in an appendix.

3.2 ■ FROM MARXIAN RESERVE ARMY TO SCHUMPETER'S COMPETITIVE SOCIALISM AND BEYOND

We start from the hypothesis that Goodwin's (1967) classical growth cycle, modeling the Marxian reserve-army mechanism, does not represent a process of social reproduction that can be considered adequate and sustainable in a democratic society in the long run.[2] On this background, the chapter builds a basic macrodynamic framework where this capitalist form of cyclical growth and economic reproduction is modified by use of an employer of "first" resort, added to an economic reproduction process that is highly competitive and flexible and thus not of the type of the past in Eastern socialism.

Instead, this economy experiences high capital and labor mobility (concerning hiring and firing in particular), and, thus, flexibility; fluctuations of employment in this first labor market of the economy (the private sector) become socially acceptable because of the security aspect of the flexicurity concept, that is, by a second labor market in which all remaining workers (and even pensioners) find a meaningful occupation. The resulting model of flexicurity capitalism with its detailed transfer-payment schemes is, in its essence, comparable to the flexicurity models developed for the Nordic welfare states, Denmark in particular.

We show that this economy exhibits a balanced growth path that is globally attracting. We also show that credit-financed investment, and thus more-flexible investment behavior, can be easily added without disturbing the prevailing stable full-capacity growth. However, we deal with only supply-driven business fluctuations with both factors of production always fully employed; we do not deal with demand-driven fluctuations. This model combines flexible factor adjustments in the private sector with high employment security for the labor force and shows that the flexicurity variety of a capitalist economy, protected by the government, can work in a fairly balanced manner.

A similar framework for flexicurity capitalism is proposed in Flaschel, Greiner, Luchtenberg, and Nell (2008). Here we expand that model by considering two types of workers in the first labor market and in the public labor market: skilled and highly skilled workers (as baseline representation of a full set of skill differentials). This change makes the model comparable in discussion of unskilled versus skilled labor under contemporary capitalism and is intended to show that there is no systematic need for unskilled labor in a model of flexicurity growth. We acknowledge, however, that there may also be an employer of last resort (in addition to the employer of first resort) in such a framework, because there may always be some people unwilling to work or incapable of working within the schemes in this model.

The primary task of the school system is to provide equal opportunities for all school students in primary and secondary education and, thereby, to minimize the number of people who, for one reason or another, including illness, do not contribute to labor markets of the flexicurity model—though refusal to work may occur after schooling is completed. Here we consider only the situation in which everybody passes successfully through the school system (as detailed in a later section of the chapter); thus the issue of an employer of last resort will need further research. However, we add a tertiary education component to the model in which access is limited, and which is responsible for educating highly skilled workers.

Solow's (1956) famous growth model, to a certain degree, fits the flexicurity type, because competitive firms always operate on their profit-maximizing activity level and because the labor market is assumed to always guarantee full employment. The Solow model thus provides employment flexibility coupled with wage-income security, through the assumed behavior of firms and the assumption of perfectly flexible money wages (which may give rise to wage-income fluctuations). The monetarist critique of Keynesianism and recent work by Blanchard and Katz (1999) and others suggest, however, a wage PC that, when coupled with the assumption of myopic perfect foresight regarding the price inflation rate, for example, implies a real-wage PC in which the growth rate of real wages depends positively on the employment rate and negatively on the level of the real-wage rate.

Adding such empirically supported real-wage rigidity to the Solow model gives rise to two laws of motion, for labor intensity and for the real wage, a dynamic system that approaches the situation of the overshooting of the Goodwin growth-cycle mechanism if factor substitution in production is sufficiently inelastic and if the Blanchard and Katz (1999) real-wage error-correction term in the PC is sufficiently weak. Solow's growth model thus becomes a variant of the classical distributive growth cycle and its overshooting reserve-army mechanism, the adequacy of which, for a democratic society, we question in this chapter. An empirical example of what we mean is provided by figure 3.1 (here for the US economy in place of the UK example considered in chapter 1).

In its upper part, figure 3.1 shows the decomposition from penalized splines of US time series of the wage share and the employment rate into a long-phase and a short-phase (business-cycle) component.[3] As can be clearly observed, the long-phase Goodwinian wage share/employment rate cycle describes, by and large, a pronounced counterclockwise orientation (in the e, v phase space), showing that the long-phase dynamics in the labor markets are negatively correlated with the wage share in the US economy on an average and in an overshooting manner.

Generating order and economic viability (profitability) in market economies by large swings in the unemployment rate (mass unemployment, with its accompanying degradation of the families that form the society), as shown earlier and as described and analyzed in detail in Marx (1954, chapter 23), is one way to make capitalism work, but it must surely be criticized with respect to its social consequences (social segmentation or even class clashes). Such a reproduction mechanism is not compatible with an educated and democratic society in the long run, as we describe it in this chapter, which is supposed to provide equal opportunity to all of its citizens.

This kind of society must, therefore, be contrasted with an alternative social structure of accumulation that allows one to combine a highly competitive market economy with a set of human rights that includes the right (as well as the obligation) to work and to make income from this work that, at the least, supports basic needs and basic happiness.

Criticizing the Eastern state socialism of his time as immature, Schumpeter (1942) developed a concept of mature socialism for countries that can be characterized as competitive socialism built on foundations erected unconsciously through the big enterprises created by the Rockefellers, the Vanderbilts and other famous economic dynasties in Western industrialized countries. In part 2 of his book, Schumpeter discusses the question of whether this type of socialism can work, what the corresponding socialist blueprints should look like, and to what extent they are superior to the capitalist "mark II" blueprints that Schumpeter saw as having made obsolescent the entrepreneurial functioning of capitalism "mark I," or the dynamic entrepreneur and the process of creative destruction conducted by this leading form of economic agent.

Monopolistic practices, vanishing investment opportunities, and growing hostility in the social structure of capitalism are among factors that characterized the decomposition of capitalism in his analysis of capitalism, socialism, and democracy in 1942. Against this form of capitalism he proposes as superior the Western competitive type of socialist blueprint, and he describes a transition to this form of social structure of accumulation, and the comparative efficiency of such economies. He discusses as well the human element in this type of

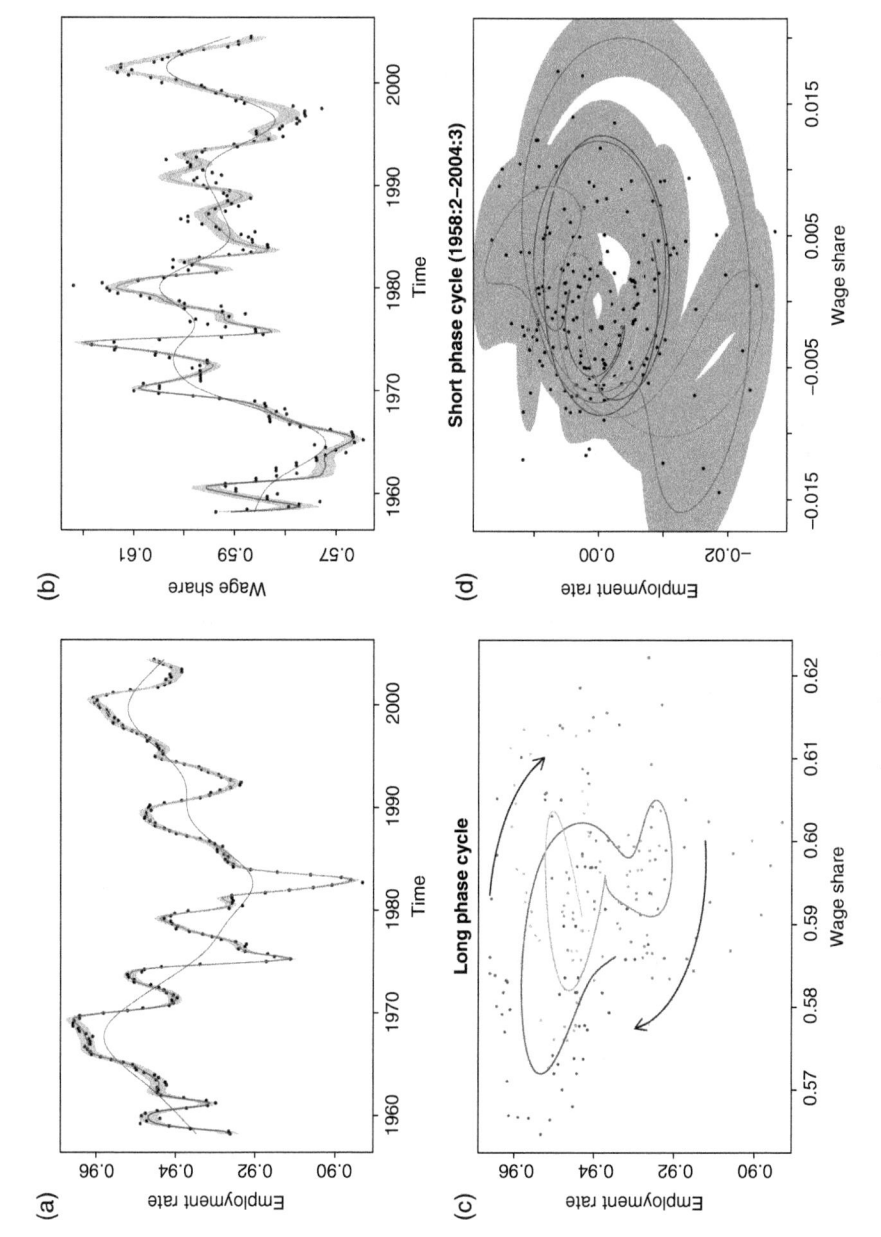

Figure 3.1 Separating the US distributive dynamics into short and long cycles.

economy—the problem of organizing work and integrating bourgeois forms of management under capitalism into this type of socialism and the incentive problems this creates for the behavior of these economic agents.

The central message of Schumpeter's (1942) work on *Capitalism, Socialism and Democracy* is that effective socialism arises from Western capitalist economies, not from the (now past) Eastern type of socialism (which he characterized as "the case of premature adoption of the principle of socialism," p. 223). Instead, socialism had to be competitively organized through large production units and their efficient—though bureaucratic—management, a form of management developed out of the principles used under capitalism in the efficient conduct of large (internationally oriented) enterprises.

Schumpeter viewed his type of socialism as culturally indeterminate, but he discussed extensively the possibility of democracy under socialism, organized as dynamic competition for political leadership under majority voting, leading to specific rules for a strong government. One of the great contributions of Schumpeter's (1942) book was not only to initiate a new concept of socialism but also to establish a new theory of democracy and its principles under a socialist accumulation structure.

However, after World War II, the discussion of how to incorporate welfare principles into the conduct of existing capitalist economies became the focus of interest, formulated particularly as "social market economy" by Ludwig Erhard in Germany. The rise of the welfare state was thus the central way European market economies responded to the increased influence of Eastern socialist economies on world politics and on the evolution of socialism in various parts of the world. Types of welfare states were, for example, discussed in detail in Esping-Anderson's (1990) *The Three Worlds of Welfare Capitalism*, among others.

But Kalecki (1943) had already pointed to limitations in the evolution of the welfare state and its full employment concept in his essay on the "Political Aspects of Full Employment." Deregulation principles and the fall of the welfare state indeed took place in Western market economies after the stagflationary period of the 1970s more or less intensively, with the gradual fall of the welfare state often being associated with insufficient recovery from the inflationary episodes and their resulting unemployment after World War II.

Labor market deregulation theories and policy proposals have, meanwhile, raised questions about the social consequences of such policies when they are implemented as "cold turkey" strategies, as is often suggested by neoclassical mainstream economists. Social degradation, social segmentation processes, and the progressive evolution of social conflicts based on them may indeed be incompatible with the proper conduct of democracy in the Western type of economies, where labor market deregulation processes and the cutback of the welfare state have occurred to a significant degree—at least in the long run. *Workfare* has, therefore, become one of the keywords that attempts to combine efficient labor market performance with welfare state principles (see for example Vis [2007] on "States of Welfare or States of Workfare? Welfare State Restructuring in 16 Capitalist Democracies, 1985–2002").

In this chapter, however, we discuss another concept that attempts to overcome the deficiencies of the purely economically oriented process of labor-market deregulations—the concept of flexicurity capitalism (in place of the Schumpeterian concept of competitive socialism, to which it is, in fact, not related either in the literature or in the current numerous political discussions of flexicurity principles; see, for example, the report "Towards Common Principles of Flexicurity—Council Conclusions" of the Council on Employment, Social Policy, Health and Consumer Affairs of the European Union [2007]).

Discussion of the Danish flexicurity system offers a typical example of such an alternative (see for example the issue of the newsletter *Future Watch* for October 2006, "Flexicurity Denmark-Style" of the Center for Strategic and International Studies [CSIS]). However, the discussion, so far, lacks a rigorous and formal model incorporating the principles, economic structure, and dynamics of flexicurity capitalism. To build a model of the reproduction schemes of this proposed type of economy requires a presentation of its system of national accounts and the behavior of economic agents within such a system. Adjustment processes in the markets for labor and goods as well as the functioning of financial markets in such an economy also need detailed study. Analysis of this type is surely at best still in its infancy.

We intend in this chapter to contribute to such an analysis against the background of the models of capitalism we have developed in Flaschel (2008), particularly concerning Marx's general law of capitalist accumulation. In modeling our proposed economy in this way, we demonstrate that there is a variety of capitalism that not only pays respect to the United Nations' *Universal Declaration of Human Rights*—particularly article 23[4]—but that is compatible with the evolution of democracy in the long run.

By contrast, a laissez-faire capitalistic society that harms family structures to a considerable degree (through alienating work, degrading unemployment, and visual media devoid of educational content and values) is not compatible with a democratic society in the long run, because it leads to conflicts that may range from social segmentation to class conflicts, racial clashes, and other types of social unrest. We argue in this chapter that stable balanced reproduction is possible under a social regime of flexicurity capitalism that is also backed by implementation of solid educational principles concerning skill formation, equal opportunity, and citizenship education in a democratic society.

The abstract vision of the new reproduction scheme of capitalism as it is formulated in this chapter can be compared—as we already have in part—with the work of Quesnay, Marx, Schumpeter, and Keynes. It may be considered as being as radical and fundamental (but also as unfeasible) as Quesnay's design of the Tableau Économique for the French economy, an ideal system centering on the productive sector and in which all taxes were paid out of rent (by the landlords). It may be compared with Marx's reproduction schemes, in *Capital,* volume 2, for a capitalist economy of his times (which he did not consider viable under capitalism).

It may also be compared to Schumpeter's vision in his work *Capitalism, Socialism and Democracy,* in which he claimed that effective socialism would be the consequence of Western-type capitalism (as created by the Rockefellers and other industrial dynasties) and not the result of the Eastern socialism that existed in his time. Also, it may finally be compared with the social philosophy of Keynes's general theory and his discussion of the means by which the trade cycle of conventional Western capitalism might be tamed. All these aspects are reflected in the model of flexicurity capitalism that we design in this chapter.

3.3 ■ FLEXICURITY CAPITALISM: BUDGET EQUATIONS, CONSUMPTION, AND INVESTMENT

In this section we consider first some basic features of a baseline macromodel of a flexicurity economy. Next, we discuss the model's budget equations and economic behavior within those equations. We then examine the stability of balanced growth paths of such an economy and its sustainability as far as the generation of sufficient income and pension payments.

3.3.1 Full-Employment Capitalism: Ideal, Status-Quo, and Compromises

Let us start here from a definition of the concept of flexicurity as it is discussed in the European Union:

> The concept of 'flexicurity' attempts to find a balance between flexibility for employers (and employees) and security for employees. The Commission's 1997 Green Paper on 'Partnership for a new organization of work' stressed the importance of both flexibility and security to competitiveness and the modernization of work organization. The idea also features prominently in the 'adaptability pillar' of the EU employment guidelines, where 'the social partners are invited to negotiate at all appropriate levels agreements to modernize the organization of work, including flexible working arrangements, with the aim of making undertakings productive and competitive and achieving the required balance between flexibility and security.' This 'balance' is also consistently referred to in the Commission's Social Policy Agenda 2000-2005 COM (2000) 379 final, Brussels, 28 June 2000).[5]

The concept of "flexicurity" was introduced on the political level in Denmark by the social democratic prime minister Poul Nyrup Rasmussen in the 1990s,[6] and it was introduced into the academic literature by Ton Wilthagen (see Wilthagen [1998; Wilthagen & Tros, 2004] on the Dutch origins of the flexicurity model). The role of the flexicurity approach in the performance of the Danish economy is critically examined in Andersen and Svarer (2007); for further critical assessments of the proposals for and the discussion on a flexicurity economy, see also recent contributions by Funk (2008) and Viebrock and J. Clasen (2009). We stress in this context that our approach to flexicurity is an abstract and primarily macroeconomic one and that it does not address the practical difficulties of implementing flexicurity coordination and incentive principles on the microlevel in light of economic, social, and juristic considerations.

Our approach to labor-market institutions of the flexicurity type differs significantly from approaches emphasizing the basic income guarantee (BIG) and employer of last resort (ELR) in the literature, for example in Tchernova and Wray (2005), though these approaches and ours have many things in common. Our approach can be characterized as an abstract modeling of a full-employment economy comparable in spirit to the Tableau Economique of Quesnay. It, therefore, represents an ideal economy we can compare with actual developed capitalist economies. Such a comparison should then allow us to formulate compromises between the ideal and actual economies, like those of the United States or Australia, as described in Tchernova and Wray, in the first case, and in Quirk et al. (2006) with respect to job guarantee (JG) principles, in the second case. We would, however, argue here that these latter approaches are, in fact, presenting compromises without really formulating an ideal on the basis of which they can be discussed.[7]

We do just the opposite here, and our approach may, therefore, be considered complementary to the ELR and JG approaches. However, in the ideal, we do not include unskilled or low-skilled labor as a significant portion of the working population, because we believe that an ideal school system can greatly ameliorate lack of skills among that population.[8] We thus have an employer of first resort (EFR) in our model required to provide employment guarantees (not JGs) to skilled or even highly skilled persons, while the buffer stock principle of an ELR must take account of the actual situations in the labor markets of capitalist economies.

Generally, we share the view of Tchernova and Wray (2005) of the superiority of ELR procedures over BIG procedures, but we propose in addition EFR modeling of the interaction of the labor markets in the private sector and the public one. Moreover, we think that the design of the educational system, as well as the selection of elites (as we describe in section 3.10), are decisively important for a flexicurity-based social structure of capital accumulation to work properly. Nevertheless, the JG system, as proposed by Quirk et al. (2006), for example, also represents a valuable perspective for flexicurity modeling on our abstract macroeconomic level.

3.3.2 Basic Principles and Problems

The flexicurity concept—primarily discussed with respect to the Nordic economies—combines two labor-market components, which—as many economists might argue—cannot be reconciled with each other, namely, workplace flexibility in a very competitive environment and income and employment (but not job) security for workers in this economy. The problem is to find the appropriate mix of these two aspects of labor-market institutions, and thus overcome both flexibility without much security (free hiring-and-firing capitalism) and security without much flexibility (historic Eastern socialism).

The basic aspects, questions, and problems of the search for such a combination of flexibility with security (many alternative ways of solving this task are conceivable) include:

1 How much flexibility in:

   1.1 Hiring and firing and job interruptions?
   1.2 Wage and price setting, and wage differentials?
   1.3 Technical change (creative destruction) and lifelong learning?
   1.4 Coping with the forces of globalization and financialization?

2 How much security in:

   2.1 Base income payments?
   2.2 Employment protection?
   2.3 Location of workplaces (workplace mobility)?
   2.4 The gestation of atypical employment and skill preservation?

To achieve social acceptance for such a combination that would fulfill the needs of capital and the needs of labor, the following problems must also find an adequate solution:

3 Basic aspects of social cohesion in a modern democratic market economy:

   3.1 Consent-based cooperation between capital and skilled and high-skilled labor.
   3.2 Acceptance of vertical job differentiation, status differences, and the selection of elites.
   3.3 Equal opportunities in primary and secondary schools as well as differentiated skill profiles and processes of elite formation later on.
   3.4 Proper citizenship education and democratic evolution.
   3.5 Reflected and controlled institutional evolution.

In this chapter, we provide a theoretical model that reconciles aspects 1.1 and 1.2 with problems 2.1 and 2.2, though we exclude other aspects of the enumerated points. Moreover, we assume here that the societal issues in the last block are developed to such an extent that not only is the proposed model transparent to the citizens of the capitalist society considered but there is basic agreement on how the economy has to be organized and the society further developed.

3.3.3 Sectoral Accounts, Consumption, and Investment

We begin by designing as an alternative to the Goodwin growth cycle, which depends on overaccumulation (in the prosperity phase) and mass unemployment (in the stagnant phase), a model of economic growth based on a second labor market, which, through its institutional setup, guarantees full employment by its interaction with the first labor market, namely, employment in the industrial sector of the economy, which is modeled as highly flexible and competitive. This model of flexicurity capitalism extends the approach of Flaschel et al. (2008) to include a treatment of heterogeneous skills and the required skill formation processes in an advanced market economy. In its basic framework, we are considering an economy in which the workforce and all of its components are given magnitudes (the given natural rate of growth is equal to zero). We assume that the uniform rate of labor productivity in the industrial sector $\hat{z}$ is positive, and that the output-capital ratio is a given magnitude, that is, we assume Harrod-neutral technical change with respect to the industrial sector of the economy.

We first reconsider the sector comprising firms in such an economy, indexed by 1:

Firms: Production and Income Account

Uses	Resources
$\delta_k K$	$\delta_k K$
$\omega_{1a} L_{1a}^d$, $\quad L_{1a}^d = Y^p/z$, $\hat{z} = m$	$C_1 + C_2 + C_r$
$\omega_{1b} L_{1b}^d$, $\quad L_{1b}^d = Y^p/z$, $\omega_{1b} = \alpha_{1b}\omega_{1a}$	G
$\Pi \quad (= Y^f)$	$I \quad (= Y^f)$
$\delta_r R + \dot{R}$	S_1
$Y^p + S_1$	$Y^p + S_1$

This account is still a simple one. Firms use their capital stock (at full capacity utilization Y^p, as we show later) to employ the amount of highly skilled labor (in hours, indexed by A), $L_{1a}^d = Y^p/z_a$, at the real wage ω_{1a}, the law of motion of which will be determined later from a model of the wage-price interaction in the manufacturing sector. In addition, companies employ a normal (skilled) labor force (in hours, indexed by B), $L_{1b}^d = Y^p/z_b$ at the wage ω_{1b}, which is a constant fraction α_{1b} of the market wage in the highly skilled labor market. Both skilled and highly skilled workers are working overtime or undertime, depending on the size of the capital stock in comparison to the amount of skilled and highly skilled workers currently employed by firms. The rate $u_x^w = L_{1x}^d/L_{1x}^w$, $x = A, B$ is the utilization rate of the workforce L_{1x}^w in the primary labor markets, those comprising the industrial workers of the economy (all other employment originates from the work of households, funded in the second labor market by the government). We assume that there is exogenous technical progress of a Harrod-neutral type at the rate $m = \hat{z} = \dot{z}/z$ with respect to the output employment ratios of both types of workers and a given output capital ratio $y^p = Y^p/K$.

Besides the primary labor market (in the privately organized industrial sector), we have a second labor market for both skilled and highly skilled workers (one organized by government agencies and indexed by 2) and indirectly also a third labor market (where the government acts as employer of first resort, indexed by 3). This third labor market, however, operates under the same remuneration and workload conditions as the second labor market (which is the reason we do not consider the government as being an employer of last resort).

Firms produce full capacity output (augmented by company pension payments $\delta_r R$) $Y^p + \delta_r R = C_1 + C_2 + C_r + I + \delta_k K + G$, output sold to the three types of worker households—the industrial workers, who pay all taxes and government transfer out of their salaries, the workers in the public sector, and the retired households—as well as to the investing firms and to the government. The demand side of the model is formulated in such a way that this full capacity output can indeed be sold. Deducting from this output Y^p of firms their real-wage payments to skilled and highly skilled workers (and depreciation)[9], we get the profits of firms, which we assume to be fully invested into capital-stock growth $\dot{K} = I = \Pi$. We thus have classical (direct) investment habits in this model with an employer of first resort.

We have assumed a fixed-proportions technology with $y^p = Y^p/K$ the potential output-capital ratio and with $z = Y^p/L_{1x}^d$, $x = A, B$ the output-labor time ratios (which determine the employment L_{1x}^d of the workforce L_x^w of firms and which grow at a uniform given rate m).

The skilled and highly skilled household sectors are composed of two types of workers: one working in the private sector and the other in the public sector. The total number of highly skilled workers is $L_a^w = \alpha_s t_a L_o$ and that of skilled workers is $L_b^w = (1 - \alpha_s)t_b L_o$. We assume here a given population L with constant deterministic age structure $L = tL_o$, where T is the given lifetime of an individual household and where L_o denotes the number of people of a certain age. This number is assumed as constant for all ages between 0 and T.[10] Moreover, we assume here that the work life of skilled workers is t_b years and that of highly skilled ones $t_a (< t_b)$ years. Finally, we assume that there is a given ratio α_s of students[11] having just finished their (comprehensive and all day) schooling years who are (by exit or entry exams) qualified to enter higher education (leading to degrees in highly skilled areas at universities and other tertiary educational institutions). Given the constant age structure within the stationary population we thus have a workforce $L_b^w = (1 - \alpha_s) t_b L_o$ of skilled workers in the economy, who start their working life directly after completing secondary schooling, while $L_a^w = \alpha_s t_a L_o$ is the number of highly skilled workers in the model. Year-in, year-out, the economy has a given amount of school students L_s, university students L_u, highly skilled workers L_a^w, skilled workers L_b^w, and retired workers L_r (contributing work according to their willingness and capability) for which it must organize education and work in the primary and secondary labor markets (including government activities as an employer of first resort).

Households 1: Highly skilled (A) and skilled (B) workers in the primary labor market

Income Account (Households A, B):

Uses	Resources
$C_1 = c_1(1 - \tau_1)(\omega_{1a} L_{1a}^d + \omega_{1b} L_{1b}^d)$	
$T = \tau_1 (\omega_{1a} L_{1a}^d + \omega_{1b} L_{1b}^d)$	
$\omega_{2a} L_{3a}^w, \ L_{3a}^w = L_a^w - (L_{1a}^w + L_{2a}^w)$	
$\omega_{2b} L_{3b}^w, \ L_{3b}^w = L_b^w - (L_{1b}^w + L_{2b}^w)$	
$\omega_{2b} L_r, \ L_r = t_r L_o$	
S_1	$\omega_{1a} L_{1a}^d + \omega_{1b} L_{1b}^d$
$Y_1^w = \omega_{1a} L_{1a}^d + \omega_{1b} L_{1b}^d$	Y_1^w

Households 2: Highly skilled (A) and skilled (B) workers in the secondary labor market

Income Account (Households A, B):

Uses	Resources
C_{2a}	$\omega_{2a}(L_{2a}^w + L_{3a}^w) = Y_{2a}^w, \ \omega_{2a} = \alpha_{2a} \omega_{1a}$
C_{2b}	$\omega_{2b}(L_{2b}^w + L_{3b}^w) = Y_{2b}^w, \ \omega_{2b} = \alpha_{2b} \omega_{1b}$
$Y_2^w = Y_{2a}^w + Y_{2b}^w$	$Y_2^w = Y_{2a}^w + Y_{2b}^w$

Both households of type 1 are taxed at the same tax rate τ_1 and consume with the same marginal propensity to consume c_1 goods of amount C_1. They pay (all) income taxes T and they pay in addition—via further transfers—all workers' incomes in the labor markets that is not coming from firms and from government tax revenues (funding thus equivalent to an unemployment insurance and, therefore, indexed by 3). Moreover, they pay the pensions of retired households ($\omega_{2b} L_r$) and accumulate their remaining income S_1 in the form of company pensions paid into a fund R that is administered by firms (with inflow S_1 [households sector] and with outflow $\delta_r R$). Wage rates are determined by wage negotiations of highly skilled workers in the industrial sector, whereas all other real wages are constant fractions of these negotiated wages and are uniform for all skilled workers in the government sector and for retired persons (who, however, receive extra company pension payments based on their accumulated contributions to work, that is, their time working in the primary sector).

The transfers $\omega_{2a}(L_a^w - (L_{1a}^w + L_{2a}^w))$ and $\omega_{2b}(L_b^w - (L_{1b}^w + L_{2b}^w))$ can be considered as solidarity payments, because workers from the primary labor markets who lose their jobs will automatically be employed in the second labor market, where full employment is guaranteed by the government (as employer of first resort). We consider this employment as skill preserving, because it can be viewed as ordinary office or handicraft work (subject to further on-the-job learning when such workers return to the first labor market).

The secondary sector of households is modeled in the simplest way available: Households employed in the secondary labor markets, that is, $L_{2a}^w + L_{3a}^w$, $L_{2b}^w + L_{3b}^w$, pay no taxes[12] and totally consume their income. This household sector thus exhibits classical saving habits, whereas households of type A may have positive or negative savings S_1 residual from their income and expenditures. We assume as the law of motion for pension funds R:

$$\dot{R} = S_1 - \delta_r R$$

where δ_r is the rate by which these funds are depreciated through company pension payments to the "officially retired" workers L_r assumed to be a constant fraction of the active workforce L^w. These worker households are considered not really inactive, because they offer work according to their remaining capabilities and their willingness to work, which can be considered an addition to the supply of work already organized by the government $L_{2a}^w + L_{3a}^w + L_{2b}^w + L_{3b}^w$, that is, the working potential of officially retired persons remains an active and valuable contribution to working hours supplied by members of the society. It is obvious that the proper allocation of work hours under the control of the government needs thorough study from microeconomic and social perspectives, which is outside the scope of our discussion here on the macroeconomics of such an economy.

The income account of retired households, shown in the following table, indicates that they receive pension payments as if they were working in the secondary skilled segment of the economy, and they receive, in addition, individual transfer income (i.e., company pensions) from the accumulated funds R in proportion to the time (and type of job) in which they were active in the first labor market as a portion of $\delta_r R$ by which the pension funds R are reduced in each period.

Income Account (Retired Households)

Uses	Resources
C_r	$\omega_{2b} L_r + \delta_r R,\ L_r = t_r L_o$
Y^r	Y^r

Finally, the government sector is also formulated in a very simple way:

The Government Income Account: Fiscal Authority/Employer of First Resort

Uses	Resources
$G = \alpha_g T$	$T = \tau_1(\omega_{1a} L_{1a}^d + \omega_{1b} L_{1b}^d)$
$\omega_{2a} L_{2a}^w = \alpha_a T$	
$\omega_{2b} L_{2b}^w = ((1-\alpha_g) - \alpha_a)T$	
$\omega_{2a} L_{3a}^w,\ L_{3a}^w = L_a^w - (L_{1a}^w + L_{2a}^w)$	$\omega_{2a} L_{3a}^w$
$\omega_{2b} L_{3b}^w,\ L_{3b}^w = L_b^w - (L_{1b}^w + L_{2b}^w)$	$\omega_{2a} L_{3a}^w$
$\omega_{2b} L_r^w$	$\omega_{2b} L_r^w$
Y^g	Y^g

The government receives income taxes, in the form of the solidarity payments (employment benefits) of workers in the primary labor market for the secondary labor market and old-age pension payments. It uses these taxes to finance government goods demand G and the surplus of taxes over these government expenditures to actively employ both skilled and highly skilled workers in the government sector. In addition it employs workers receiving unemployment benefits and "retired" persons to the extent they can still contribute to various employment activities. Therefore, the total labor force in the secondary labor market is employed through the government, in a program administered by the government in the way it does in all modern market economies.

We assume that real wages in the public sector are limited by the following conditions

$$\omega_{2a} \geq \bar{\omega}_{2a}, \quad \omega_{2b} \geq \bar{\omega}_{2b},$$

where $\bar{\omega}_{2a}, \bar{\omega}_{2b}$ are the levels of real wages where the expressions L_{3a}^w, L_{3b}^w are zero, that is, where planned employment in the private and public sectors is just sufficient to clear the labor market. This condition, therefore, provides a lower bound for public real wages that prevents supply constraints from the labor market in this flexicurity model.

In sum, workers are employed either in the primary labor market or in the government sector comprising public administration, infrastructure services, educational services, or other public services. (In addition, there is a potential labor supply L_r from retired households, which, because of the long life expectancy in modern societies, can remain effective suppliers of specific work over a considerable time.) In this way the whole workforce is always fully employed in this model of social growth (including retired persons according to their capabilities and willingness to work) and thus does not suffer human degradation resulting from unemployment. Of course, there are a variety of problems with work organized by the state, but all such problems also exist in all actual industrialized market economies in one way or another. We thus have a classical growth model in which full employment is not assumed but actively constructed, and one in which—because of the assumed expenditure structure—Say's law holds true; that is, the capital stock of firms is also always fully utilized, since all savings are additions to the pension fund, in terms of goods, and all profits are invested. For the inclusion of debt-financed investment (which is excluded here), see Flaschel et al. (2008).

3.4 DYNAMICS: STABILITY AND SUSTAINABILITY ISSUES

3.4.1 Stability of Balanced Reproduction

For expositional simplicity, we assume in this section that labor productivity z is constant; that is, we do not augment what follows with growth in labor productivity which would require the use of wage shares instead of the real wage, which represents only a simple switch in the choice of the state variable to be used. (However, a positive natural rate of growth is necessary for a steady-state solution of the model.) We return to a consideration of technical change in the section on Schumpeterian creative destruction.

As in Flaschel et al. (2008), we assume in this model type a real-wage PC, relating the growth rate of real wages to the current state of the first labor market, specifically the utilization rate of the highly skilled workforce of firms.[13] The real wage has a negative influence on its rate of growth, representing the Blanchard and Katz (1999) real-wage error-correction term, and a second influence comes from the utilization rate of the highly skilled workforce employed by firms, which simply indicates that real-wage dynamics depends positively on the utilization rate of highly skilled workers of firms in its deviation from a normal utilization rate. We stress again that all other types of work exhibit fixed-wage differentials with respect to the highly skilled workers of the primary labor market. This allows us to consider only their real wage in the dynamical study that follows, rather than a full array of real-wage dynamics, represented by growth laws for $0 < \omega_{2b} < \omega_{2a} < \omega_{1b} < \omega_{1a}$.

The growth rate of the highly skilled workforce of firms (the recruitment of new highly skilled workers), $\hat{L}_{1a}^w$, also depends positively on the rate of capacity utilization $u_w = l^d/l_1^w$, more precisely on the previously shown utilization gap, as suggested by Okun's law, and thus also negatively on its own level. Moreover, because one state variable of the model l_{1a}^w, the workforce of the type employed in industry, is defined per unit of capital, the rate of profit has a negative effect on the growth rate of this state variable (through the investment behavior of firms), and there is a positive effect of real wages of highly skilled workers in the law of motion of l_{1a}^w. Therefore, we derive a law of motion for real wages ω_{1a} and for the workforce l_{1a}^w employed by firms per unit of capital equipment.

Our modest assumptions imply that the preceding two laws of motion of the economy indeed exhibit a unique interior steady-state position, where there is balanced growth of all levels of magnitude.

The two-dimensional dynamics we consider allow for the application of the Liapunov function H shown in figure 3.2 and used in the stability proof of appendix 1. This function describes by its graph a three-dimensional sink with the steady state of the economy as its lowest point, obtained through appropriate integration of the two laws of motion of the flexicurity economy. For the first

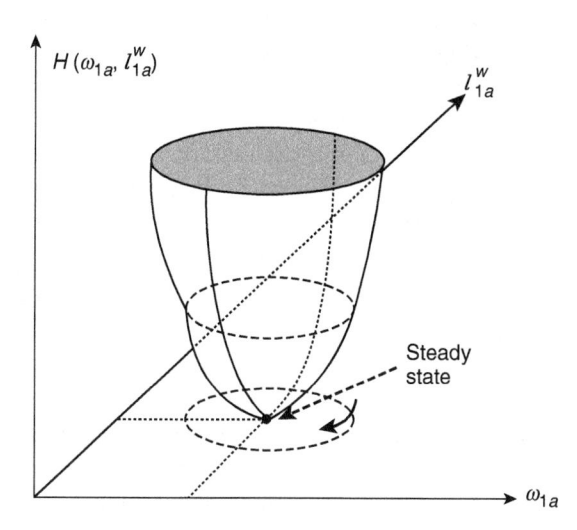

Figure 3.2 A Liapunov sink where the orbits of the dynamics lose height and are thus moving inside toward the steady state.

derivative of this Liapunov function along the trajectories of this dynamical system, we can show that it must be negative, that is, the movement along the trajectories is accompanied by a loss of height of the Liapunov function H depicted in figure 3.2. In other words, the trajectories must be moving inside with respect to the level curves of the shown sink (the dashed closed orbits in figure 3.2). This proves that there holds (see appendix 1 for details):

Proposition 1

> The interior steady state of the dynamics is a global sink of the function H, defined on the positive orthant of the phase space, and is attracting in this domain, since the function H is strictly decreasing along the trajectories of the dynamics in the positive orthant of the phase space, that is, the economic part of this phase space.

We can even show that these convergent dynamics of income distribution and growth become monotonically convergent if the speed of adjustment of the workforce of firms becomes sufficiently large, that is, if the process of hiring and firing in the industrial part of the economy is sufficiently flexible (see Flaschel et al. [2008] for details). The stability results depend in particular on the negative feedback between labor intensity and its rate of growth as implied by the conventional type of Okun's law here assumed to govern the recruitment policy of firms. The obtained stability results, however, do not imply that the economy is really a prosperous one, characterized by steady-state levels of the real wage and pension payments that can be considered adequate for such a society. We focus on this topic in the next subsection.

3.4.2 Sustainability of Balanced Reproduction

There is one further law of motion in the background of the model that needs to be considered in order to provide a complete statement of the model's *economic sustainability*. This law of motion describes the evolution of the company pension fund per unit of the capital stock $\eta = \frac{R}{K}$, and it is obtained from the equation that relates growth of these funds to the savings of households occupied in the primary labor market (minus current pension payments to the retired). This equation requires use of many components of the accounting structure of the economy and leads to a lengthy expression for a single law of motion for the variable η. For this law of motion, see appendix 2:

Proposition 2

> The steady state of the law of motion for the state variable η is a global attractor. The economy is, therefore, also converging to a steady state ratio of company pension funds per unit of capital, which is higher the higher the capital intensity of the economy.

The important issue here is whether this state level of pension funds R per unit of capital K is sufficiently large to allow, for example, a ratio of company pension payments to base pension payments of 1 (100 percent). In this situation, the economy would be endowed with enough capital and would exhibit a sufficiently high level of labor productivity that workers who have spent part of their worktime in the first labor market are rewarded not only by higher real wages, but also by higher pension payments when they retire. Such incentives are necessary in such an economy so that workers want to work in the private sector for part of their life (probably in the first part) and do not settle for just being employed by the employer of first resort (EFR). In this case, the EFR principle could, in fact, not work properly, but would instead give rise to conditions an employer of last resort has to cope with.

The steady-state ratio of η is sufficiently positive if the ratio between retired workers and workers in the first labor market is sufficiently small, that is, there are enough workers engaged in work in the industrial sector of the economy. A closer analysis here reveals that we need a condition that limits the ratio $L_r/L = t_r L_o/L = t_r/t$, mentioned earlier, in combination with conditions that limit (also earlier) real wages $\omega_{2a}^o \geq \bar{\omega}_{2a}$, $\omega_{2b}^o \geq \bar{\omega}_{2b}$ paid in the government sector in order to get a sufficiently positive ratio η in the steady state (an η−value that is sufficiently high).

The establishment of a desired ratio between company pension payments and base pension payments, therefore, requires (besides a viable ratio t_r concerning the age structure of the economy) the choice of appropriate real wages in the public sector, which can be obtained if labor productivity in the first labor market is sufficiently high (see Flaschel [2009, chapter 10] for details).

Stability and sustainability are important economic requirements for the functioning of a flexicurity society, but in this model still work in an environment that is not subject to Keynesian demand rationing in the market for goods. In a setup with Keynesian demand problems and the resulting fluctuations in economic activity, the institutional structures of a flexicurity society have to cope with significantly more difficult labor market problems than are so far present in this model (see Flaschel et al. [2008] for the details of such a Keynesian business cycle scenario). Therefore, our brief informal discussion of the stability and sustainability of our flexicurity approach shows that there are conditions under which the structure erected in subsection 2.2 can be considered a workable framework for flexicurity growth.

The obtained sustainability results are important foundations for social cohesion as well as social acceptance of the flexicurity system by the society's citizens. They must, however, be supplemented by an educational system that supports the understanding of, as well as participation in the new social structure of accumulation provided by the flexicurity idea. We consider this topic in detail in section 3.6.

In the next section we augment the flexicurity model with the possibility of credit financed investment, a financial mechanism considered central in Schumpeter's understanding of the dynamics of capitalism and in the process of creative destruction. First, however, we will formulate this additional feature in purely real terms (where no Keynesian demand problem can arise, because the validity of Say's Law is still ensured). We add Keynesian goods-demand restrictions to the model in section 3.7 as one of the important challenges an employer of first resort has to cope with. The next section is still a fairly unproblematic extension of the supply-side dynamics so far considered.

3.5 ■ PENSION FUNDS AND CREDIT

In this section we consider implications of using existing pension funds for real capital formation (instead of their remaining idle except for being used for company pension payments of amount $\delta_r R$ at each moment). For this productive use of part of the existing pension fund R, we assume a constant interest rate r applied to the debt level D accumulated by firms in the private sector.

In order to simplify our presentation, we assume that tertiary education is provided to all members of the workforce (during their schooling). The generalization to two types of workers in the industrial as well as the government sector is straightforward, but makes presentation of the model more complex (since we have to distinguish between workers of type A and B and their income and consumption patterns).

Accounting Relationships

Pension funds here act as quasi commercial banks that give credit to firms from their funds and thus allow firms in good times to invest far more than their retained earnings, that is, profits net of interest payments on loans.

Firms: Production and Income Account

Uses	Resources
$\delta_k K$	$\delta_k K$
$\omega_1 L_1^d = \omega_1 Y^p/z$	$C_1 + C_2 + C_r$
rD	$\tilde{G}$
Π	$I = (i_\rho(\rho - \rho_o) - i_d(d - d_o) + \bar{a})K$
Y^p	Y^p

The behavior and financing of gross investment is shown in the next account.

Investment and Credit

Uses	Resources
$\delta_k K$	$\delta_k K$
$I = (i_\rho(\rho - \rho_0) - i_d(d - d_0) + \bar{a})K$	Π
	$\dot{D} = I - \Pi$
I^g	I^g

We assume as investment behavior of firms the functional relationship:

$$I/K = i_\rho(\rho - \rho_0) - i_d(d - d_0) + \bar{a}$$

In this investment schedule, investment plans depend positively on the deviation of the profit rate from its steady-state level and negatively on the deviation of the debt-to-capital ratio from its steady-state value. The exogenous trend term in investment is $\bar{a}$, and we again assume that it represents the influence of investing firms' "animal spirits" on their investment activities.

Firms' Net Worth

Assets	Liabilities
K	D
	Real Net Worth
K	K

In the management of pension funds, we assume that a portion of them, sR, is held as minimum reserves and that a larger portion of them has been given as credit D to firms. The remaining amount is idle reserves D^s, not yet allocated to any interest-bearing activity.

Pension Funds and Credit (stocks)

Assets	Liabilities
R	sR
	D
	X excess reserves
R	R

Pension funds receive the savings of households of type 1 (the other households do not save) as well as the interest payments of firms. They allocate this funding into required reserve increases, payments to pensioners, and new credit demands of firms, and the rest as an addition or subtraction to their idle reserves.

Pension Funds and Credit (flows)

Resources	Uses
S_1	$\delta_r R + rD$
rD	$s\dot{R}$
	$\dot{D}(= I - \Pi)$
	$\dot{R}$
$S_1 + rD$	$S_1 + rD$

This representation of the flows of funds in the pension-funds system implies the following relationship for the time derivative of accumulated funds R

$$\dot{R} = S_1 - \delta_r R - (I - \Pi) = S_1 + \Pi - \delta_r R - I$$

that is, it is given by the excess of savings of households of type 1 over current company pension-funds payments to retired households and the new credit that is given to firms to finance the excess of investment over retained profits. We note that any excess of goods demand over goods supply is served from pension funds through new debt of firms, whereas insufficient goods demand is accompanied by the repayment of debt by firms using their excess supply of goods.

Households 1 and 2 (primary and secondary labor markets)—Income Account (Households 1)

Uses	Resources
$C_1 = c_{h1}(1 - \tau_h)Y_1^w$	
$\omega_2 L_{2h}^w = c_{h2}(1 - \tau_h)Y_1^w$	
$T = \tau_h Y_1^w$	
$\omega_2(L - (L_1^w + L_{2h}^w + L_{2g}^w))$	
$\omega_2 L^r$	
S_1	$\omega_1 L_1^d$
Y_1^w	Y_1^w

Households in the first labor market consume with a constant marginal propensity out of income after primary taxes, and they employ household services in constant proportions to consumption habits. They pay the wages of workers in the second labor market not employed by firms, along with government contributions, as a quasi unemployment benefit insurance (a generational solidarity contribution), and they pay the common base rent of all pensioners (as an intergenerational contribution). The remainder represents their contribution to the pension scheme of the economy, from which they will receive $\delta_r R + rD$ when retired. We consider this a possible scheme of funding excess employment and pensioners, but not necessarily the only one.

Income Account Households 2

Uses	Resources
C_2	$\omega_2 L_2^w$
Y_2^w	Y_2^w

Income Account (Retired Households)

Uses	Resources
C_r	$\omega_2 L^r + \delta_r R + rD$
Y^r	Y^r

The Government: Income Account—Fiscal Authority/Employer of First Resort

Uses	Resources
$G = \alpha_g \tau_h Y_1^w$	$T = \tau_h Y_1^w$
$\omega_2 L_{2g}^w = (1-\alpha_g)\tau_h Y_1^w$	
$\omega_2 L_x^w$	$\omega_2(L - (L_1^w + L_{2h}^w + L_{2g}^w))$
$\omega_2 L^r$	$\omega_2 L^r$
Y^g	Y^g

The government gets primary taxes and spends them on goods as well as services in the government sector (which are determined residually). It administers common base rent payments as well as payments to those not yet employed in the other sectors. This sector's workforce consists of all workers not employed by firms of households of type 1 and all pensioners still capable of working. The model, therefore, assumes not only that there is work guaranteed for all but also an obligation to work for all members in the workforce, including those who are retired but are still able and willing to work.

Investment and Credit Dynamics in Flexicurity Growth

For simplicity, we assume again that the steady-state value of the real wage is fixed at a level that implies $m = \hat{K}$ in the steady state, as we earlier assumed in discussing the stability of the basic reproduction schemes.[14] We thus determine the steady-state value of the real wage ω_1 from the law of motion for $l = L/K$, and supply it here from the outside through a given $\omega_1^o = \bar{\omega}_1$. We can ignore the fluctuations of the state variable l outside the steady state, because they do not feed back into the rest of the dynamics.[15] This determination, however, no longer provides the steady-state value of the rate of profit, because profits are now determined net of interest payments $\rho = y^p[1 - (1 + \alpha_\omega \alpha_f)\bar{\omega}_1/z] - \delta_k - rd$, where $d = D/K$ denotes the indebtedness of firms per unit of capital. We assume as the trend term in Okun's law the growth rate of the capital stock (i.e., this part of new hiring is determined by the installation of new machines or whole plants, under the assumption of fixed proportions in production). The normal level of the rate of employment of the workforce employed by firms is again set equal to 1 for simplicity.

On the basis of these assumptions we get from what we formulated in the preceding subsection (where we assumed investment to be given by $I/K = i_\rho(\rho - \rho_o) - i_d(d - d_o) + \bar{a}$):

$$\hat{l}_1^w = H(l_1^w), \quad H' < 0$$

$$\hat{\omega}_1 = G^1\left(\frac{\omega_1}{\bar{\omega}_1}\right) + G^2\left(\frac{y^p}{l_1^w} - \bar{u}_w\right), \quad G^{1'}, G^{2'} < 0$$

$$\dot{d} = [i_\rho(\rho - \rho_o) - i_d(d - d_o) + \bar{a}](1 - d) - \rho$$

$$\hat{\eta} = s_1 + \rho - (\delta_r \eta + (1 + \eta)[i_\rho(\rho - \rho_o) - i_d(d - d_o) + \bar{a}])$$

$$= (1 - c_{h1}(1 - \tau_h) - \alpha_g \tau_h)\omega_1 y^p/z - ((1 + \alpha_r)\bar{l} - (l_1^w + \alpha_f y^p/z))\alpha_\omega \omega_1$$

$$+ [y^p[1 - (1 + \alpha_\omega \alpha_f)\bar{\omega}_1/z] - \delta_k - rd]$$

$$- (\delta_r \eta + (1 + \eta)[i_\rho(\rho - \rho_o) - i_d(d - d_o) + \bar{a}])$$

The introduction of debt financing of firms thus makes the model considerably more advanced in its economic structure, but not as advanced mathematically, because of the recursive structure that characterizes the dynamical system at this level of generality. We note that there is not yet an interest rate policy rule involved in these dynamics, but the assumption of an interest rate peg: $r =$ const.

We use the following abbreviations:

$$s_1^o = (1 - c_{h1}(1 - \tau_h) - \alpha_g \tau_h)\bar{\omega}_1 y^p/z - ((1 + \alpha_r)\bar{l} - y^p/z(1 + \alpha_f))\alpha_\omega \bar{\omega}_1$$

and

$$\rho_{max} = y^p[1 - (1 + \alpha_\omega \alpha_f)\bar{\omega}_1/z] - \delta_k$$

On the basis of such expressions we then have proposition 3.

Proposition 3

The interior steady state of the considered dynamics is given by:

$$l_1^{wo} = \frac{y^p}{z}/\bar{u}_w, \quad \omega_1^o = \bar{\omega}_1, \quad \eta_o = \frac{s_1^o + \rho_o - \bar{a}}{\delta_k + \bar{a}},$$

where d_o, ρ_o have to be determined by solving the two equations

$$\rho_o = \rho_{max} - rd_o, \quad \rho_o = \bar{a}(1 - d_o)$$

which gives for the steady state values of d, ρ, η the expressions:

$$d_o = \frac{\bar{a} - \rho_{max}}{\bar{a} - r}, \quad \rho_o = \bar{a}\frac{\rho_{max} - r}{\bar{a} - r}, \quad \eta_o = \frac{s_1^o + \bar{a}\frac{\rho_{max} - r}{\bar{a} - r}}{\delta_k + \bar{a}} = \frac{s_1^o(\bar{a} - r) - \bar{a}(\bar{a} - \rho_{max})}{(\delta_k + \bar{a})(\bar{a} - r)}$$

We assume that both the numerator and the denominator of the fraction that defines d_o are positive, that is, the trend term in investment is sufficiently strong (larger than the rate of profit before interest-rate payments ρ_{max} and larger than the rate of interest r). Moreover, we also assume that $\rho_{max} > r$ holds so that all fractions shown in proposition 3 are, in fact, positive. In the case where $\bar{a} = \rho_{max} = y^p[1 - (1 + \alpha_\omega \alpha_f)\bar{\omega}_1/z] - \delta_k$ holds, then $d_o = 0$ and $\rho_o = \bar{a}$, in which case the value of η_o is the same as in the sections on investment without debt financing. Nevertheless, the dynamics around the steady state remain debt financed and are, therefore, different from the dynamics in the preceding section. Thus, we can have a "balanced budget" of firms in the steady-state while investment remains driven by $I/K = i_\rho(\rho - \rho_o) - i_d(d - d_o) + \bar{a}$ outside the steady-state position.

For the fraction of company pension funds divided by base pension payments, we now get as the relationship in the steady state

$$\alpha_c = \frac{\delta_r \eta_o + rd_o}{\alpha_\omega \alpha_r \bar{\omega}_1 \bar{l}}$$

an expression that in general does not give rise to unambiguous results concerning comparative dynamics. In the special case $d_o = 0$ we, however, can assert that this fraction depends positively on s_o^1 (also in general) and negatively on $\bar{a}, \delta_r, \bar{l}$.

The Jacobian at the interior steady state of the four-dimensional dynamics reads

$$J^o = \begin{pmatrix} - & 0 & 0 & 0 \\ ? & - & 0 & 0 \\ ? & ? & -(i_\rho + i_d)(1 - d_o) - (\bar{a} - r) & 0 \\ ? & ? & ? & -\bar{a}(1 + \delta_k) \end{pmatrix}$$

This lower triangular form of the Jacobian immediately implies that the elements on the diagonal of the matrix J^o are just equal to the four eigenvalues of this matrix, which are all real and negative. This gives proposition 4.

Proposition 4

The interior steady state of the considered dynamics is locally asymptotically stable and is characterized by a strict hierarchy in the state variables of the dynamics.

Because of the specific form of the considered laws of motion, we conjecture that the steady state is also a global attractor in the economically relevant part of the four-dimensional phase space. We then would get monotonically convergent trajectories from any starting point of this part of the phase space and thus fairly simple adjustment processes for the case in which investment is jointly financed by profits (retained earnings) and credit.

The stability of the steady state is increased (i.e., the eigenvalues of its Jacobian matrix become more negative) if the speed parameter characterizing hiring and firing is increased, if Blanchard and Katz type error correction becomes more pronounced, and if the parameters $i_\rho, i_d, \bar{a}$ in the investment function are increased.

Summing up, we can see that the adjustment processes and their stability properties remain very supportive of the working of our flexicurity model, which is generally monotonically convergent with full-capacity utilization of both capital and labor to a steady-state position with a sustainable distribution of income among firms, our three types of households, and the government. We conclude that flexicurity capitalism may be a workable alternative to current forms of capitalism. In particular, it can avoid severe social deformations and human degradation caused by the reserve-army mechanism and the mass unemployment that mechanism implies for certain stages in a long-phase distributive and welfare-state cycle, which in the United States and the United Kingdom would be more of a neoclassical cold turkey type and in Germany and in France more gradualistic in nature.[16]

However, there are two challenges with which a flexicurity economy must be capable of coping. We consider these challenges in sections 3.7 and 3.8. The first challenge concerns the possibility that effective demand problems may strain the EFR mechanism of the flexicurity system to a much larger extent than the supply-side dynamics we have studied so far. The second challenge involves Schumpeterian-type productivity shocks, which may also lead to much higher fluctuations in the employment rate of the industrial sector than we have considered until now. But before we treat these challenges, we study, in the next section, the educational foundations of flexicurity capitalism, which are of great importance and involve individual acceptance and the process of social cohesion.

3.6 ■ EDUCATION AND SCHOOLING

3.6.1 The Educational System: Basic Structure and Implications

In this section we extend the flexicurity model toward the integration of an educational sector designed to implement the objectives of such a society. We assume as in section 3.3 that there are only two types of workers—skilled ones (B) and highly skilled ones (a)—and assume again a stationary population $L = tL_o$ in an environment exhibiting exogenous Harrod-neutral technical change. The natural rate of growth found in section 3.4 is thus set equal to 0 for reasons of simplicity, labor productivity z is assumed to be growing at a constant rate, and the output-capital ratio is a given magnitude (see discussion of the firms sector in section 3.3).

The expression L_o represents the stationary number of people of age τ, $\tau = 1, \cdots, t$, with t denoting the given lifespan of each individual agent of the economy. There are $L_r = t_r L_o$ retired people in each given year, $L_s = t_s L_o$ students on the primary and secondary education levels, $L_u = \alpha_g t_u L_o$ students on the tertiary education level, $L_b = t_b L_o$ skilled workers, and $L_a = t_a L_o$ highly skilled workers (and $L_c = t_c L_o$ children in the background of the model).

The t_x-coefficients express the number of years an agent will be part of this population group.[17] Finally, we assume that the current system allows a fraction α_s of $t_s L_o$ to go to university to become highly skilled workers, whereas the remainder enters the workforce as a member of L_b^w after finishing school with a final certificate. To keep the model simple, we do not consider vocational schools, apprenticeships, or dual systems.

Before we come to a graphical representation and analysis of such a stylized educational system, figure 3.3[18] provides a brief representation of an existing example: the Finnish educational structure as described by the National Board of Education in Finland (we give a more detailed explanation of this educational structure later). Distinguishing marks of this school system are:

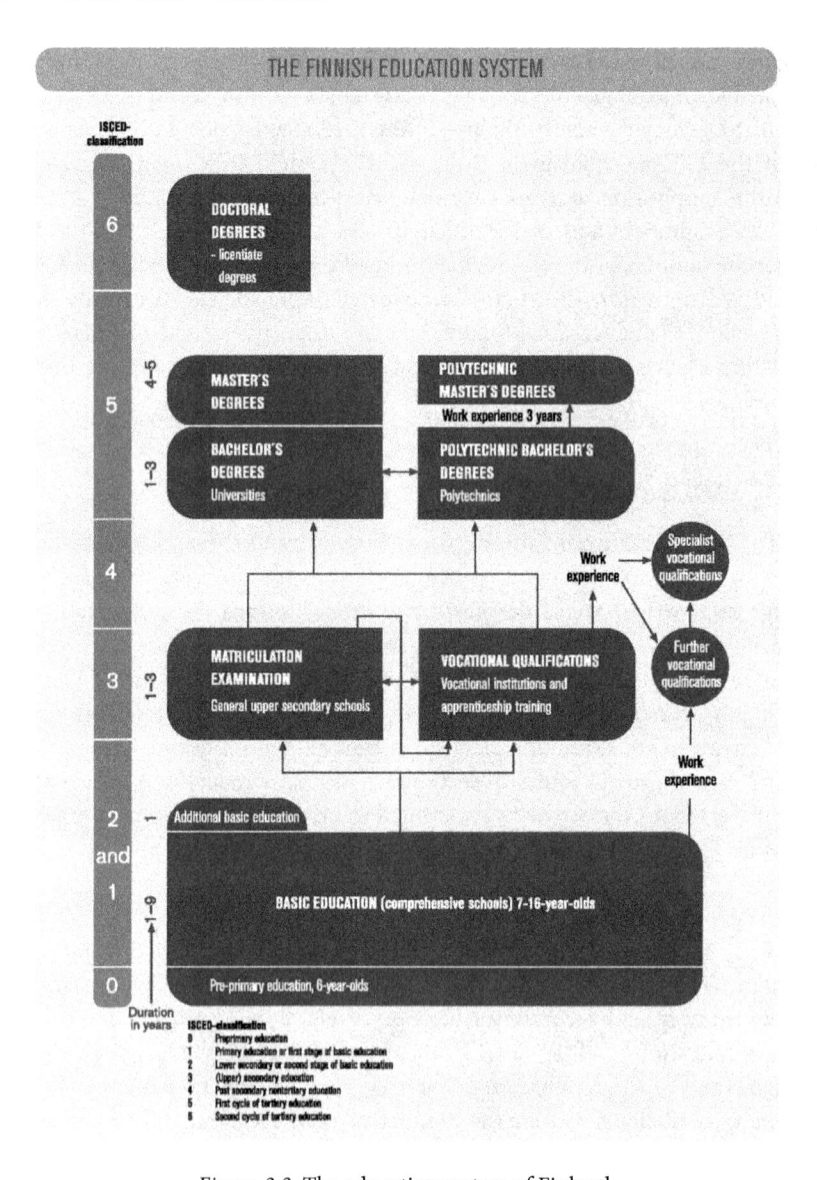

Figure 3.3 The education system of Finland.

1. A comprehensive compulsory school for all students, with no differentiation between good learners and those with learning difficulties.
2. Two ways to finish secondary school; both can lead to higher qualification (to enter universities or polytechnics).
3. Further aspects that are not shown in this figure, such as the absence of grading until the last two years of basic education.

Figure 3.4

Education and Occupations in the Flexicurity Model

Elected Executive Persons (Elites)

Occupation by firms	Occupation by firms	Public Occupation	Public Occupation	EFR Occupation
1A	*1B*	*2A*	*2B*	*3A* / *3B*

plus officially retired workers: Complementary -- Voluntary Contributions

Tertiary Education (Occupations Type A)
ACCESS BY CERTIFICATE RESULTS OR ENTRY EXAMS

Secondary Education (Occupations Type B)
ALL DAY COMPREHENSIVE SCHOOL:
TECHNICAL OR ACADEMIC ORIENTATION (AGE 15/16 TO 18/19)

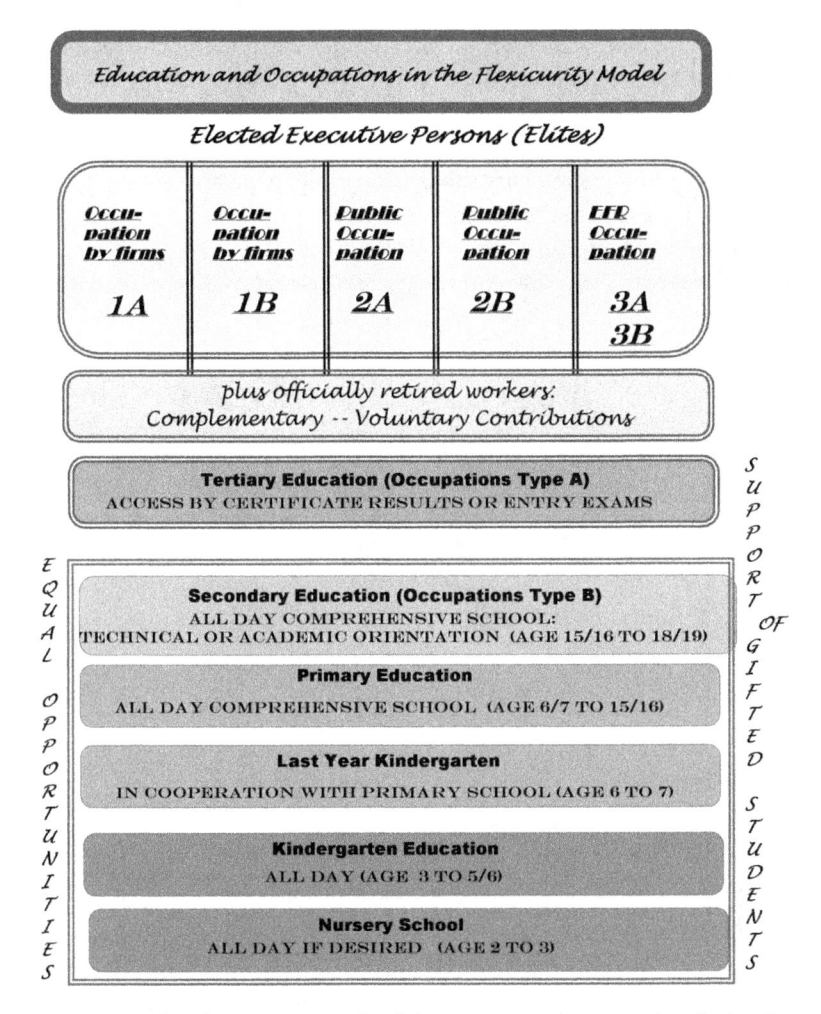

Primary Education
ALL DAY COMPREHENSIVE SCHOOL (AGE 6/7 TO 15/16)

Last Year Kindergarten
IN COOPERATION WITH PRIMARY SCHOOL (AGE 6 TO 7)

Kindergarten Education
ALL DAY (AGE 3 TO 5/6)

Nursery School
ALL DAY IF DESIRED (AGE 2 TO 3)

EQUAL OPPORTUNITIES — SUPPORT OF GIFTED STUDENTS

Figure 3.4 The education system (and the occupational structure) in flexicurity economies: stylized representation.

For our purposes, however, we use a somewhat simpler structure for an educational system underlying flexicurity capitalism, which has to be augmented now, in light of the three labor markets that can exist under flexicurity for both workers of type a and B. With respect to our model of flexicurity capitalism, we thus modify figure 3.3 even further and obtain the structure shown in figure 3.4.

Note with respect to this figure that type B workers can fit only two categories of salary group, because employment of first resort is remunerated at the same level as type B workers who are actively employed in the government sector. Type a workers, however, in this structure can be in one of three salary states, because they are paid higher wages when employed in the public sector. Note that we consider only a steady-state situation in the following discussion and thus examine the implications of balanced reproduction in this type of capitalism (shown to be an attractor of situations of unbalanced growth in section 3.4).

With respect to this stationary subdivision of the population of the economy, let us consider the case in this workforce reproduction scheme in which there is no employment of first resort needed for the workforce of type a. If $\alpha_s L_o$ is the number of students that go from primary and secondary education to tertiary education, after finishing school, we get for the parameter α_s the definitional relationship:

$$L_a^w = \alpha_s t_a L_o, \quad L_b^w = (1 - \alpha_s) t_b L_o$$

We have the following as active employment rules for type a workers:

$$L_{1a}^w = Y^p/z, \quad L_{2a}^w = \alpha_h T/\omega_{2a} = \alpha_h \tau_h \left(\frac{\omega_{1a}}{\omega_{2a}} L_{1a}^w + \frac{\omega_{1b}}{\omega_{2a}} L_{1b}^w \right)$$

The equilibrium condition $L_a^w = L_{1a}^w + L_{2a}^w$ then implies

$$\alpha_s t_a L_o = Y^p/z \left(1 + \alpha_h \tau_h \left(\frac{\omega_{1a}}{\omega_{2a}} + \frac{\omega_{1b}}{\omega_{2a}} \right) \right)$$

which in turn gives:[19]

$$\boxed{\alpha_s = \left(1 + \alpha_h \tau_h \left(\frac{\omega_{1a}}{\omega_{2a}} + \frac{\omega_{1b}}{\omega_{2a}} \right) \right) \frac{L_{1a}^d}{t_a L_o}}$$

This ratio must be applied to access to universities if the training of highly skilled workers is such that no first resort employment is necessary for them. A numerical example may help to explain this condition in more detail. Because workers employed in the industrial sector pay all taxes, we may assume the following crude estimates for the expressions that determine the equilibrium α_s:

$$\alpha_h = 1/3, \quad \tau_h = 0.5, \quad \frac{\omega_{1a}}{\omega_{2a}} = 4, \quad \frac{\omega_{1b}}{\omega_{2a}} = 2, \quad \frac{L_{1a}^d}{t_a L_o} = 0.5$$

This gives for α_s the value $\alpha_s = 0.5$, a value that coincides with what is suggested by studies of the Organization for Economic Co-operation and Development (OECD). The preceding formula for the access ratio α_s clearly shows the possibilities by which this ratio may be increased (if desirable).

Even though we divide the working population into two groups—skilled and highly skilled workers—skilled workers have finished their time in school on the same level as highly skilled ones, but with lower scores on their final examinations, which are equivalent to "Abitur" in Germany, "Baccalaureat" in France, or "A-Levels" in Great Britain. Thus, the workforce as a whole is guaranteed to be well educated and trained far above basic skills. Such high qualifications might seem impossible to attain, but examples, especially from the Scandinavian countries, show that a strict concept of "demand and support" can get such results in the school population.

3.6.2 Equal Opportunities and Lifelong Learning

In this section, we first discuss the characteristics of a suitable educational system, including preschool, but with an emphasis on school education. To attain the desired results requires strict enforcement of equal opportunities in order to eliminate any hindrances to children in participation in an education that matches their abilities and allows them to meet the schools' requirements. We also discuss the competitive way in which students in their final exams either gain or fail to gain university access.

Second, we deal with the demand for lifelong learning, assuming that part of leisure time for all people is used for keeping skills up to date, as well as accepting skill enhancement offered by their employers. A generally accepted necessity of lifelong learning allows for a continuously maintained high skill level in all sectors employing skilled or highly skilled workers, but it also holds true for all pensioners who still feel able to take an active part in the workforce.

Finally we broaden our discussion of education to the role of equal opportunities as human rights, which are strongly related to democracy. We further discuss democracy and citizenship education as well as human rights education, though here we can only outline the questions that we will discuss in more detail in future work.

The School System

To become and remain a member of the workforce demands great engagement even if employment is guaranteed. Although the industrial sector is free to hire and fire, the employer of first resort will take over the dismissed workers who are both skilled and highly skilled. All workers owe their education and welfare expenses to the taxpayers—the industrial workers in this model. Thus, the system is extremely supportive of its citizens by giving work to all, but it is also highly demanding of them by expecting full commitment by everyone, since the system's success depends on mutual give and take. This requires a high consensus within the society about the necessity of work and working conditions.

The task of education is not only to provide students in (pre)schools with the necessary skills to become adequate workers in their later professions but also to help them understand this system and integrate themselves into it.

This kind of integration is not to be misunderstood as a simple adaptation, but it requires — as does socialization—the development of an independent, mature, and responsible personality, which is part of the aim of education, as described in this chapter. A positive view toward work is a necessity in a society in which all persons are assumed to find work, but are also obliged to engage in their work, even (voluntarily) after their retirement. A negative attitude toward work in public and media discourse, where consumption and leisure time are often more favored than work, is not compatible with the demands of our model. Based on these underlying assumptions, skills are here understood in a broad sense, which transcends intellectual or technical competencies to include work attitudes, teamwork, and so on.

As we have already made clear, all students will be required to complete school on the level of "Abitur." This requirement demands a good education from the very beginning, because in its evolution, a child's brain requires a lot of attention and exercise from the very beginning of life. Such evolution may be achieved by parents taking care of their children at an early age. Often, however, parents work and may not have the time to do that. Therefore, in our ideal society "school" may start at an early stage, considering that mothers normally return to work two years after the birth of a child.

Our educational system—which we call the school system for simplicity—may begin for children at the age of two, though nursery schools may be available for younger children if parents want them. All forms of schooling are all-day institutions, though families may choose shorter schedules until the child reaches a certain age. In nursery schools children are cared for by trained personnel. Even if the children receive no formal training, they first learn social skills, which include rules of behavior in a community, such as how to share toys, how to behave during meals in an age-appropriate way, and so forth.

Other skills that are learned at this age are linguistic and communicative ones. These skills are taught in families, too, but sometimes in a (voluntary) educational setting such as a nursery school more effective support can be given through guiding the children. By the age of two, children have already learned to use materials and thus train their fine motor skills. They are also trained to use and exercise their bodies. This kind of early education demands caretakers with good university training.

This is also true for the following (also voluntary) kindergarten period, which should last for three years. Skills introduced in the nursery schools will now be honed in a more and more systematic way, though the stages of development of a child have to be kept in mind, as well as the necessity for formal and informal play. The last kindergarten year is either moved to primary schools or organized together with them, to allow for a gradual transition into school.

Following the Scandinavian model of schooling, all children will attend a general school at least until grade 8 or 9, when they are about 15 or 16 years old (see, e.g., Ministry of Education and Science of Sweden [2004]). Any earlier division into different types of school would lead to a selection before all of a child's abilities can be developed, depriving young people of the chance to evolve into the skilled person they are capable of becoming. Longer time learning together will help develop social skills.

Finally, a selection before or just as they have reached puberty would probably intensify the general problems of that age. When students have to opt for different types of secondary or high school, they can be assured that all types will lead them to a matriculation certificate but with different focuses (either more academic or more technical) and different lengths of schooling (between two and four years, depending on the preferences of the student), so that they are able to plan their secondary school time with the help of their teachers, based on their individual abilities and interests.

This school system needs to discover all abilities and interests of children; otherwise the ambitious aim of a final certificate for all cannot be reached. This means that the school education must work in a way that supports differently talented students while obeying the principle of equal opportunities for all.

In providing such a nurturing environment, it is important to eliminate social or structural hindrances, such as family income, level of education of the parents, social stratum, migration background, and so forth. In our system, these forms of disadvantage should become less prevalent when all—or at least most—parents are skilled or highly skilled persons with an adequate income. However, disadvantages, which are often connected with discrimination, may remain, such as those due to the social, regional, or political background of a family. An important task of all forms of schooling is to overcome such disadvantages by providing sufficient support.

Although this task must be fulfilled by the state and the society, the schools must find the special abilities of a child and develop them. Education thus must improve its didactic philosophy and methods, so that each child is supported in discovering and nurturing his or her special competencies, and furthermore that each child can be supported individually and pass a successful school career.

This focus on individual support with the aim of attaining a final certificate requires not only a well-equipped school in teaching staff, social workers, psychologists, librarians, medical helpers, and professionals from outside the school, such as sport trainers, artists, and so on; it also calls for a well-equipped school building with attractive rooms and other interior spaces. Special support is given to students with disabilities within integrated classes (see Report 2006). Equal opportunities are thus not just an aim of the school system but also the best way in which the ambitious aim of a final certificate for all can be reached.

In a competitive school, when only those with the best results (about 50 percent) will be allowed to go to a university, how is the concept of equal opportunity compatible with competition? Competition is part of school life and, in most cases, it is a planned part of education, for example, in sports where a winner will be declared and not all students are equally talented athletically. In schools where individual abilities are detected and supported, competition in this sense does no harm because students learn that they have different abilities, making them winners in different disciplines. The real challenge of education is to make sure that there are no obvious losers.

This intention is implemented when students are not ranked within their class but measured by their individual progress. Thus there is a winner after the 100 meter sprint, but each child learns about his or her individual successes or is supported in further improvement. All children will take part in sports even if their main abilities are not athletic. The competition after school is a different matter. There are not enough university spaces and subsequent job opportunities for all, in line with the idea that the society needs only a certain number of highly skilled persons with university degrees.

Tertiary Education, Lifelong Learning, and Equal Opportunities

This is not the place to discuss the question of whether a society and workforce can be conceived in which all persons might go to university mainly to complete their personal education, though without the society abandoning the division into skilled and highly skilled positions. The graded high school, where students attend different types of classes, either mainly academic or mainly technical, will already lead to a kind of preliminary decision between those who want to go to a university and those who will enter the skilled workforce after receiving their final certificate. It will certainly be a task of education to prepare students for such competition and the possibility of not gaining the most desired position. Schools must compensate for this situation by developing individual abilities and skills, some of which may be more valid for leisure time (e.g., playing an instrument without reaching the top level of orchestra music).

The selection for university is based on school results recorded with the final certificate, though entry exams are also an option. According to recent results by OECD, about 50 percent of students wanting to go to a university have realistic expectations (see OECD 2007). About half of the students with a final certificate can thus be expected to become highly skilled workers in our model. We will not go into the details of a university education and how students are distributed among different courses of study, but we want to conclude this discussion of the school system by stressing again the necessity of an education that allows individual development and support under the principles of equal opportunities.

Students who finish school with a final certificate and enter the workforce as well as those who do so after having finishing a university education are already well trained in organizing their learning processes, because one of the principles of teaching is to teach students how to adopt learning competencies, that is, how to organize a learning program, how to work together with others, and how to discover special skills and weak points. The aim is to lead students to an independent learning style that best fits the individual learner. Learning portfolios may be a suitable way to keep records of this learning process. We can assume that young adults will be able to continue with this procedure, as well as continue documenting it.

The European Union declared the year 1996 as the European year of lifelong learning and passed a resolution on "Lifelong Learning" in 2002 (Council 2002). The resolution emphasizes that learning starts during the preschool years and lasts until postretirement. Furthermore, the resolution refers to all kinds of learning, including the entire spectrum of formal, nonformal, and informal learning and establishes the aim of learning as not being restricted to skills and competencies that relate to later employment. Instead it regards learning as important within a personal, civic, or social perspective as well.

Although schools follow a common, general curriculum that also achieves the highest possible grade of individualization and interest, lifelong learning after high school and college is far more guided by individual interests and needs, though there will also be on-the-job training in most professions. Skills and knowledge have to be updated on a regular basis.

The idea of lifelong learning builds on the concept of equal opportunities. Personal access to knowledge and competencies is increased by the possibility of learning independent of age or position. Therefore, the educational system must offer a variety of learning procedures after schools and universities, such as adult education centers, and also access to arts, museums, and nature and its opportunities for learning. Mobility will add to lifelong learning of languages and cultures, but also of professional skills. Lifelong learning includes all forms of social learning, and it also includes the highly important subject of "political learning."

Political learning plays an important role in education, especially in a model where the state has a major role as employer and provider of social services. Political learning, which is often referred to as citizenship education, is highly relevant to a system that depends on individual skills and knowledge of its workforce but, at the same time, demands a high level of social commitment and the acceptance of different workplaces without unemployment. Furthermore, the principles of equal opportunities on which we have commented are integrated into political concepts such as human rights, again emphasizing the necessity of political learning.

Political learning will be part of both schooling and lifelong learning. Human rights education provides all the necessary instruction and skills to enable effective participation in a democratic society, especially since human rights and democracy are inseparably interconnected. Thus, democracy as the underlying state model and equal opportunities as the foundational principle for social justice are implied by the concept of human rights. Democracy education, citizenship education, and human rights education are well-established and partly overlapping forms of education that provide not only an introduction into the necessary knowledge of political structures but often preparation for different kinds of participation in democratic procedures. Additionally they intend to increase media competence to allow students as well as adult learners to understand actual political decision-making processes.

The Educational System of Finland

In Finland,[20] the basic right to education and culture is stated in the country's constitution. Public authorities must ensure equal opportunities for every resident of Finland for an education, including postcompulsory education, and to develop themselves, irrespective of their financial standing. Legislation provides for compulsory education and the right to free preprimary and basic education. Most other qualifying education is also free of charge for students, including postgraduate education at universities. The key words in Finnish educational policy are *quality, efficiency, equity*, and *internationalization*.

Education is a factor in competitiveness. The current priorities in educational development are to raise the level of education and upgrade competencies among the population and the workforce, to improve the efficiency of the educational system, to prevent exclusion among children and young people, and to expand adult learning opportunities. The government also pays special attention to enhancing the quality of education, to training and research, and to internationalization. The success of Finland in education builds on the following principles:

Equal Opportunities

The Finnish educational system offers everybody equal opportunities for education, irrespective of domicile, sex, economic situation, or linguistic and cultural background. The school network is regionally extensive, and there are no sex-specific school services. Basic education is free of charge (including instruction, school materials, school meals, health care, dental care, commuting, special-needs education, and remedial teaching).

Comprehensiveness of Education

Basic education encompasses nine years and caters to all those between seven and sixteen years of age. Schools do not select their students, but every student goes to the school in his or her own school district. Students are neither channeled to different schools nor streamed.

Competent Teachers

On all school levels, teachers are highly qualified and committed. Masters degrees are required, and teacher education includes teaching practice. The teaching profession is very popular in Finland, and, hence, universities can select the most motivated and talented applicants. Teachers work independently and enjoy full autonomy in the classroom.

Student Counseling and Special Needs Education

Individual support for the learning and welfare of pupils is well accommodated, and the national core curriculum contains guidelines for this purpose. Special-needs education is integrated into regular education as far as possible. Guidance counselors support upper-grade students in their choice of studies and choice of further education.

Encouraging Assessment and Evaluation

Student assessment and evaluation of learning outcomes are encouraging and supportive by nature. The aim is to produce information that supports schools and enables students to develop. National testing, school ranking lists, and inspection systems do not exist.

Significance of Education in Society

Finnish society strongly favors education, and the population is highly educated by international standards. Education is appreciated and there is a broad political consensus on education policy.

A Flexible System Based on Empowerment

The educational system is flexible and the administration based on the principle of centralized direction and local implementation. Direction is conducted through legislation, establishment of norms and core curricula, government planning, and provision of information. Municipalities are responsible for providing education and implementing the system. Schools and teachers, however, enjoy a large amount of autonomy.

Cooperation

Interaction and partnerships are built into all levels of activity. There is cooperation in developing education among various levels of administration, among schools, and among other social actors and schools. Educational authorities cooperate with teachers' organizations, pedagogical subject associations, and school leadership organizations. This provides strong support for development of the system.

A Student-Oriented, Active Conception of Learning

The organization of schoolwork is based on a conception of learning that focuses on students' activities and interaction with the teacher, with other students, and with the learning environment.

3.7 ■ CHALLENGE I: KEYNESIAN BUSINESS FLUCTUATIONS

So far, the economy has been purely supply driven, with the growth of capital stock driven by net profits and credit from pension funds such that Say's law has remained true; that is, aggregate demand has always been equal to potential output because of the expenditure behavior of households, the government, and firms. In this section we now briefly sketch a situation in which capacity utilization problems, as well as stability problems, may arise within the flexicurity variant of a capitalistic economy. We modify the baseline credit model of section 3.5 in a minimal way in order to obtain such results. In place of its pension funds, as well as the credits they give to firms, we now consider a situation in which firms finance their investment plans through their profits and through the issuing of corporate paper bonds. We assume these bonds to be of the fixed price variety, and we also keep the rate of interest paid on these bonds fixed for simplicity.

With this simple change, actual goods-market equilibrium departs from potential output (here reinterpreted by a normal rate of capacity utilization of potential output) and may fluctuate around the assumed normal capacity output. Therefore, we have the first real problem here on the macrolevel: the flexicurity society has to cope with the possibility of severe recessions or even depressions when aggregate demand is behaving accordingly, and also the possibility of an overheated economy. Clearly, there is now a need for economic policy, that is, fiscal, monetary, or even income distribution policy in order to avoid large swings in economic activity and thus large imbalances between the industrial and the public labor markets. This section, however, only provides the basics for such an analysis and leaves policy consideration for future research.

The amount of corporate bonds that firms are now assumed to have issued in the past is denoted by B and their price is 1 in nominal units. Firms thus have to pay rB as interest currently, and they intend to use their real profits net of interest-rate payments for investments. In addition they issue $\dot{B}^s/p$ to finance their rate of investment $I/K = i_\rho(\rho - \rho_o) - i_b(\frac{B}{pK} - (\frac{B}{pK})_o) + \bar{a}$. This rate of investment is assumed to depend positively on excess profitability compared to the steady-state rate of profit and negatively on the deviation of firms' debt from its steady-state level.

Firms: Production and Income Account

Uses	Resources
$\delta_k K$	$\delta_k K$
$\omega_1 L_1^d, L_1^d = Y/z$	$C_1 + C_2 + C_r$
	G
rB/p	$I = i_\rho(\rho - \rho_o)K - i_b\left(\frac{B}{P} - \left(\frac{B}{P}\right)_o\right) + \bar{a}K$
$\Pi(= Y^f)$	$[I = \Pi + \dot{B}^s/p]$
Y	Y

Type-1 households behave as we have assumed so far, but now attempt to channel their real savings into corporate bond holdings as shown below. They will be able to exactly satisfy their demand for new bonds when there is goods-market equilibrium prevailing ($I = S$), because only firms and these households act on this market, whereas all other economic units just spend what they get (with balanced transfer payments organized by the government). The real return from savings in corporate bonds rB/p, at each moment, will be added below to the base rent payments of retired households, who receive these benefits in proportion to the bonds they have allocated during their work life in the private sector of the economy. The bonds allocated in this way thus only generate a return when their holders are retired and then—as in the pension fund scheme of section 3.3—at the then prevailing market rate of interest (which is still a given rate here). The pension fund model is, therefore, reformulated only in terms of nominal paper holdings (coupons) and thus no longer based on the storage of physical products. Hence, corporate bonds are not only of a fixed-price variety; they also provide their return only after retirement. This is shown in the income account of retired persons. The income account of the workers in the second labor market is unchanged and, therefore, not shown again.

Households 1 (primary labor market) and Retired Households: Income Account (Households 1)

Uses	Resources
$C_1 = c_{h1}(1 - \tau_h)\omega_1 L_1^d$	
$\omega_2 L_{2h}^w = c_{h2}(1 - \tau_h)\omega_1 L_1^d$	
$T = \tau_h \omega_1 L_1^d$	
$\omega_2(L - (L_1^w + L_{2h}^w + L_{2g}^w))$	
$\omega_2 L^r, L^r = \alpha_r L$	
$S_1[= \dot{B}^d/p]$	$\omega_1 L_1^d$
$Y_1^w = \omega_1 L_1^d$	$Y_1^w = \omega_1 L_1^d$

Income Account (Retired Households)

Uses	Resources
C_r	$\omega_2 L^r + rB/p$, $L^r = \alpha_r L$
Y^r	Y^r

The government income account (not shown) is also kept unchanged, and it is balanced in the way used in the preceding models. The modifications to the model in section 3.3 are, therefore, minimal, largely involving a different type of investment behavior of firms and a new way of organization of the company pension funds. However, the assumed flexicurity system becomes now of real importance, because the dynamics implied by the model will produce demand-determined (Keynesian) business-cycle fluctuations, whereas firms did not face capacity under- or overutilization problems in the earlier models. Keynesian IS-equilibrium determination has to be considered now and gives rise to the following equation for the effective output per unit of capital (characterizing goods market equilibrium):[21]

$$Y/K = y = C_1/K + C_2/K + C_r/K + \delta_k + I/K + G/K$$

$$= c_h(1-\tau_h)\omega_1\frac{y}{z} + \alpha_\omega\omega_1(\bar{l}-l_1^w) + \alpha_\omega\alpha_r\omega_1\bar{l} + rb$$

$$+ \delta_k + i_\rho(\rho-\rho_o) - i_b(b-b_o) + \bar{a} + \alpha_g\tau_h\omega_1 y/z$$

$$\rho = y - (1+\alpha_f\alpha_\omega)\omega_1 y/z - \delta_k - rb, \qquad b = B/(pK)$$

which taken together give:

$$y = \frac{\alpha_\omega\omega_1(\bar{l}-l_1^w) + \alpha_\omega\alpha_r\omega_1\bar{l} + (rb+\delta_k)(1-i_\rho) - i_\rho\rho_o - i_b(b-b_o) + \bar{a}}{1 - [c_h(1-\tau_h) + \alpha_g\tau_h - i_\rho(1+\alpha_f\alpha_\omega)]\omega_1/z - i_\rho}$$

$$= y(l_1^w, \omega_1, b, \dots)$$

Note that we have modified the investment function in this section to $i(\cdot) = i_\rho(\rho-\rho_o) - i_b(b-b_o) + \bar{a}$. Note also that we have assumed that natural growth n is always adjusted to the growth rate of the capital stock $\hat{K}$ (through migration). We also assume that the denominator in the foregoing fraction is positive, with the important result that output per unit of capital is no longer equal to its potential value, but now depends on the marginal propensity to spend as well as on other parameters of the model. This is due to the new situation in which firms use corporate bonds to finance their excess investment (exceeding their profits) or buy back such bonds in the opposite case, and type-1 households buy such bonds from their savings (and thus do not buy goods in this amount anymore to increase the pension fund). Thus we have independent real investment and real savings decisions, which, when coordinated with the achievement of goods market equilibrium as shown earlier, lead to a supply of new corporate bonds that is exactly equal to the demand for such bonds at this level of output and income. This follows from the fact that only firms and type 1 households are saving, and all other budgets are balanced. Type-1 households thus must accept the amount of the fixed-price bonds offered by firms and thereby accumulate these bonds (whose interest-rate payments are paid out to retired people according to the percentage they have achieved at retirement).

Assuming the accumulation of corporate bonds in the place of real commodities and an investment function that is independent from these savings conditions thus implies that the economy is subject to Keynesian demand rationing processes (at least close to its steady state). We derive these demand problems on the assumption of IS-equilibrium and thus represent them in static terms instead of a dynamic multiplier approach that can also be augmented further by means of Metzlerian inventory adjustment processes. We stress once again that the possibility of full capacity output is prevented through the Keynesian type of underconsumption assumed as characterizing the type 1 household sector and the fact that there is only one income level that allows savings in bonds to become equal to bond-financed investment in this simple credit market. This credit market characterizes this modification of the flexicurity model, because of the existing effective demand schedule $y(l_1^w, \omega_1, b, \ldots)$. We assume that the parameters are chosen such that the partial derivatives of the effective demand function y are:

$$y_{l_1^w}(l_1^w, \omega_1, b, \ldots) < 0, \quad y_{\omega_1}(l_1^w, \omega_1, b, \ldots) > 0, \quad y_b(l_1^w, \omega_1, b, \ldots) < 0$$

This is fulfilled, for example, if the expression in the denominator of the effective demand function is negative and if the parameter i_b is chosen sufficiently large. Effective demand is then wage led, and flexible wages are, therefore, dangerous for this economy.

The interacting laws of motion now are:

$$\hat{l}_1^w = H\left(\frac{y}{zl_1^w} - \bar{u}_w\right), \quad H' > 0$$

$$\hat{\omega}_1 = G^1\left(\frac{\omega_1}{\bar{\omega}_1}\right) + G^2\left(\frac{y}{l_1^w} - \bar{u}_w\right), \quad G^{1'}, G^{2'} < 0$$

$$\dot{b} = (1-b)(i_\rho(\rho - \rho_o) - i_b(b - b_o) + \bar{a}) - \rho - \hat{p}b$$

$$\hat{p} = \kappa\left[\beta_{py}\left(\frac{y}{y^p} - \bar{u}_c\right) + \beta_{p\omega}\ln\left(\frac{\omega_1}{\omega_1^o}\right) + \kappa_p\left(\beta_{wu}\left(\frac{y}{zl_1^w} - 1\right) - \beta_{w\omega}\ln\left(\frac{\omega_1}{\omega_1^o}\right)\right)\right] + \pi^c$$

where $\hat{p}$ has to be inserted into the other equations (where necessary) in order to arrive at an autonomous system of four ordinary differential equations.

This particular formulation of the debt financing of firms thus makes the model considerably more advanced from the mathematical as well as the economic point of view. We note that these dynamics do not yet involve an interest rate policy rule, but that the assumption of an interest rate peg is maintained: $r = \text{const.}$

Because the model is formulated partly in nominal terms, we need to consider the price inflation rate explicitly. We do this on the basis of a wage-price spiral mechanism as it has been formulated in Flaschel et al. (2008) with respect to the industrial sector of the economy:

$$\hat{w} = \beta_{wu}\left(\frac{y}{zl_1^w} - \bar{u}_w\right) - \beta_{w\omega}\ln\left(\frac{\omega}{\omega^o}\right) + \kappa_w \hat{p} + (1-\kappa_w)\pi^c$$

$$\hat{p} = \beta_{py}\left(\frac{y}{y^p} - \bar{u}_c\right) + \beta_{p\omega}\ln\left(\frac{\omega}{\omega^o}\right) + \kappa_p \hat{w} + (1-\kappa_p)\pi^c$$

In these equations, $\hat{w}, \hat{p}$ denote the growth rates of nominal wages w and the price level p (their inflation rates) and π^c a medium-term inflation-climate expression, which, however, is of no relevance in the following discussion because of our neglect of real-interest-rate effects on the demand side of the model (and thus is set equal to zero). We denote again by $\bar{u}_w$ the normal ratio of utilization of the workforce within firms and now by $\bar{u}_c$ the corresponding utilization of the capital stock. Deviations from these normal ratios measure the demand pressure on the labor market and the goods market respectively. In the wage PC, as well as in the price PC, we also employ a real-wage error-correction term $\ln(\omega/\omega_0)$ as in Blanchard and Katz (1999) (see Flaschel and Krolzig [2006] for details) and as cost pressure term a weighted average of short-term (perfectly anticipated) wage of price inflation $\hat{w}, \hat{p}$, respectively and the medium-term inflation climate π^c in which the economy is operating.

The preceding structural equations of a wage-price spiral read in reduced form as follows:

$$\hat{w} = \kappa\left[\beta_{wu}\left(\frac{y}{zl_1^w} - \bar{u}_w\right) - \beta_{w\omega}\ln\left(\frac{\omega_1}{\omega_1^o}\right) + \kappa_w\left(\beta_{py}\left(\frac{y}{y^p} - \bar{u}_c\right) + \beta_{p\omega}\ln\left(\frac{\omega_1}{\omega_1^o}\right)\right)\right] + \pi^c$$

$$\hat{p} = \kappa\left[\beta_{py}\left(\frac{y}{y^p} - \bar{u}_c\right) + \beta_{p\omega}\ln\left(\frac{\omega_1}{\omega_1^o}\right) + \kappa_p\left(\beta_{wu}\left(\frac{y}{zl_1^w} - \bar{u}_w\right) - \beta_{w\omega}\ln\left(\frac{\omega_1}{\omega_1^o}\right)\right)\right] + \pi^c$$

which give the previous equations for the price inflation rate and also the real dynamics when the price equation is deducted from the wage equation.

Note that our model only considers the utilization rate of insiders (within firms) in the wage dynamics, since the markets for labor are always cleared in flexicurity capitalism. We thus now use the output-capital ratio $y = Y/K$ to measure the output gap in the price inflation PC and the deviation of the real wage $\omega = w/p$ from the steady-state real wage ω^o as the error-correction expression, also in the price PC. Cost pressure in this price PC is formulated as a weighted average of short-term (perfectly anticipated) wage inflation and our concept of an inflationary climate π^c (see Flaschel and Krolzig [2006] for details). In this price PC we have three elements of cost pressure interacting with one another, a medium-term element (the inflationary climate) and two short-term elements, basically the level of real unit-wage labor costs—a Blanchard and Katz (1999) error-correction term—and the current rate of wage inflation, which, taken by itself, would represent a constant markup pricing rule. This basic rule is, however, modified by these other cost-pressure terms and in particular also made dependent on the state of the business cycle by way of the demand pressure term $y/y^p - \bar{u}_c$ in the market for goods.

The laws of motion describe again (in this order) our formulation of Okun's law, the real wage dynamics as it applies in a Keynesian environment (see section 3.3), the debt dynamics of firms, and a simple regressive-expectations scheme concerning the inflationary climate surrounding the wage-price spiral where it is assumed (and, in fact, is also taking place) that inflation converges back to a constant price level. There is, therefore, not yet an inflation accelerator present in the formulation of the dynamics of the four state variables of the model. Nevertheless, price-level inflation is now explicitly accounted for, indeed for the first time in this chapter.

Steady-state and stability analysis is no longer straightforward in this Keynesian variant of flexicurity capitalism. With respect to steady-state positions, we have to solve now a simultaneous equation system in the variables ω_1, ρ, b. Because of the structure of the effective demand function, we no longer have zero entries in the Jacobian of the dynamics at the steady state of the first three state variables (the last law of motion is a completely trivial one). We can identify as an economic mechanism a real-wage channel as in the Kaleckian dynamics of Flaschel et al. (2008) (working here in a wage-led environment by assumption). Furthermore, there is the dynamic of the debt-to-capital ratio of firms. These feedback channels can be tamed through appropriate assumptions, but even then work in an environment that gives no straightforward economically plausible stability assertions, due to the strong interactions present in the dynamics. Therefore, we leave stability analysis for future research.

We conclude that effective demand problems can make flexicurity capitalism significantly more difficult to analyze (and to handle), and they demand a treatment of much more depth—including inflation and interest-rate-policy rules, government deficits, and fiscal-policy rules, and so on—than was possible in this short section. Moreover, we can look for credit relationships that avoid the more complex dynamics described in this section.

3.8 ■ CHALLENGE II: SCHUMPETERIAN PROCESSES OF "CREATIVE DESTRUCTION"

After considering the macroeconomic problems a flexicurity economy might face, we now briefly discuss the microeconomic problems it is intended to solve, namely, the socially acceptable handling of exit and entry problems with respect to the real capital stock as well as the labor supply. The most remarkable feature of existing capitalism is definitely its property to revolutionize the technological foundations and the product frame of market economies. The first in-depth treatment of this fundamental tendency was Marx's (1954) *Capital,* volume 1, based on what he called the law of value. Schumpeter knew Marx's work very well but developed his own vision of the microdynamics of capitalism, which, in lieu of some questionable monotonic tendencies asserted by Marx, with the exception of the secular law of increasing labor productivity, led him to the consideration of long waves in his work on business cycles (see Schumpeter [1939]). Marx, of course, had not lived long enough to become aware of long-phase cyclical changes in the economic and social structure of capitalist economies, but he was, nevertheless, able, on the basis of his value theory, to discuss the secular tendencies of the concentration and centralization of capital, even on a global scale.

Schumpeter's (1912) *Theory of Economic Development* started from quite a different theoretical perspective compared to the classical theory of labor values and production prices, namely, from the Walrasian concept of a perfectly competitive market economy, which, for him, described the circular flow of economic life in given circumstances. To this he then added economic development and credit, and most fundamentally, the dynamic character of the entrepreneur who is initiating spontaneous and discontinuous changes that forever alter and displace the previously existing equilibrium state.

> These spontaneous and discontinuous changes in the channel of the circular flow and these disturbances in the center of equilibrium appear in the sphere of industrial and commercial life, not in the sphere of the wants of the consumer of final products.
>
> Schumpeter (1912, p. 65)

Compared to today's Walrasian theory of general equilibrium in which production is but an appendix to consumption theory, this is a totally different perspective, and may be one reason why Schumpeter (1942) later used the theory of monopolistic competition as the starting point for his analysis of the dynamics of capitalism. Defining development as driven by the spontaneous action of the dynamic entrepreneur, Schumpeter (1912, p. 66) then classifies the possibilities for such actions as follows:

> Development in our sense is then defined by the carrying out of new combinations. This concept covers the following five cases: (1) The introduction of a new good— that is one with which consumers are not yet familiar—or of a new quality of a good.

(2) The introduction of a new method of production, that is one not yet tested by experience in the branch of manufacture concerned, which need by no means be founded upon a discovery scientifically new, and can also exist in a new way of handling a commodity commercially. (3) The opening of a new market, that is a market into which the particular branch of manufacture of the country in question has not previously entered, whether or not this market has existed before. (4) The conquest of a new source of supply of raw materials or half-manufactured goods, again irrespective of whether this source already exists or whether it has first to be created. (5) The carrying out of the new organization of any industry, like the creation of a monopoly position (for example through trustification) or the breaking up of a monopoly position.

To realize the various activities, the role of credit plays is essential, because it allows such projects to start with a degree of innovation, often created by new ideas of new entrants in certain markets. Credit helps to redirect labor and capital from old combinations to new ones through process or product innovation, and the other kinds discussed by Schumpeter. Entrepreneurs, therefore, do not just use idle resources of the economy but redirect employed resources toward new projects and the extra profits they can generate in comparison to their competitors. A typical example is the "railroadization" discussed at length in Schumpeter (1939).

The innovative character of the Schumpeterian entrepreneurs thus alters the way the economy has been functioning so far, and the larger the scale on which such entrepreneurs enter the scene, the more rapidly it does so. Of course, there are subsequent processes for the diffusion of the newly created technology or products, which, over time, reduce extra profits and become routine economic activity. Yet processes of innovation and diffusion may cluster and thus lead to the long-phase evolution of social structures of accumulation, described historically in Schumpeter (1939) as three Kondratieff waves (superimposed by shorter cycles).

We do not intend here to discuss in detail Schumpeter's analysis of the forces that drive the evolution of capitalist economies. For more on that analysis, see Swedberg (1991) on Schumpeter's work and biography and the voluminous edition on Schumpeter and neo-Schumpeterian economics edited by Hanusch and Pyka (2007a). Here we go from Schumpeter's analysis of capitalism to his analysis of competitive socialism and the implications it may have for the model of flexicurity capitalism we discuss in this chapter.

Questioning the sustainability of existing (at his time) Eastern state socialism because of its immaturity, Schumpeter (1942) developed a concept of socialism for mature Western countries characterized as a type of competitive socialism built on foundations erected unconsciously through the big enterprises created by the Rockefellers, the Vanderbilts, and other famous dynasties in Western industrialized countries. Schumpeter discusses whether this type of socialism can work, what the corresponding socialist blueprints should look like, and to what extent they are superior to the mark II capitalist blueprints (of the megacorporations) that Schumpeter thought made obsolescent the entrepreneurial function in mark I capitalism, the dynamic entrepreneur, and the process of creative destruction conducted by this leading form of economic agent.

Monopolistic practices, vanishing investment opportunities, and growing hostility in the social structure of capitalism were some of the reasons that caused what Schumpeter saw as the decomposition of capitalism as he studied it in 1942. Against this background he described the superiority of the Western competitive type of socialist blueprint, the transition to this form of social structure of accumulation, and the comparative efficiency of such economies. He also discusses the human element in this type of economy, the problem of work organization, and the integration of bourgeois forms of management under capitalism into this type of socialism, including the incentive problems involved in the behavior of these economic agents.

In a typical statement with respect to this last issue, Schumpeter asserts:

> It is not difficult however to insert the stock of bourgeois extraction into its proper place within that machine and to reshape its habits of work. . . . Rational treatments of the ex-bourgeois elements with a view to securing a maximum performance from them will then not require anything that is not just as necessary in the case of managerial personnel of any other extraction.
>
> Schumpeter (1942, p. 65)

It may appear, from today's perspective, that his focused and provocative discussion of these points in section 3 of the chapter "The Human Element" can be denied to a certain degree. However, the managerial element in existing Western capitalism has become more and more the focus of public debate, over topics ranging from the salaries to the ethics the (top) managerial personnel should receive and adopt, respectively. Therefore, actual discussions of the behavior of industrial management are already preparing the ground for a situation in which these people may be given an appropriate level of exclusiveness that may motivate them sufficiently. We do not, however, claim that such broad examinations suffice as considerations of the issue. On the contrary, detailed microeconomic studies and other kinds of work are essential in dealing with actual capitalist management issues. The important point in Schumpeter's arguments is that Western capitalism may transform itself automatically into some kind of competitive socialism on the basis of Western management principles. Such a statement can be applied to the evolution of the Nordic European countries, which may be en route to the kind of social structure of accumulation we have described as flexicurity capitalism in this chapter.

With respect to the workforce of firms—in both capitalism and this type of socialism—he describes, Schumpeter (1942, p. 213) argues:

> Second, closely allied to the necessity of incessant training of the normal is the necessity of dealing with the subnormal performer. This term does not refer to isolated

pathological cases, but to a broad fringe of perhaps 25% of the population. So far as subnormal performance is due to moral or volitional defects, it is perfectly unrealistic to expect that it will vanish with capitalism. The great problem and the great enemy of humanity, the subnormal, will be as much with us as he is now. He can hardly be dealt with by *unaided* group discipline alone—although of course the machinery of authoritarian discipline can be so constructed as to work, partly at least, through the group of which the subnormal is an element.

In view of our discussion of the working of Marx's general law of accumulation under today's conditions in Western economies, we would point here to the fact that capitalism itself is in part responsible for the existence of the "subnormal" element as characterized by Schumpeter. Mass unemployment and its consequences for family life far beyond workers' current status on the labor market, alienation from human types of work organization, degradation of part of the workforce as the unskilled element in an otherwise flourishing economy, the rise and the fall of the welfare state, and the latter's consequences for basic income needs, health care, care for children and the elderly, and school systems are just some of the reasons the "subnormal" element in the population is a persistent fact of life. In this respect, we would argue that the social acceptance of a system of flexicurity and its educational substructure—as we have sketched it in this chapter—would be one way to eliminate the "subnormal" segment from the population gradually, though maybe not totally.

Therefore, we assert here that a system of flexicurity capitalism, based on the principles we have modeled in this chapter, would increasingly gain social acceptance and result in social learning that would put it on a path toward viable economic reproduction, sufficient income, and care for everybody. Furthermore, if such security is developed well enough to coexist with flexibility of a Schumpeterian kind (creative destruction), such flexicurity capitalism can indeed compete with societies subject to the Marxian reserve-army mechanism and the ruthless capitalism that results from it.

The central message of Schumpeter's (1942) work, *Capitalism, Socialism and Democracy*, is that socialism is created out of Western capitalist economies, and not on the basis of (the now defunct) Eastern type of socialism. This can be carried over to the current debate on the possibility of flexicurity capitalism. This form of socioeconomic reproduction may be organized through large production units and their efficient, though bureaucratic, management, a form of management developed out of the principles used under capitalism in the efficient conduct of large (internationally oriented) enterprises. Also, as we currently experience this condition in the service sector (both for industrial production and private consumption), there may be sufficient room for the Schumpeterian type of dynamic entrepreneur, particularly through the flexible entry and exit conditions the flexicurity variant of capitalism may allow.

It is certainly true that contemporaneous capitalism (often of the ruthless type, but in certain countries also of a socially acceptable kind) is not likely to be forced into a defensive position, at least from its performance in the goods market and the labor market (though the current operation of financial markets may produce extremely undesirable results). Yet the consciousness that ruthless, unrestricted capitalism is producing significant negative external social and environmental effects is growing throughout the world, raising hope that an alternative form of capitalism—based on flexicurity principles—may be superior in its socioeconomic performance, at least when that form is mature, Schumpeter considered necessary for his vision of a democratic society based on competitive socialism.

To a certain extent, this alternative variety of capitalism is also ruthless, if Schumpeterian creative-destruction processes are allowed, but, as in any democratic society there are more or less close limits to the choice of techniques (for example, in biogenetics) and the choice of products (for example, in wargames) that are set by the elected political leadership of each country.

Marx viewed the general law of accumulation and its perpetual reserve-army mechanism as the element that not only allowed but was also needed for the reproduction of capitalism. Schumpeter considered changes toward a competitive socialism as providing a possible alternative to the form of capitalism of his times. We think there is a chance for an alternative to current forms of ruthless capitalism that not only adopts some welfare principles but also is founded on a coherently based socioeconomic structure that is socially accepted, and is flexible enough to quickly adjust to changing world market conditions. The foundations of such a system are social acceptance in an educated democratic society. Its problems involve mastering Keynesian types of business fluctuations and Schumpeterian types of creative process and product revolutions and controlling financial markets such that the real activities of an economy do not just become the side product of a casino, as Keynes's (1936) *General Theory* warned.

3.9 ■ THE FUTURE OF CAPITALISM: A BRIEF APPRAISAL

Starting from the problematic features and the social consequences of the reserve-army dynamics characterizing the evolution of the labor markets of many contemporaneous developed capitalist economies, we have tried to demonstrate that a combination of ideas of Marx, Keynes, and Schumpeter on the future of capitalism can provide an alternative to the ruthless form of competition that is currently ruling the world (in developed as well as developing countries). Instead of the multilayered degradation of a significant proportion of the population in democratically governed societies, we have designed economic reproduction models (including education and skill formation) of a competitive form of capitalism that combines flexicurity of a very high degree with security of income as well as employment for the workforce. We thus carry Schumpeter's study of the workability of a competitive type of socialism one step further toward a social vision that preserves, to a great extent, the advantages of existing capitalist forms of production and circulation, but that nevertheless creates a social structure of accumulation that, in its essence, is liberated from the human degradation we observe even in leading industrialized countries in the world economy.

The essential ingredients for such a social structure are not only a basic income guarantee based on work (which includes the obligation to work) but also a reorganization of the labor market so that an employer of first (not last) resort organizes, in a decentralized way, the work of all people not employed within privately run industries, and includes the work of officially retired persons who are still willing to offer their human capital on the labor markets of the economy. The workability of flexicurity type designed reproduction depends—in the same way as many other actual organizational problems—on detailed microeconomic analysis of labor relations within large, medium-sized, and small business firms, as well as in the public sector. Economic incentives need to be coupled with an educational system that not only creates the basis for skill formation but also provides the proper foundations for citizenship education in a democratic society, in which citizens essentially approve the high degree of flexibility in the industrial part of the economy (as well as elsewhere) on the basis of this system's security aspects and the equal opportunity principles implemented in primary and secondary education.

There are many micro problems to be solved in properly designing the Schumpeterian process of creative destruction in the flexicurity economy, problems we have only touched on in our presentation of the bare bones of flexicurity capitalism. There are, also, many macro problems to be solved, since Keynesian effective-demand constraints may lead to unwanted fluctuations in the industrial sector of the economy, caused particularly by malfunctions in the financial sector of the economy. It is far from clear whether these micro and macro problems can indeed all be solved and thus a well-educated democratic society created that provides income and employment guarantees (and interrelated obligations), though no guarantees of specific jobs, workers might experience significant job discontinuities, coupled with a process of lifelong learning.

The main argument for such a flexicurity society in our view is that the currently existing alternative reproduction models of capitalism do not provide a social structure of accumulation compatible with an educated and democratic society in the long run, because recurring episodes of mass unemployment undermine social cohesion in many ways in such societies, leading to social segmentation, social class clashes, and other problems.

The evolution of the Nordic states of the European Union provides examples of how to go about developing a socially accepted flexicurity economy based on a modern schooling system. We close the chapter, however, with the observation that it is not yet clear how this model can, in fact, be implemented in actual economies, such as those in the Nordic countries currently. We simply assume that individual experience with progress in educational systems (regarding equal opportunities in particular), perception of the need for flexibility as well as security during the working life of individuals, and the necessity of democratic institutions on all levels of society will cause effects in individual- and social-choice mechanisms that prevent a return to the Marxian reserve-army mechanism, as described in the many contributions to the original Goodwin growth-cycle model that take account of what has happened in actual capitalist economies.

Goodwin has proposed (see Flaschel [2009], appendix to chapter 10) to construct a M(arx)K(eynes)S(chumpeter) system to analyze the functioning and evolution of actual capitalism. We have proposed a similar idea with respect to ideal constructions by Marx (1954) and Schumpeter (1942), namely, the so-called reproduction schemes of Marx's and Schumpeter's visions of a competitive (Western, not Eastern) type of socialism, with both constructions confronted with Keynesian effective-demand problems. This MKS system may be regarded as the attempt to introduce a social structure of accumulation that is not of the ruthless competitive type of functioning capitalism, particularly as we observe it now.

> Le laissez-faire, c'est fini.
>
> Nicolas Sarkozy (*Le Monde*, September 27, 2008)

But what comes next? A detailed answer to this question was provided more than fifteen years ago by Roemer (1994) in his study of the future of socialism. In the first section of his book he starts from the observation (p. 11):

> I believe that socialists want equality of opportunity for:
>
> - self-realization and welfare,
> - political influence, and
> - social status.

And in the final section of the book, Roemer argues:

> At the least, I hope that readers will take away from this essay two crucial ideas. The first is the view that the goal of socialism is best thought of as a kind of egalitarianism, not the implementation of a specific property relation. I am saying, in other words, that property relations must be evaluated by socialists with respect to their ability to deliver that kind of egalitarianism.... The second idea is that modern capitalism provides us with many fertile possibilities for designing the next wave of socialist experiments.
>
> J. E. Roemer (*A Future for Socialism*, 1994, pp. 124–125)

We believe that the flexicurity concept is one possible response to these two points, meaning that we need not necessarily pursue the Western type of socialism proposed by Schumpeter (1942). Instead the work of Roemer (1994) may be taken as a starting point for the discussion of the future of capitalism, because many of the details of his book are compatible with what we have discussed under the name of a flexicurity system so far. However, such a flexicurity system must solve the issue of property rights and of control rights appropriately, issues that we approach next.

3.10 ELITES IN FLEXICURITY SOCIETIES

This section considers an important (in our view indispensable) human component for the proper working of (advanced) flexicurity societies, a component that needs to be integrated into the model of this chapter, primarily by considering incentive-compatible reward systems for a group of elites who are of decisive importance for the conduct of the society.

Elites are not only distinguished or even exceptional in their decision-shaping power, but they will also differ—in actual economies as well as in our model of a flexicurity society—with respect to rewards from the skilled and highly skilled persons in this society. In Schumpeter's discussion of the Western (competitive) type of socialism that he envisaged as a possible future of capitalism, he expressed not only these rewards in categories of income and wealth (where Schumpeter thought that much less was indeed necessary than was prevalent in the capitalist economies of his time) but also in terms of social distance. We believe that Schumpeter's statement on the integration of the ex-bourgeoisie into his Western type of competitive socialism can be meaningfully extended to the flexicurity societies we are considering:

> In capitalist society, social recognition of performance or social prestige carries a strongly economic connotation both because pecuniary gain is the typical index of success, according to capitalist standards, and because most of the paraphernalia of social prestige—in particular, that most subtle of all economic goods, Social Distance—have to be bought. This prestige or distinction value of private wealth has of course always been recognized by economists.... And it is clear that among the incentives to supernormal performance this is one of the most important.... Moreover the prestige motive, more than any other, can be molded by simple reconditioning: Successful performers may conceivably be satisfied nearly as well with the privilege—if granted with judicious economy—of being allowed to stick a penny stamp on their trousers as they are by receiving a million a year.
>
> Schumpeter (1942, p. 208)

3.10.1 Basic Aspects

Elites (and their sub-elites) are a crucial component of societal development processes, because, by and large, they determine the rules for decision making, make and evaluate decisions, and decide sanctions in the case of failure. They are crucial for the maintenance of stable and systematically improving labor productivity, capital productivity, and capital depreciation rates, by appropriately solving coordination as well as microlevel incentives problems.

Their structure, formation processes, reproduction (i.e., how elite status is attained and transmitted to others), leadership role (i.e., how their power is exercised and controlled), and ethics (i.e., how consistency between the goals of elites and national objectives can be obtained) within democracies (as well as within nondemocratic societies) and, also, within our ideal model of a flexicurity society needs detailed discussion.

From a historical sociological point of view, Hartmann (2007) studied the role of elites in detail. In this section, our approach must proceed against the background of such actual studies, but we must go from there to the partly constructive as well as normative considerations of the formation and reproduction of elite, subelite, and (for completeness and as a contrast), also, prominence structures in our flexicurity model. In the flexicurity context of this chapter, we assume, in particular, the democratic societal structure sketched in figure 3.1, which involves majority voting as the much more efficient way to generate political structures (i.e., governments) capable of acting consistently and efficiently than (we think) is possible under a percentage voting system.

The basic task for elites is decision framing, particularly the most important decision making, by and large in the inner domains shown in figure 3.5. There is also decision making in the domains outside the rectangle shown, but we consider this area more as an environment within which elites are operating. This is an environment that is not only formed by elites, in the narrower sense of the word, but also more broadly by prominent people in general. Elites make the most important decisions, but it is by no means obvious that their performance can be considered as always excellent or even adequate in this respect. Their selection process should, in principle, rest on the best education available within the school system, but it may still well be that social origin and habitus play a role when new elite members are selected through the established elite.

The current condition of worldwide capitalism, in democratic as well as nondemocratic societies, is characterized by massive failures in elite behavior, particularly in sectors related to commercial banking and automobile production, but also in other areas involving primarily economic and financial management processes. This raises the question of how elites should be educated, selected, and disciplined (in the case of elite failures). In order to discuss this, we need a structure describing elite categories, elite selection processes, and positive or negative elite reward systems (incentives and sanctions). In the following— based on figure 3.5—we attempt to provide a sketch of such a structure, as the foundation for an analysis both of how elites have behaved in actual economies and societies and how they should behave in the ideal flexicurity society of this chapter.

We observe in figure 3.5 that it contains more structure than has been considered so far in our flexicurity model. There is, on the one hand, not only the question of the demand of elites for income and goods and services, which must be integrated into the formal structure of the model, but also the way elites

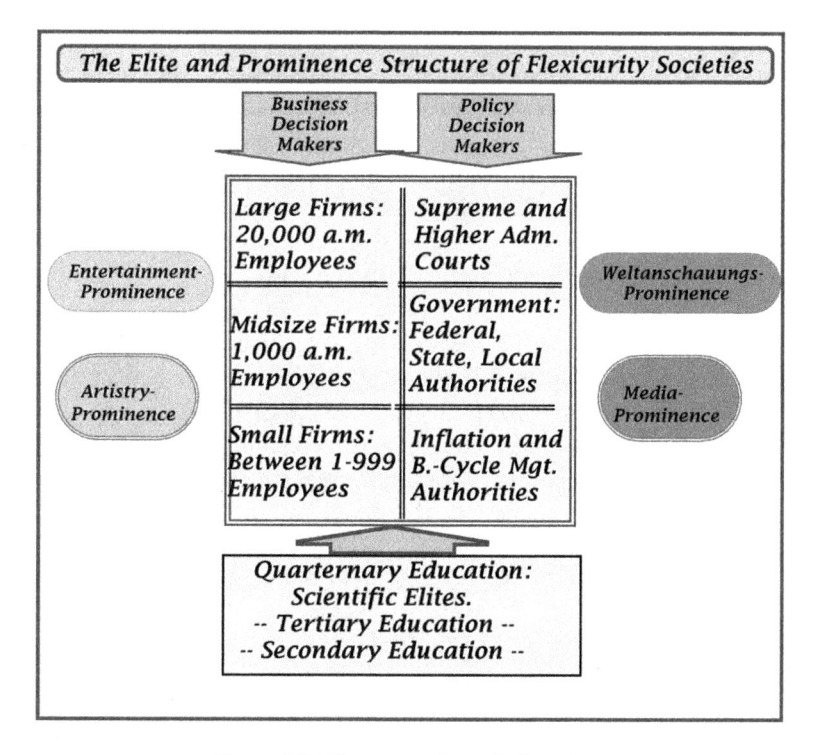

```
┌─────────────────────────────────────────────────────────┐
│      The Elite and Prominence Structure of Flexicurity Societies │
│                  Business      Policy                    │
│                  Decision      Decision                  │
│                  Makers        Makers                    │
│                    ▼             ▼                       │
│   ┌──────────────┬──────────────┬──────────────┐        │
│   │ Entertainment-│ Large Firms: │ Supreme and  │ Weltanschauungs- │
│   │ Prominence   │ 20,000 a.m.  │ Higher Adm.  │ Prominence       │
│   │              │ Employees    │ Courts       │                  │
│   │              ├──────────────┼──────────────┤        │
│   │              │ Midsize Firms:│Government:  │        │
│   │ Artistry-    │ 1,000 a.m.   │ Federal,     │ Media-           │
│   │ Prominence   │ Employees    │ State, Local │ Prominence       │
│   │              │              │ Authorities  │        │
│   │              ├──────────────┼──────────────┤        │
│   │              │ Small Firms: │ Inflation and│        │
│   │              │ Between 1-999│ B.-Cycle Mgt.│        │
│   │              │ Employees    │ Authorities  │        │
│   └──────────────┴──────────────┴──────────────┘        │
│                          ▲                               │
│              ┌───────────────────────────┐              │
│              │ Quarternary Education:    │              │
│              │   Scientific Elites.      │              │
│              │ -- Tertiary Education --  │              │
│              │ -- Secondary Education -- │              │
│              └───────────────────────────┘              │
└─────────────────────────────────────────────────────────┘
```

Figure 3.5 Elite categories and education.

in the business sector shape the course of the economy. There is, on the other hand, the role of political elites in ensuring the separation of powers in a modern democratic state. The normal division of political estates is into an executive, a legislature, and a judiciary. In this respect, we distinguish government on federal, state, and local levels and its interactions with various forms of "parliaments" on these three levels, and with respect to the judiciary, the supreme court and higher administrative courts. In addition, we consider not only the (by-and-large) conventional role of a central bank (for controlling inflation) but also a new fiscal authority (for controlling the business cycle) and the cooperative interaction between these two authorities. Thus, there is a reduced role for the government itself with regard to fiscal policy (here concentrated on infrastructure evolution and growth), because we assume that business-cycle-oriented fiscal policy is to be conducted—similarly to how the central bank does so independently—by an independent fiscal institution in our flexicurity model.

The main task in discussing the elite structure of a flexicurity society is to understand how people (should) attain, use, and preserve or transmit their status in the elite group and the social desirability of this top-level structure. That is, how should these processes of elite formation be further developed (or modified) in order to achieve a rationally founded balance between efficient elite-conducted economic and political decision-making processes and processes that guarantee socially adequate performance? This also includes discussion of property rights as well as control rights (which may be of a residual nature, if credit is involved).

There is or can be private property in small firms (defined as having under 100 employees). However, the role of the proprietors is restricted, after some limited extraction of profits for personal income, to choosing the direction of investment made with profits (and possibly also investments financed by credit). Large firms, by contrast, have a board of managing directors (top managers, controlled by an independent supervisory board), who conduct the investment (and employment) decisions of their companies and who assume liability for their decisions to a certain degree. In the middle range of firms shown in figure 3.4 there may be some mix of the two possibilities just considered. We do not go into details here but leave these issues for future work on property rights under flexicurity (concerning the details of property rights and defined liabilities).

3.10.2 Elite Groups and Areas of Operation

We start examining the formation and role of elites by describing elite categories and their areas of operation, a supplement to the occupational structure we have already considered in figures 3.1 and 3.4. The main categories involve economic decision processes, political decision mechanisms, and the social and cultural environments in which these processes are embedded, but also the occurrence of negative elites, most notably in oligarchies and under dictatorships. We observe that the structures to be discussed are not yet formally integrated into the flexicurity society we have modeled so far. This modification will only be sketched here and, therefore, will remain a task for future research. Our categories are:

- Business administration and economics (agriculture, manufacturing, services, trade, and banking):
  - National and international decision-making leadership
  - Top administration
  - Innovation conduct and Schumpeterian creative destruction
  - Ownership elites in the sector of small (and partially medium-sized) firms
- Politics and political administration:
  - National and international decision-making leadership
  - Political representation
  - Top administration
  - High nobility and state representation

- Culture and value formation (prominence):
    - Outstanding ethical figures, religious leaders
    - Scientific leadership
    - Arts and high-level entertainment

This structure gives a survey of the possible types of elites in modern democratic societies, including flexicurity systems, but in more or less nondemocratic societies as well, such as plutocratic systems, one-party systems, dictatorships, and even worse, that is, societies with state terrorism, particularly those engaging in so-called ethnic cleansing and the like. Also, study of the influence of elites—whether good or bad—is not restricted to the consideration of leading figures solely; it also includes lower-level elites (sub-elites), particularly in business administration, and focuses on how such elites are molded and cared for in the attempt to recruit from them the highest elite members when needed.

The structure described accounts for functional elites as well as educational elites, and, to a certain degree, simply prominent people. Of course members of the elite (or subelite) can have multiple identities within the sketched structures. We stress, however, that we focus on functional elites (power elites) primarily and consider other types of elites as being largely having the (less important) status of prominence, particularly in the domain of arts and the media, and even more in the range of well-established people within entertainment and weltanschauung perception. An important exception may occur in the area we have called quaternary education in which world-class research groups are formed and work together under the guidance of leading scientists. Notable further exceptions are state representatives (presidents, kings, and queens) and leaders of the dominant religions (who to a certain degree are also the top managers of large enterprises).

3.10.3 Education: Foundation for Administrative Authority and Social Behavior

The following list describes the educational steps in the formation of (new members of) elites in a flexicurity society, primarily from the common perspective of the society's members. There are exceptions to these rules, such as allowing university education for the skilled segment of the labor market (based possibly on persons having part-time work or simply voluntarily using their leisure time as accordingly motivated members of the skilled workforce). Such ability to advance within the societal structure applies in our model economy quite generally to political careers, which all members of the workforce should have access to (but not to state secretary positions and those of comparable levels in similar political state agencies, for which extra skills are required).

- No child left behind, no talent wasted:
  - Qualified education of all teachers and educators at a university
  - Equal opportunities, but also the promotion of individual gifts of students in primary and secondary school (and preschool)
  - Detection of special talents of students in school
  - Positive recognition of talents in school by all participants
- Foundations of elite careers:
  - Basing of normal elite careers (major exception: politicians) on tertiary education as the prerequisite and including advancement through the group of highly skilled workers
  - Reflection of social backgrounds and the social origin of elites
  - Existence of elite universities and related educational institutions
  - Cultivation of elite character traits
  - Cultivation of citizenship awareness
  - Establishment of ethical norms relating to the conduct of social power
  - Emphasis on regional, national, and international aspects of education

Elites, particularly in a flexicurity society, must be well educated, well trained, and well aware of their citizenship obligations and in their roles as leading decision makers, and leading representatives of moral institutions and the political and cultural system they belong to. Education of elites is a crucial element in any society, not only from the point of view of preparing talented people for their adult occupations but also with respect to their moral and ethical conduct in a multifaceted, pluralistic democratic society.

There is no way to predict whether a child will become a member of the elites as an adult, even if the social and intellectual background of his or her family may indicate that path. Therefore, it is absolutely necessary to support all children in their progress so that they can develop all their skills, competencies, and talents. This demands an educational system as we described briefly in section 3.6. That education starts early and is capable of supporting each child in his or her individual progress. The need for early support of developing children is one of the reasons why not only teachers but all educators need a tertiary education at a university.

The individual support of all children in preschool and school grows out of the underlying concept of equal opportunity, but also includes the support of gifted and highly gifted children. Because there is a consensus in most societies about the necessity of elites, it is also a duty of schools to keep in mind that some children might not develop the skills, behavior, and responsible commitment to belong to this group until their later adult life. The slogan "no child left behind" stems from an American concept of advancing all students by promoting their skills and talents. Although this is not the place to evaluate the success of the implementation of this concept in the United States (which may be questionable), it is obvious that its underlying idea of equal opportunity can only be realized in an open school system that allows individual support for all students by respecting the pace of each child (see the description of a possible model school system in section 3.6).

Although it is a task of schools to detect and support students—among them those who will be elites later on—it is mainly tertiary education where students get the chance to proceed in their development of skills and competencies toward later (top-level) executive or managerial responsibilities. In most cases, elites will finish their studies with a PhD. Many countries have schools and universities—often titled elite schools and universities—that mostly (should) provide not only an excellent education but also (currently too much?) access to a network that will be helpful in the careers of the students.

In section 3.3 we proposed one task of the educational system as taking care that the social background of a child does not hinder his or her school career. In the case of elites, we face a different situation: Often it is the social background that determines—or at least strongly influences—the development of a student toward a later position as an elite, not least by enabling him or her to attend an elite school and university. These experiences may influence elites later on. We regard it as an important task of the school and university to help these students to reflect on the positions of social power they may gain later on, and deepen their responsibility in those positions. Dealing with human rights will be as important as establishing a citizenship awareness to prevent elites from separating from the rest of the society by losing their commitment and ignoring their responsibility in this area.

Education in the twenty-first century is no longer a regional or national matter, though regional and national aspects remain part of education, especially with regard to the demands of a particular society. Education in the twenty-first century is a global matter, and international connections and responsibilities have to be taken into account. This is also a fact to be considered in the education of elites.

To conclude, we again stress that elite education does not exist in the sense of the expression, because a society cannot predict whether a student may become a member of the elite, even if social background indicates so. Therefore, it remains the task of schools to provide the best education to all students so that those with the best skills and competencies may develop as members of the elite after their university studies. We believe that both these demands, equal opportunities and the development of elites, can and must be fulfilled.

3.10.4 Career Advancement and Decent Paths

This section briefly discusses the standard procedures in the selection of members of the elite (and also their dismissal) in a flexicurity system. We have already pointed to the fact that there must be exceptional careers at least for certain types of functional or educational elites, most notably political ones. In addition, there must exist a system of sanctions in the case of failure or misconduct that can be accepted by the members of the elite as well as the ordinary citizens of the society.

- Career paths of elites include:

    - Tertiary education normally required for all professions enumerated in figure 3.4
    - Political elites drawn from both skilled and highly skilled persons through majority voting
    - Professional elites chosen through qualified majority voting of selected representatives of both skilled and highly skilled persons
    - Exceptions made for very specifically talented persons like artists
    - High-, medium-, and low-level elites formed and corresponding selection principles established
    - Positions filled on regional, national, and supranational levels
    - Elites include company owners, chief executive officers, judges on supreme court, members of other supreme decision-making bodies, party leaders, prime ministers and cabinet members, top researchers, and leading personalities engaged in the cultural sector
    - Conduct criteria and control criteria established (incentives, sanctions, and status removal)

Career paths of individual elites are very different depending on the elite category. For example, the path of a top manager is different than the path of a top politician. In the first case, the role of elite character formation and an informal selection process may be typical, whereas in the latter case, there may be a path through party stages with selection processes depending less on elite formation and more on popularity, though this applies more to percentage voting systems than to majority voting systems (which we prefer because of the likelihood of effective action). In universities the selection process is also less dependent on elite background and more on formal screening criteria (publication records, for example). In arts and entertainment there may be very personalized selection processes that also depend on fashions and the media. We have, however, already stressed that such groups of society may be considered more adequately as celebrities than as elites, because of the lack of power they have in their decisions for affecting larger segments of the society. Career paths of elites and elite formation processes can vary significantly even within democratic societies such as the United Kingdom and Germany (see Hartmann [2007] for detailed studies of five major democratic countries). Access to elite positions will be organized in different ways as far as economic and political leadership is concerned. In the former case, it is professional education that is of high importance, whereas political leadership should, in principle, be open to all members of the voting population, excluding persons whose integrity is in doubt. By contrast, in arts and entertainment individual performance is the basis for success and the attainment of elite status. In this area, however, we distinguish between elite and celebrity people, with the former group being fairly small and the latter group characterized less by their media presence than by extraordinary achievements or performances.

3.10.5 Preferences, Incentives, and Responsibilities

The preferences of the various members of the elite—with respect to status, authority, respect of others, for example—are endogenous, formed by their families, by the educational system, and, later on, in interaction with one another (and not only in a flexicurity society). Particularly in interactions with one another, there may be self-supporting processes at work that influence the professional and moral integrity of members of the elite, and sometimes negatively—as the current world financial crisis has shown. It is important, therefore, to consider the preference formation of elites in detail, in particular at the early stage (within education) where their membership in such a segment of the societal structure is not yet a real issue. Points of importance in this area in particular are the following ones.

- Preferences, incentives, and responsibilities:
    - Income levels sufficiently above skilled and highly skilled workers, but in addition the provision of "social distance" (not based on million euros of income and extraordinary wealth, but on good reputation)
    - Exclusiveness provisions à la Schumpeter (1942)
    - The need for preferences not based on extreme personal wealth, and unchecked personal power as core personal objectives
    - Ethical obligations and citizenship awareness
    - Paths of progress in elite formation and elite performance processes
    - Responsible real-wage management in interaction with both skilled and highly skilled workers and their representatives
    - Possibility of losing elite status when personal failures occur

Preferences of the members of an elite of a particular occupation are of central importance for the conduct of such elites in forming their personal goals, which are, at best, when they are in accordance with human rights, the national objectives, and the public interest of the considered society. Yet preferences—even if they are not distorted by excessive income, wealth, and power objectives—can be in conflict with such objectives, for the right or for the wrong reasons. A society thus needs a mechanism that can detect what is right or wrong socially, and it needs to establish both incentives and sanctions that encourage actions producing positive economic and social results.

Preferences in elite groups are far from being exogenously determined, because there is intensive interpersonal preference interaction on this level of decision making. Preferences also change with the age and experience of elite people. Schumpeter (1942)—discussing how to integrate the ex-bourgeois element into his model of a Western type of socialism—provides examples that demonstrate that the incentives to motivate elites need not be extreme income payments and the prospect of becoming very wealthy in the course of their careers, but may indeed consist in a certain level of exclusiveness related to their elite status. In fact, the power elites in economics and business administration may have objective functions that are not conducive to the best interests of the countries or companies they are directing.

3.10.6 Elite Failures

We restrict our discussion here to the case of democratic societies as they are assumed to underlie the flexicurity systems of this chapter. The following list provides only some overall points, which need elaborating in detailed societal mechanisms in order to minimize the occurrence of such possibilities. This includes the establishment and enforcement of independent standards of professional conduct for supervisory boards (i.e., in business administration, the board of managers) and for politicians.

- Elite failures:
    - Malfunctions and incompetence with respect to leadership and accomplishment
    - Misuse of elite positions
    - Corruption, corrupted utility functions
    - Unreasonable or even illegitimate enrichment
    - Risk and gambling motivations instead of thorough screening of investment opportunities (commercial banks)
    - Inadequate human resource management
    - Inadequate environmental resource management
    - Inadequate management of the Schumpeterian process of creative destruction of production technologies

The fact that elites can fail on a grand scale is an obvious fact when evaluating the current economic situation, and that failure relates primarily to the inappropriate conduct of commercial banks (and other financial institutions) and the bad loans they generated on a worldwide scale. In industry, too, most notably in the automobile industry, top decision makers favored outcomes that had little to do with an innovative Schumpeterian process of creative destruction of processes or products, but more with short-sighted preservation of their elite status through routines and noninnovative behavior that primarily supported the power and income position of the elites in question. Globalization trends were simply ignored, especially under political regimes that were, by and large, blind to the interaction of innovation and environmental protection.

3.10.7 The Remuneration of Elites under Flexicurity: A Baseline Proposal

In light of the discussion in the preceding subsections, we formulate here a baseline proposal for the remuneration of elites in the private (and public) sector. We believe that this proposal will help prevent to a significant degree the behavior of the elite members observed before and after the world financial crisis that began in 2008, since it in particular removes inducement for elites to gamble on financial markets, provides gain to them as individuals if successful, but socializes the risk if they fail.

We also briefly indicate here how our accounts of the groups forming the elites can be integrated into the formal structure in section 3.3. We consider again a stationary population and assume that the number of people in an elite position L_{1e} in the industrial sector of the economy is a constant fraction of the number of highly skilled workers L_{1a} in that sector (who represent, by and large, the stock of people from whom elites in the business sector are recruited). As gross income of the group L_{1e} (based on—and deducted from—the profits or losses of firms), we assume the following situation Y_e for elites in the private sector:

$$Y_e = \max\left[(1 + \gamma_{1e})\omega_{1a}L_{1e} + \phi_{1e}\Pi, \quad \omega_{1a}L_{1e}\right]$$

This group of the working population therefore exhibits two sources of income, wage income $(1 + \gamma_{1e})\omega_{1a}L_{1e}$, which is increased by the factor $1 + \gamma_{1e}$ compared to the wage income of highly skilled workers, and profit income $\phi_{1e}\Pi$, which is a constant fraction of the profits of firms, yet also of the losses of firms if profits become negative. There are thus deductions from the wage income of business elites when their firms face a loss, but these deductions are limited from below by the wage sum that elites would receive when remunerated solely as highly skilled workers.

Elites L_{2e} in the public sector—a constant proportion of the stock of labor L_{2a}—exhibit as gross income equation the expression

$$(1 + \gamma_{2e})\omega_{2a}L_{2e}$$

They therefore do not bear here any risk for the performance of the public sector in the form of income losses (but can of course lose their status as a member of their elite). Moreover remuneration may be significantly (but not extremely) lower than the remuneration of elites in the business sector. We stress here that this discussion concerns only the basics of the remunerations of elites, and that further incentives and further sanctions may be established in line with current public discussion on the failure of elites after the subprime/banking crisis.

3.10.8 Summing Up

Following Higley (2006) we now define elites—against the background of what we have discussed in this chapter—as

> persons, who by virtue of their strategic locations in large or otherwise pivotal organizations and movements, are able to affect political outcomes regularly and substantially.

We should here include the direction of firms (above a certain size) besides the conduct of the state on its three levels (beginning at a certain level of responsibility) and also—though rarely—independent and publicly financed research-and-development units with a significant impact on the society. Elites are, therefore, defined by the (democratically controlled) power they possess with respect to decentralized as well as centralized economic and political management problems. There may be a small educational elite, in addition, but surely not in the same numbers that occur in commerce and political decision making. We note again that elements in this discussion of elites are not yet firmly integrated into our formal model, especially in regard to the income (and other rewards) of elites, as well as their spending propensities. We have not considered sub-elites (handling some types of work rather than the elite), either. We have, however, reached a stage at which the characteristics of elite structures are visible enough to discuss their reproduction in time and in specific societies, such as the one considered in this chapter.

On the basis of what has already been discussed, the following central topics need to be solved in research on actual elites and their integration into a flexicurity society, as it may arise as part of progress from welfare states to workfare systems and from there to flexicurity societies.[22] Such progress depends on how preferences are formed among voters and among the political elites as a result of voting decisions. Work to be done includes:

1. International comparisons of how persons get, use, and perpetuate (or not) their elite status or power position in actual capitalist democracies
2. Implications of this analysis for the formation of elites in flexicurity economies in which income, wealth, and personal power over large institutions, especially over social (re-)production processes, are not the main motives that drive elite behavior
3. Institutional reforms that make decision processes in all areas of the society more transparent, more responsible, and more effective socially.

It is a bit surprising that there is not much research effort in this central area of the future development of capitalism, be it from the conceptual, theoretical, or empirical point of view. For a historical perspective, see the classic work of Pareto (1935, 1968), as well as the various, also classic contributions of Pierre Bourdieu (see Hartmann [2007] for a discussion), Mills (1959), Rothkopf (2009). See also Schumpeter (1942), who discussed the formation of elites on the basis of his views on Western-type socialism and the superiority of majority-voting democracies in forming competent political elites in such a framework. A large collection of essays with a wide range of topics in the sociology of elites is also provided by Scott (1990).

Elites, in flexicurity systems, (should) have significant competencies in shaping the course of such societies in an economically efficient and socially sensible way; accordingly, they should be rewarded with appropriate social status. With this status, they would—in a carefully managed way—have the power (from the individual perspective, temporary) of quasi ownership of the means of production as well as of the political apparatus. Control of elites can be to a certain degree intrinsically organized, but must also depend on straightforward selection mechanisms controlled by the legislature as well as policymakers and thus indirectly by the voting population. We consider such a scenario a significant step forward from what Schumpeter (1942) proposed in his analysis of capitalism, socialism and (majority-voting) democracy, building on his work on economies under the impact of World War II and the socialism of his time. Eventually this may lead to a theoretical structure (the M[arx]-K[eynes]-S[chumpeter] system, as Goodwin [1989] called it) where the Marxian conflict over income distribution has become a rationally controlled one, though one in which Keynesian effective demand may still restrict the working of the economy and a modernized type of Western type socialism exists, as envisaged by Schumpeter.

We close this section by quoting again from Roemer's (1994) book on the future of socialism:

Yet for any end state of a social process to be feasible, a path must exist from here to there, and so at least a rough sketch of possible routes, if not a precise map, may reasonably be asked of someone attempting to describe the final destination. I preface the remarks that follow with the caveat that recent history has shown we tread on thin ice when trying to predict the future.

Roemer (1994, p. 126)

In this respect we believe (or hope) that the endogenous evolution of the preferences of the citizens may be such that democratic ratchet effects develop in the political decision processes and lead to progress toward a path-dependent flexicurity society. This, of course, is more likely to happen the more developed the welfare state (and its workfare complement) of the society has become already. We will return to a discussion of the structure of firms, the related issue of property rights, and the control rights of elites in the final chapter of this book.

3.11 ■ PRICE FORMATION: TIME DEPENDENT MARK-UP PRICING AROUND LONG-PERIOD PRICES OF PRODUCTION

In this section[23] we start from the seminal article of Alchian (1950) and develop an economic and mathematical framework that describes price-setting rules of firms that allow them to calculate market prices based solely on their local knowledge (i.e., based on the set of technological blueprints they control). Thus, they are able to adjust their prices for the commodities they produce in every period by a procedure that also allows for exogenously given influences from the business cycle currently characterizing the macroeconomy, as well as for the introduction of aggregate inflation or deflation dynamics.

3.11.1 Profit Maximization Not a Guide to Action

Assuming that firms maximize profits—as is common in the economics literature—implies that analysis of the actual behavior of firms starts from the wrong end of the situation firms generally face. Firms—in any given period—choose their actions in a given institutional framework, which in the early days of capitalism may have been maladjusted or even hostile to their behavior, but which gives their actions a frame from which they have to start and which they understand in a more or less perfect way. Nevertheless, even at the beginning of capitalism, there was more uncertainty than certainty surrounding firms' production and pricing decisions, be it uncertainty over demand, price inflation, profitable investments or profitability. The rational response of firms in such an environment is not to establish huge optimization routines to guide their daily actions and try to reduce uncertainty to subjective risk, but instead to attempt to find and develop routines or rules of behavior to ensure they are making profits over the long run.

3.11.2 Success Based on Satisfying Rules

In this respect cost calculations and markup price-setting behavior follow one simple rule, which enables firms to avoid having to specify large optimization programs (based on probability distributions) in order to choose their action today, tomorrow, the day after tomorrow, and so on. The costs of such optimization procedures may be enormous and add to other costs of having to use technology in ways firms would rather avoid. Choosing appropriate behavioral rules in place of actions or in addition to those actions that can be optimized easily may thus be a rational way to conduct a business in a world of uncertainty. Markup pricing and subsequent adjustment procedures provide an example of practical importance (rather than the numerous marginal conditions of academic theory), and the sales value method of calculating the costs of single items in a joint production technology system may be another such example (allowing firms to relate costs and profits in a neutral, nondistorting way without using complicated techniques from linear programming and the like).

Profits in the long run may thus be better ensured through adjustable simple markup pricing rules (that test the market) than through expensive market studies of a possibly questionable reliability.

3.11.3 Success in Competition with Other Firms Selects the Rules with Satisfactory Results

Which rules survive and become established is a matter of a Darwinian selection process. Techniques for running a firm are chosen and developed in economic history on the basis of maintaining profitability. Their choice is therefore path dependent, that is, at least partly to be explained through the lessons of economic history, as, for example, the historic arrangement of the keys on a keyboard that remains in use today (the economics of QWERTY). Knowledge and procedures for running a firm are thus not only based on individual firms' learning by doing but also on a collective learning by doing in conducting capitalist enterprises. Which rules are indeed successful and workable in the long run, and which may improve the performance of innovating firms, is a difficult subject and we only treat it in the following formal analysis in a preliminary way, by providing an analytical example that shows that a specific type of markup pricing by firms need not be in conflict with long-period equilibrium prices that ensure positive profits for cost-minimizing techniques and perhaps also balanced growth.

3.11.4 Business Cycle Dependent Choice of Technique and Mark-up Pricing

The economy we examine is characterized by the following assumptions. There are n branches in the economy each producing a single commodity; in other words, the commodity space consists of n goods. We leave open the question of the market form of each branch, but assume in the following that the choice of technique in each branch is always cost-minimizing. The technology set in branch i is given by a collection of linear production activities $A_i, \ell_i \in T_i$. We consider only circulation capital (only intermediate inputs) and assume that each process has to employ labor in order to become activated. There are n branches $T_1, \ldots, T_n$. With respect to labor we assume a given wage basket $c = (c_1, \ldots, c_n)'$ and assume for reasons of mathematical simplicity that all c_i are strictly positive. We consider markup determined price vectors $p = (p_1, \ldots, p_n)$ and get on this basis for the money wage the expression $w = pc$.

On the basis of these data we define a function $C_i(p) : \mathfrak{R}_+^n \to \mathfrak{R}$ by

$$C_i(p) = \min\{pA_i + w\ell_i \text{ s.t. } (A_i, \ell_i) \in T_i\}$$

We note that $pA_i + w\ell_i$ can be rewritten as $p(A_i + c\ell_i)$. We define on this basis a mapping $C(p) : \mathfrak{R}_+^n \to \mathfrak{R}_+^n$ that is given by $C(p) = (C_1(p), \ldots, C_n(p))$. This mapping is positively homogeneous, primitive, and concave, according to Krause and Nesemann (1999), and therefore allows the application of the concave Perron theorem (proposition 6.6 in Krause and Nesemann [1999]).

On this basis we now define the following markup pricing rule for the n sectors of the economy:

$$p_{t+1} = \mu_t C(p_t) \in \mathfrak{R}_+^n$$

where μ_t is a positive scalar (larger than 1 in fact) that depends on the state of the business cycle. In good conditions of overall economic activity this scalar may be higher than in bad conditions, but for the markup pricing process under consideration it is given exogenously (as a term that drives the nominal price level and thus inflation). The question now is, what are the limit properties of such a uniform marking up of the minimal input costs of the n firms?

3.11.5 Existence and Limit Propositions

We define a measure for inflation by starting from the definition $\|p\| = \sum_{i=1}^n p_i c_i = pc$, and employ on this basis as definition of the rate of inflation over a certain period t the expression

$$\pi_t = \frac{\|p_{t+1}\| - \|p_t\|}{\|p_t\|} = \frac{(p_{t+1} - p_t)c}{p_t c}$$

which is a well defined expression for all semipositive price vectors p, since we have assumed that the consumption basket c is strictly positive. Under the assumptions made we then get the following proposition for the limit properties of the cost minimizing mapping $C(p)$ and the vector of markup prices p based on this mapping.

Proposition 5:

1. There exists a unique strictly positive solution p*, λ* with $\|p\|= 1$ of the equation $C(p) = \lambda p$ which fulfills

$$\lim_{t\to\infty} \frac{C(p_t)}{\|C(p_t)\|} = \lim_{t\to\infty} \frac{C^t(p_o)}{\|C^t(p_o)\|} = p^* > 0$$

   for any semipositive starting price vector p_o.

2. Furthermore, there holds:

$$\lim_{t\to\infty} \frac{p_t}{\|p_t\|} = \lim_{t\to\infty} \frac{C^t(p_o)}{\|C^t(p_o)\|} = p^* > 0$$

   for any semipositive starting price vector p_o.

3. Finally we have for the sectoral rates of profit

$$r_i^* := \frac{p_i^* - C_i(p^*)}{C_i(p^*)} \; : \; r_i^* = \frac{\lambda^* - 1}{\lambda^*} = r^*$$

Proof:
See Krause and Nesemann (1999).

Markup pricing thus leads us in the limit to a system of production prices, not yet necessarily one with a positive rate of profit r*, however.

3.11.6 Equalizing Positive Profit Rates and Inflation Dynamics

The given set of technologies is called productive if there are choices of technique $A_i, \ell_i \in T_i$ and nonnegative activity levels x_i for the n sectors of our economy (i = 1, ..., n) such that there is nowhere excess demand for the n commodities and at least in one sector excess supply with respect to the input vectors $A_i + c\ell_i, i = 1, \ldots, n$:

$$\sum_{i=1}^n A_{ij}x_i + \sum_{i=1}^n c_j\ell_i x_i \leq x_j, \quad j = 1, \ldots, n$$

In matrix notation this implies—with activities as columns in the implied matrix A—for the selected activities: $(A + c\ell)x \leq x$, with at least one strict inequality sign. Multiplying this inequality from the left with the determined strictly positive vector of production prices then gives the inequality

$$p^*(A + c\ell)x < p^*x, \quad \text{and} \quad \lambda^*p^*x = C(p^*)x \leq p^*(A + c\ell)x, \quad \text{i.e.} \quad \lambda^* < 1$$

because of the properties of the mapping C(p).

Proposition 6:

1. Under the above assumption of a productive technology system we have $r^* = (1 - \lambda^*)/\lambda^* > 0$, i.e., the uniform rate of profit is then positive.
2. Furthermore, there holds for the deflated rates of profit $r_i = \frac{\frac{p_{i,t+1}}{\|p_{t+1}\|} - \frac{C_i(p_t)}{\|p_t\|}}{\frac{C_i(p_t)}{\|p_t\|}}$:

$$\lim_{t \to \infty} r_{it} := \lim_{t \to \infty} \frac{\frac{p_{i,t+1}}{\|p_{t+1}\|} - \frac{C_i(p_t)}{\|p_t\|}}{\frac{C_i(p_t)}{\|p_t\|}} = \frac{\lambda^* - 1}{\lambda^*} = r^* \quad \text{for} \quad i = 1, \ldots, n,$$

Proof:
See Krause and Nesemann (1999).

Taken together, we thus have considered a markup pricing dynamics of the type

$$p_{t+1} = \mu_t \cdot \ldots \cdot \mu_o C^t(p_o), \quad t \in \mathbb{N},$$

where C^t is the t-times iterated mapping C. Depending on the evolution of the markup factor μ_t this process may be characterized by longer periods of inflation or deflation (caused through the business cycle that drives the markup factor μ). Normalizing these prices by means of the price index $\| p \|$, based on the consumption basket c of workers, then allows for various limit considerations that show that such normalized prices tend to equally normalized prices of production and that their deflated rates of profit (for the n sectors of the economy) tend toward the uniform rate of profit of the obtained production prices. We are thus considering an economy where nominal wages fluctuate with nominal prices in order to allow the consumption of a given subsistence wage by the workers and where nominal prices may fluctuate with the state of the business cycle, but where nevertheless relative prices tend to a price system that allows uniform profitability with respect to the n activities chosen by the n sectors.

3.11.7 Demand and Supply Side Driven Output Levels

In this subsection we provide an example of how the quantity side of the considered economy may evolve through time, dependent on the markup pricing strategies of firms and on their choice of technology. We emphasize here that the formulated dynamics of the activity levels of firms do not yet feed back into their pricing decision in this particular closure of the dynamics of an economy with n sectors. From the preceding subsections we take the assumption that the cost-minimizing choice of techniques by the n firms leads to a square system matrix $A(p_t)$ that depends—as shown—on the currently prevailing price vector. Similarly, we have a scalar function $\ell(p_t)$ describing the labor input corresponding to the system $A(p_t)$. Next we assume that there is a vector g_t that represents the growth rates intended by firms with respect to their input requirement in the next period, that is, $A(p_t) < g_t > x$ describes the total net investment demand that firms plan in the current period (depending on their willingness to take risks on the evolution of the economy). These growth rates can be made dependent on the past performance of the economy, but are here given as an exogenous time-dependent process.

On the basis of these data we can then formulate the final net demand that firms will have to satisfy as:

$$f(x_t, p_t) = A(p_t) < g_t > x_t + c\ell(p_t)x_t$$

As net supply function we simply have:

$$y_t = (I - A(p_t))x_t + s_t$$

where s_t represent the inventories of all commodities that firms have accumulated over the history of the economy. The change in inventories from period t to t + 1 is given by

$$s_{t+1} = y_t - f_t = s_t + (I - A(p_t))x_t - f_t, \quad f_t = f(x_t, p_t)$$

We assume that s_{t+1} stays nonnegative over time (otherwise, the inventory policy of firms must be formulated as an active one). The supply decisions by firms for the next period are assumed to be given by

$$x_{t+1} = A(p_t)x_{t+1} + f_t,$$

that is, they want to satisfy the net final demand observed in this period in the next period, based on this period's choice of technique, but next period's intermediate inputs necessary to supply this demand.

For actual current profits from sales we have the defining equation and as the implied result

$$\Pi := p_t f_t + p_t A(p_t) x_t - p_t A(p_t) x_t - p_t c\ell_t x_t = p_t A(p_t) < g_t > x_t$$

by the definition of net final demand and actual sales. Firms thus get what they spend and can exactly finance the amount of net investment they desire.

As resulting dynamics of activity levels, one therefore gets

$$x_{t+1} = (I - A(p_t))^{-1} f_t = (I - A(p_t))^{-1}(A(p_t) < g_t > x_t + c\ell(p_t)x_t)$$

which represents a nonautonomous system of difference equations for the evolution of x_t in time. We note that the Leontief inverse $(I - A(p_t))^{-1}$ will always exist and will be given by

$$(I - A(p_t))^{-1} = \sum_{k=0}^{\infty} A(p_t)^k \geq 0$$

On this basis the inventory process is then obtained as

$$s_{t+1} = y_t - f_t = s_t + x_t - (A(p_t)(I+ <g_t>)x_t + c\ell(p_t)x_t)$$

These processes in sum describe a still simple output dynamics driven by Keynesian aggregate demand and thus a meaningful supplement to a Keynesian price-setter framework.

We consider this as a more satisfactory starting point for a Keynesian approach to price quantity dynamics than the ones discussed so far in this chapter, though we have no optimizing firms in this setup (in regard to their output and investment decisions), a situation we consider adequate if one follows Alchian (1950) and starts from complete uncertainty in place of certainty (and also considers subjective or objective risk behavior).

We briefly observe before closing this subsection that the assumption c of balanced growth implies for the activity levels of firms (if g_t is assumed to be constant in time and a vector of uniform rates of growth)

$$x = (1+s)(I - A(p^*))^{-1}[gA(p^*) + c\ell(p^*)]x$$

where s may be smaller or larger than zero. It will be larger than zero if we assume that there holds

$$\lambda[gA(p^*) + c\ell(p^*] > 1 - \lambda^*$$

for the positive eigenvalues that characterize the semipositive matrices $[gA(p^*) + c\ell(p^*)]$, $A(p^*)$.

3.11.8 Concluding Remarks

We have established in this section a simple Keynesian price-quantity dynamics (where price dynamics dominates the quantity dynamics) and where relative prices tend toward long-period prices of production. Depending on the economy-wide technique $A(p_t)$, $\ell(p_t)$ chosen by n firms from a local cost-minimizing perspective, we may then also add labor values to such a framework by means of the definition

$$v_t = v_t A(p_t) + \ell(p_t) = \ell(p_t)(I - A(p_t))^{-1} = \ell(p_t)\sum_{k=0}^{\infty}A(p_t)^k = \sum_{k=0}^{\infty}\ell(p_t)A(p_t)^k$$

This definition can be used to derive the consequences of cost-minimizing technical change for labor productivity indices $1/v_{it}$, the inverse of the full labor costs imputed in the production of one unit of commodity i, as in the United Nations' System of National Accounts. Such relationships have been derived in this chapter for arbitrary actual price vectors guaranteeing positive profits and may be even more powerful in their application if markup prices are used: $p_{t+1} = \mu_t(p_t A(p_t) + p_t c\ell(p_t))$. Moreover, the ratio

$$\epsilon = \frac{\ell x - vc\ell x}{vc\ell x} = \frac{1 - vc}{vc}$$

can again be used to express a percentage of how much labor is used up for producing the consumption goods of workers in comparison to the labor time they spend for producing the whole net product of the economy and how this ratio will change over time.[24]

3.12 ■ CONCLUSIONS AND OUTLOOK

Starting from the problematic features and the social consequences of the reserve army of unemployed workers characterizing the evolution of the labor markets of many contemporaneous capitalist economies, we have tried in this chapter to demonstrate that there is—on the theoretical level—an alternative to the unleashed capitalism currently ruling the world (in developed as well as developing countries). As a substitute for the considerable degradation of a significant proportion of the working population of democratically governed societies, we have designed an economic reproduction model (including education, skill development, and elite formation) of a competitive form of capitalism that combines flexibility to a very high degree with security of income, as well as employment for members of the workforce. Schumpeter's work on the viability of a competitive type of socialism is thereby carried one step further toward a social vision that preserves to a great extent the advantages of existing capitalist forms of production and circulation but nevertheless creates a social structure of accumulation that in its essence is liberated from the human degradation we observe even in leading industrialized countries.

We believe that Schumpeter's process of creative destruction can also be implemented in such an economy, in particular on the level of the smaller firms shown in figure 3.5, since it has figured in the evolution of capitalism after World War II. It has continued to play a role in the processes we have observed in the last twenty years. One of the tasks of the elite structure shown in figure 3.5 (to the left in the middle box) is to foster such processes of creative destruction. This process of innovation and diffusion may create long waves in the evolution of the potential output-capital ratio, as well as of the growth rate of labor productivity on the macrolevel (including significant irregularities in these two time series), driven by bunching productivity shocks. The employer of first resort must address the problems this process creates for the first labor market, as well as the processes that drive effective demand and the actual output capital ratio (as implied in Keynes's explanation of the trade cycle mechanism, also present in a flexicurity system).

The essential ingredients for progress toward such a social structure are not only a basic income guarantee of the workfare type (including the obligation to work) but also reorganization of the labor market to create an employer of first resort who organizes, in a decentralized way, the work of all people not employed within privately run industries and of officially retired persons still willing to offer their human capital in the labor markets. The workability of the designed flexicurity model depends—in the same way that proposed solutions to many other actual organizational problems in contemporary market economies do—on detailed microeconomic analysis of labor relations within large, medium-sized, and small business firms as well as in the public sector. Here, economic incentives as discussed in Schumpeter (1942) need to be coupled with an educational system that not only fosters skill development and elite formation but also provides the proper foundations for citizenship education in a democratic society, where citizens essentially approve the high degree of flexibility in the industrial part of the economy (and elsewhere) because of the security aspects of the flexicurity concept and the equal opportunity principles it is based on during primary and secondary education.

Elites play an important, even central role in models of flexicurity capitalism, and their formation must therefore be carefully incorporated into the educational system. Malfunctioning elites have currently caused a worldwide crisis in capitalism, particularly since they have illustrated Keynes's statement:

> When the capital development of a country becomes a by-product of the activities of a casino, the job is likely to be ill-done.
>
> John Maynard Keynes (1936, p. 159)

It is therefore of outmost importance that the accumulation of wealth—and the power accompanying it—by individuals for selfish purposes, risk-loving individuals and financial institutions primarily using financial markets to gamble on them on a worldwide scale, and other types of malfunctioning elite behavior based on wealth and power as the main objectives give way to a process of elite formation—as described in section 3.10—that focuses on citizenship education, including ethics, competence, and responsibility in place of "greedy" elite behavior as we currently often observe it. Incredible wealth is not really necessary to induce talented persons to do excellent work, as Schumpeter (1942, p. 208) observed in his discussion of integrating the ex-bourgeois element properly into his model of competitive socialism. Exclusiveness and distinctiveness may appropriate rewards for elites under flexicurity capitalism, but there may also be many concrete incentives for elites to play their proper role in assuring the well-being of their societies.

One additional problem concerns the microlevel extensively discussed in Schumpeter's (1942) chapters 16 and 17 on competitive Western socialism. This problem involves the design of mechanisms by which prices and quantities are determined in the industrial sector. Schumpter asserts that the abstract concept of perfect competition should not be used to determine the principles that govern the formation of prices, quantities, and incomes, but rather the actual mechanisms adopted by big business under capitalism that will carry out this task (183). This idea applies in a flexicurity system, which we view as an organic evolution from unleashed forms of capitalism to socially controllable ones, achieved by steadily building on principles that are already being discussed, but in isolation from each other, in Western capitalist democracies.

The basic mechanisms of the price-quantity dynamics of capitalism are of a classical cross-dual type and they are interacting with Keynesian dual price-quantity adjustment processes in general. The latter include, on the quantity side, the Keynesian dynamic multiplier process and, on the price side, a dynamic Kaleckian markup pricing process. Cross-dual elements in this conceptually separated quantity and price dynamics are thus, on the one hand, the flow of capital into sectors of high profitability and its effects on the supply of commodities and, on the other hand, the price reactions to these quantity changes. We cannot consider these interacting price and quantity adjustment mechanisms here any further; for an initial formal discussion of them, see appendix 1. In any case, this dynamic poses no problem for the working of a flexicurity economy, since it basically performs in the way it has under big business capitalism. A discussion of the Lange-Lerner type is therefore not necessary here.

The essential changes under a flexicurity system most notably affect the labor market and result in the abolishment of the reserve-army mechanism. Our discussion of elites has furthermore shown that property rights will also be changed to make use of elected boards of managers, leaving room for private ownership only in the smaller segments of the economy. This is not a huge step away from what we already find in practice. It is in any case a change much easier to enact than the labor market reforms we need in the transition to a flexicurity society. Moreover, there may then be a greater role for the credit channel to play under flexicurity and less or even no role to play anymore for equities in financing the investments of firms, in line with Schumpeter's views on the role of credit in an entrepreneurial framework. The public discussion of stricter regulation of financial markets is currently very active and is therefore a good starting point for further analysis of the role credit, stocks, and bonds should play in contemporary globalized conditions.

Central to the transition to a new form of capitalism is the human element: workforce behavior in efficiently organized production and elite behavior in leading the society, including creation of an educational system that fosters the necessary skills and ethics needed for a democratic form of capitalism to evolve that serves the interest of the majority of people, not just a minority class of elites in the business sector. Gaining control over the Marxian distributive cycle mechanism in a Keynesian trade cycle framework, in which Schumpeterian waves of technical change occur, is the challenge management and workers have to meet together, democratically, as capitalist market economies evolve further.

APPENDIX 1: STABILITY OF BALANCED REPRODUCTION

As in Flaschel et al. (2008), we assume in this model type a real wage PC, relating the growth rate of real wages to the current state of the first labor market, specifically the utilization rate of the highly skilled workforce of firms. This PC can be represented in stylized form as follows:

$$\hat{v}_{1a} = G^1(v_{1a}) + G^2(l^w_{1a}), \quad G^{1'}, G^{2'} < 0 \qquad (3.1)$$

The first component in the growth law for $v_{1a} = \omega_{1a}/z$, z labor productivity represents the Blanchard and Katz (1999) real wage error correction term, while the second one derives from the utilization rate $u_{wa} = l^d_{1a}/l^w_{1a}$ of the highly skilled workforce employed by firms expressed in per unit of capital form, where l^d_{1a} is a given magnitude due to fixed proportions in production and full capacity growth. The assumption $G^{2'} < 0$ thus simply asserts that real wage dynamics depends positively on the utilization rate of the highly skilled workers employed by firms.

The growth rate of the highly skilled workforce of firms, $\hat{L}^w_{1a}$, is assumed to also depend positively on the rate of capacity utilization $u_{wa} = l^d_{1a}/l^w_{1a}$, as suggested by Okun's law, and thus negatively on its own level. Moreover, since the second state variable of the model l^w_{1a} is to be defined by zL^w_{1a}/K, there is a negative effect from the rate of profit on the growth rate of this state variable (through the investment behavior of firms) and thus a positive effect of real wages of highly skilled workers in the second law of motion of the economy, which in general terms therefore reads:

$$\hat{l}^w_{1a} = F^1(v_{1a}) + F^2(l^w_{1a}), \quad F^{1'} > 0, F^{2'} < 0 \qquad (3.2)$$

The two-dimensional dynamics (3.1), (3.2) allows the application of the following Liapunov function to be used in the stability proof that follows:

$$H(v_{1a}, l^w_{1a}) = \int_{v^0_{1a}}^{v_{1a}} F^1(\tilde{v}_{1a})/\tilde{v}_{1a} d\tilde{v}_{1a} + \int_{l^{wo}_{1a}}^{l^w_{1a}} -\tilde{G}^2(\tilde{l}^w_{1a})/\tilde{l}^w_{1a} d\tilde{l}^w_{1a}$$

This function describes by its graph a three-dimensional sink (see figure 3.2), with the steady state of the economy as its lowest point, since the function integrates two other functions that are negative to the left of the steady-state values and positive to their right. For the first derivative of the Liapunov function along the trajectories of the considered dynamical system, we get:

$$\begin{aligned}
\dot{H} = dH(v_{1a}(t), l_{1a}^w)/dt &= \left(F^1(v_{1a})/v_{1a}\right)\dot{v}_{1a} - \left(G^2(l_{1a}^w)/l_{1a}^w\right)\dot{l}_{1a}^w \\
&= F^1(v_{1a})\hat{v}_{1a} - G^2(l_{1a}^w)\hat{l}_{1a}^w \\
&= F^1(v_{1a})(G^1(v_{1a}) + G^2(l_{1a}^w)) - G^2(l_{1a}^w)(F^1(v_{1a}) + F^2(l_{1a}^w)) \\
&= F^1(v_{1a})G^1(v_{1a}) - G^2(l_{1a}^w)F^2(l_{1a}^w) \\
&= -F^1(v_{1a})(-G^1(v_{1a})) - (-G^2(l_{1a}^w))(-F^2(l_{1a}^w)) \\
&\leq 0 \quad [= 0 \quad \text{if and only if} \quad v_{1a} = v_{1a}^o, l_{1a}^w = l_1^{wo}]
\end{aligned}$$

since the multiplied functions have the same sign to the right and to the left of their steady-state values and thus lead to positive products with a minus sign in front of them (to the point where the economy is already sitting in the steady state). We thus have proved that there holds

Proposition 7

The interior steady state of the dynamics (3.1), (3.2) is a global sink of the function H, defined on the positive orthant of the phase space, and is attracting in this domain, since the function H is strictly decreasing along the trajectories of the dynamics in the positive orthant of the phase space, the economic part of this phase space.

APPENDIX 2: SUSTAINABILITY OF BALANCED REPRODUCTION

There is one more law of motion in the background of the model that needs to be considered in order to provide a complete statement on the economic sustainability of our model of flexicurity capitalism. This law of motion describes the evolution of the company pension fund per unit of the capital stock $\eta = R/K$, and it is obtained from the equations for $\dot{R}$ and $\dot{K}$ as follows:

$$\frac{d\eta}{dt} = \frac{S_1}{K} - (\delta_r + \rho)\eta = s_1 - (\delta_r + \rho)\eta$$

with savings of households of type 1 and profits of firms per unit of capital being given by

$$\begin{aligned}
s_1 &= (1 - c_1)(1 - \tau_1)(v_{1a} + v_{1b})y^p - v_{2b}l_r \\
&\quad - [v_{2a}l_a^w - (v_{1a} + v_{2a}\alpha_a\tau_1(v_{1a} + v_{1b}))y^p] \\
&\quad - [v_{2b}l_b^w - (v_{1b} + v_{2b}((1 - \alpha_g) - \alpha_a)\tau_1(v_{1a} + v_{1b}))y^p] \\
\rho &= y^p[1 - (v_{1a} + v_{2a})] - \delta_k
\end{aligned}$$

For the ratio of savings to GDP $\theta_1 = S_1/Y^p = s_1/y^p$ we derive in the steady state of the economy the expression

$$\theta_1^o = (1-c_1)(1-\tau_1)(v_{1a}^o + v_{1b}^o) - v_{2b}^o y_r^o$$
$$- [v_{2a}^o y_a^{wo} - (v_{1a}^o + v_{2a}^o \alpha_a \tau_1(v_{1a}^o + v_{1b}^o))]$$
$$- [v_{2b}^o y_b^{wo} - (v_{1b}^o + v_{2b}^o((1-\alpha_g) - \alpha_a)\tau_1(v_{1a}^o + v_{1b}^o))]$$

with $y_r = l_r/y^p = zL^r/Y^p$, $y_a^w = zL_a^W/Y^p$, $y_b^w = zL_b^W/Y^p$. For $v_{2a}^o = \bar{v}_{2a}$, $v_{2b}^o = \bar{v}_{2b}$, that is, the case where wages in the government sector are clearing the labor market without any need for an employer of first resort; this leads to

$$\theta_1^o = (1-c_1)(1-\tau_1)(v_{1a}^o + v_{1b}^o) - \bar{v}_{2b} l_r^o$$

This ratio is positive if $L_r/(Y^p/z) = L_r/L_{1a}^d$ is sufficiently small. We therefore need a condition that limits the ratio $L_r/L = t_r L_o/L = t_r/t$ from above in combination with conditions that limit (from above) the real wages $\omega_{2a}^o \geq \bar{\omega}_{2a}$, $\omega_{2b}^o \geq \bar{\omega}_{2b}$ paid in the government sector in order to get a positive ratio θ_1^o. This shows that such upper limits on wages in the public labor markets as well as in base pension payments are needed to provide sufficient conditions for a positive savings ratio with respect to the GDP Y^p. If this is given, we will have a positive steady state value for company pension funds per unit of capital $\eta^o = s_1^o/(\delta_r + \bar{m})$ and also a positive value for the percentage of company pension payments as a fraction of base pension payments γ_1^o, which then is given by

$$\gamma_1^o = \theta_1^o/\sigma_r \leq (1-c_1)(1-\tau_1)\frac{v_{1a}^o + v_{1b}^o}{v_{2b}^o}\frac{y^p}{y_r} - 1$$

where $\sigma_r = \omega_{2b}^o L_r/Y^p$ is the share of base pension payments in the GDP. The establishment of a desired ratio between company pension payments and base pension payments therefore requires (besides a viable ratio t_r concerning the age structure of the economy) the choice of appropriate real wages in the public sector and it is in any case limited from above by the expression on the right-hand side in this equation.

4 Unleashed Capitalism: The Starting Point for Societal Reform

4.1 ■ INTRODUCTION

In 1936, after the financial crisis in the United States and the Great Depression of the 1930s, John Maynard Keynes issued a severe warning concerning the misdirected objectives of the financial markets of his time.

> It is rare, one is told, for an American to invest, as many Englishmen still do 'for income'; and he will not readily purchase an investment except in the hope of capital appreciation. ... i.e. that he is, in the above sense, a speculator. Speculators may do no harm as bubbles on a steady stream of enterprise. But the position is serious when enterprise becomes the bubble on a whirl-pool of speculation. When the capital development of a country becomes a by-product of the activities of a casino, the job is likely to be ill-done. The measure of success attained by Wall Street, regarded as an institution of which the proper social purpose is to direct new investment into the most profitable channels in terms of future yield, cannot be claimed as one of the outstanding triumphs of *laissez-faire* capitalism—which is not surprising, if I am right in thinking that the best brains of Wall Street have been in fact directed towards a different object.
>
> Keynes (1936, p. 159)

Yet in mainstream thinking and the neoclassical synthesis of Keynes and classics theories, there was no serious debate on modeling of the causal nexus from financial markets to goods markets to labor markets envisaged (including repercussions) by Keynes; instead, there has been a move away from his theoretical insight toward supply side approaches and the theory of inflation. This (though limited) understanding of the wage-price spiral was and remains an important element in the understanding of the working of capitalism (as this chapter will show), but it very much ignores the financial accelerator mechanism and the herding behavior that characterize the dynamics in the financial markets. In 1982, Hyman Minsky argued from various perspectives that "it" can happen again, for example as follows:

> Success breeds disregard of the possibility of failures. The absence of serious financial difficulties over a substantial period leads ... to a euphoric economy in which short-term financing of long term positions becomes the normal way of life. As previous financial crisis recedes in time, it is quite natural for central bankers, government

officials, bankers, businessmen and even economists to believe that a new era has arrived.

Hyman P. Minsky (*Can "It" Happen Again?*, 1982, p. 213)

In this chapter we consider the issues raised by Keynes and Minsky, in a model with, on the one hand, a fully articulated wage-price spiral, exhibiting a variety of (in-)stability scenarios, and on the other hand, cumulative processes generating capital gain spirals, driven by capital gains expectations operating in a Keynesian quantity dynamic that is essentially shaped by profitability expectations, state-of-confidence-determined investment behavior, and the Keynesian multiplier. We find that there are a variety of primarily unstable feedback channels at work in the private sector of the modeled macroeconomy, which only under relatively sluggish economic adjustment rules imply the stability of the balanced growth path of the economy, but which more likely imply the instability of this growth path. We must therefore examine behavioral changes far off the steady state, such as downward money wage rigidity, as part of the dynamics of the economy so that they remain bounded within an economically viable domain (in case they do not simply collapse and undergo severe economic reform in order to get the economy working again).

Section 4.2 discusses the approach chosen in this chapter from the general perspective underlying this type of model building. In section 4.3 we develop the extensive form of the model and give a detailed explanation of its structure. The intensive form of the dynamics is only derived for a basic modification of the model in section 4.6, in which we use long-term bonds instead of short-term ones. This modified version—as well as the model with only short-term bonds—allows for a unique interior steady-state solution on the basis of the implied eight autonomous laws of motion of the economy. We consider the stability of the full eight-dimensional dynamical system in section 4.4 through a sequence of subsystems of increasing dimensions. We also briefly show to what extent monetary and fiscal policy can moderate the persistent fluctuations that are endogenously generated by the model. In section 4.5 we briefly consider against this background some instability scenarios for this type of real-financial model building. Sections 4.6 and 4.7 extend the model toward a treatment of risk-bearing long-term bonds in place of the risk-free short-term bonds so far considered, as well as toward the inclusion of an interest-rate policy rule rather than the constant growth rate of money supply we assumed beforehand.

4.2 ■ REAL DISEQUILIBRIA, BALANCED PORTFOLIOS, AND THE REAL-FINANCIAL MARKETS INTERACTION

In this chapter[1] we develop a model of capitalism basically descriptive of economies such as the US economy. The assumed behavioral equations are at first kept as linear as possible in order to concentrate on the intrinsic nonlinearities of such an approach to the real-financial market interaction. Semi-reduced substructures of this model type have been estimated for the US economy, the Eurozone, and other advanced capitalist economies (see for example Flaschel and Krolzig [2006] and Flaschel [2009, chapter 9]).

We formulate a Tobin (1980, 1982) type model of the stock-flow interaction of the financial markets with the real markets, assuming imperfect asset substitution and imperfect foresight. In doing so, we make use of the Keynes-Metzler-Goodwin approach developed by Chiarella and Flaschel (2000). In contrast to their basic KMG approach, we now use, as in the Blanchard (1981) stock market model, Tobin's q explicitly in the investment function as well as in the stock demand functions in the asset markets. This chapter therefore provides a synthesis of the KMG treatment of real markets with the portfolio approach of Tobin (1980, 1982), though one that departs from rational expectations models and their ideal treatment of financial markets simply by rates of return parity conditions. We expect stability (as in the six-dimensional KMG approach) in the case of imperfect asset substitution based on the gross substitute assumption if only fundamentalists are present in the financial markets, while the addition of chartists will introduce behavior that can give rise to cumulative instability if not stopped by appropriate bounding mechanisms.

The literature on the interaction of stocks and flows on the macrolevel is to a certain extent still in its infancy. Tobin's work (see in particular Tobin [1980, 1982]) has pushed this topic a decisive step forward, but the analytical treatment (not to speak of an empirical analysis) of a full interaction of the real and the financial side of the macroeconomy is by and large missing. There are works by Godley and Lavoie (see in particular Godley [1999] and Godley and Lavoie [2007]), Franke and Semmler (2000), Foley and Taylor (2006), and Docherty (2005) that attempt to improve the situation,[2] but the dominant tradition—in particular in mainstream economics—is to use return parity conditions (up to the money market) in order to study the interaction of the financial with the real markets. This chapter provides a significant step forward in the directions proposed by this literature, but in contrast to its approach by providing (in-)stability propositions for the resulting necessarily high-dimensional interaction of the stock markets for financial assets with the flow markets of the real sectors of the economy.

Our goal is to present a Keynesian macrodynamic model of a growing monetary economy that builds on the analysis of the working KMG model of Chiarella and Flaschel (2000) and Chiarella, Flaschel, Groh, and Semmler (2000). We try to explain the real—financial interaction in Keynesian dynamics more carefully than has been done in the working KMG model from which it has been derived. In this model, asset markets influence the real dynamics only in a very traditional way, by means of an LM curve that gives rise to a stable relationship between the nominal rate of interest, the output capital ratio, and real balances per unit of capital.

Furthermore, neither bond dynamics nor the evolution of the equities could influence the real part of the economy because of the lack of wealth and interest income effects on aggregate demand. This chapter introduces a portfolio theory of asset market behavior instead of a single LM curve and thereby improves the representation of asset market dynamics considerably, though we ignore wealth and interest income effects. Nevertheless bond and equity dynamics now feeds back into the real part of the economy, though still by a single route, namely through Tobin's average q as one important argument about the investment behavior of firms.

Our KMG approach to macrodynamics studies the interaction of all important markets of the macroeconomy (for labor, goods, money, bonds, and equities) in a nonstochastic environment without explicit utility maximization of households and profit maximization of firms.[3] Household behavioral equations are in the tradition of the Kaldorian approach, focusing on differentiated saving habits, and are not derived by optimizing a hypothetical utility function of workers or capitalists. On the one hand, this method reflects our skepticism about the relevance of utility maximization for aggregate behavioral relationships (in an economy with labor and goods markets disequilibrium), and on the other hand, it allows us to leave the model sufficiently simple in order to concentrate on the description and analysis of asset market dynamics.[4] Combining a full disequilibrium approach in the real part of the economy with a general equilibrium approach in the financial part raises several issues about the dynamics that drives the economy. The model therefore presents an integrated approach to macrodynamics that accounts for all budget constraints of all types of agents in the economy, and exhibits a uniquely determined steady-state solution surrounded by various propagation or feedback mechanisms in the economy. It is therefore a consistently formulated, integrated, dynamical model on the aggregate level, exhibiting a rich dynamic structure with a type of high-order dynamics that has not been studied theoretically in the macroeconomics literature.

As we mentioned, the core of the model is given by a KMG approach to integrated macrodynamics,[5] the foundations to which were laid in Flaschel, Franke, and Semmler (1997). Further work is ongoing to extend the KMG approach to the treatment of small or interacting open economies (see Asada, Chiarella, Flaschel, and Franke [2003]) and a theoretical and numerical analysis of modern macroeconometric model building (Chiarella, Flaschel, and Semmler [2000]). The level of macrodynamic modeling reached in this chapter goes significantly beyond the work just cited and represents the basis of future work on the topic firms, finance, and economic policy, in which we will continue these approaches toward a fuller treatment of the behavior of firms, influence of financial markets on the real side of the economy, and treatment of fiscal and monetary policy rules that can render more stable the volatile dynamics that typically characterizes models of KMG growth.

The main elements of this approach are, briefly, the following. The economy consists of various private agents: workers, asset holders, and firms. The public sector consists of the government and the central bank. The goods market (and the money market) is modeled in a way that draws on Keynes's (1936) general theory and other traditional Keynesian theory. A production good exclusively produced by firms can be either consumed by workers, asset holders, or the government and/or invested as business fixed capital or used for inventory investment by firms. Firms do not have perfect foresight with respect to the demand for goods and do not adjust their output instantaneously toward the level of aggregate demand. Hence, to satisfy actual and future demand, they must hold stocks of inventories of produced goods. The adjustment policy for the attainment of a desired stock of inventories is modeled in a way proposed by Metzler (1941).

We assume the labor market takes place under a Keynesian regime, in the sense that any demand can be satisfied by an always positive excess supply of labor at the actual wage rate. Goodwin's (1967) contribution to the model is the study of the dynamic interaction of employment and the real wage rate.

We want to model a monetary economy with various financial assets in order to examine their interaction with the real parts, namely the goods market and the labor market. There are three financial assets: money issued by the central bank, short-term bonds issued by the government, and equities issued by firms to finance investments. All three financial assets are exclusively held by the asset holders in the model.

4.3 ■ A PORTFOLIO APPROACH TO KMG GROWTH DYNAMICS

In this section we provide the extensive or structural form of our growth model of KMG type. It includes a portfolio equilibrium block rather than the LM theory of the short-run rate of interest and the dynamic adjustment equations for the prices of the other assets of Chiarella, Flaschel, Groh, and Semmler (2000). We split the model into appropriate modules, primarily dealing with sectors of the economy—households, firms, and the government (fiscal and monetary authority)—but also representing wage-price interaction and the asset markets.

4.3.1 Households

As discussed in the introduction, we disaggregate the sector of households in worker households and asset holder households. We begin with the description of workers' behavior:

Workers' Households

$$\omega = w/p \tag{4.1}$$

$$C_w = (1 - \tau_w)\omega L^d \tag{4.2}$$

$$S_w = 0 \qquad (4.3)$$

$$\hat{L} = n = \text{const} \qquad (4.4)$$

Equation (4.1) gives the definition of the real wage ω before taxation, where w denotes the nominal wage and p the actual price level. We operate in a Keynesian framework with sluggish wage and price adjustment processes, hence we take the real wage to be given exogenously at each moment. We further follow the Keynesian framework by assuming that the labor demand of firms can always be satisfied out of the given labor supply; in other words, we do not allow for regime switches as they are discussed in Chiarella, Flaschel, Groh, and Semmler (2000, chapter 5). According to (4.2), real income of workers equals the product of real wages times labor demand, which net of taxes $\tau_w \omega L^d$ equals workers' consumption, since we do not allow for savings of workers, as postulated in (4.3).[6] The absence of savings implies that wealth of workers is zero at all times. This means that workers do not hold any money and that they immediately spend their disposable income. As is standard in theories of economic growth, we finally assume in equation (4.4) a constant growth rate n of the labor force L based on the assumption that labor is supplied inelastically at each moment. The parameter n can be easily reinterpreted to be the growth rate of the working population plus the growth rate of labor augmenting technical progress.

The modeling of the asset holders' income, consumption, and wealth is described by the following set of equations:

Asset Holders' Households

$$r^e = (Y^e - \delta K - \omega L^d)/K \qquad (4.5)$$

$$C_c = (1 - s_c)[r^e K + iB/p - T_c], \quad 0 < s_c < 1 \qquad (4.6)$$

$$S_p = s_c[r^e K + iB/p - T_c] \qquad (4.7)$$

$$= (\dot{M} + \dot{B} + p_e \dot{E})/p \qquad (4.8)$$

$$W_c = (M + B + p_e E)/p, \quad W_c^n = pW_c \qquad (4.9)$$

The first equation, (4.5), defines the expected rate of return on real capital r^e to be the ratio of the currently expected real cash flow and the real stock of business fixed capital K. The expected cash flow is given by expected real revenues from sales Y^e diminished by real depreciation of capital δK and the real wage sum ωL^d. We assume that firms pay out all expected cash flow in the form of dividends to the asset holders, one source of income for asset holders. The second source is given by real interest payments on short-term bonds (iB/p), where i is the nominal interest rate and B the stock of such bonds. Summing up these types of interest incomes and taking account of lump sum taxes T_c in the case of asset holders (for reasons of simplicity), we get the disposable income of asset holders within the brackets of equation (4.6), which together with a postulated fixed propensity to consume $(1 - s_c)$ out of this income gives us the real consumption of asset holders.

Real savings of pure asset owners is real disposable income minus their consumption as expressed in equation (4.7). They can allocate it in the form of money $\dot{M}$, or buy other financial assets, namely short-term bonds $\dot{B}$ or equities $\dot{E}$ at the price p_e, the only financial instruments that we allow in this reformulation of KMG growth. Hence, savings of asset holders must be distributed to these assets as shown in equation (4.8). Real wealth of pure asset holders is defined on this basis in equation (4.9) as the sum of the real cash balance, real short-term bond holdings, and real equity holdings of asset holders. Short-term bonds are assumed to be fixed-price bonds with a price of 1, $p_b = 1$, and a flexible interest rate i.

To describe the demand equations of asset owning households for financial assets, we follow Tobin's general equilibrium approach (Tobin [1969]):

$$M^d = f_m(i, r_e^e)W_c^n \qquad (4.10)$$

$$B^d = f_b(i, r_e^e)W_c^n \qquad (4.11)$$

$$p_e E^d = f_e(i, r_e^e)W_c^n \qquad (4.12)$$

$$W_c^n = M^d + B^d + p_e E^d \qquad (4.13)$$

The demand for money balances of asset holders M^d is determined by a function $f_m(i, r_e^e)$, which depends on the interest rate on short-term bonds i and the expected rate of return on equities r_e^e. The value of this function times the nominal wealth W^n gives the nominal demand for money M^d, that is, f_m describes the portion of nominal wealth allocated to pure money holdings. This formulation of money demand is not based on a transaction motive, since the holding of transaction balances is the job of firms in this chapter. We also do not assume that the financial assets of the economy are perfect substitutes, but indeed assume that financial assets are imperfect substitutes in the approach that underlies the block of equations just presented. But what is the motive for asset holders to hold a fraction of their wealth in the form of money, when there is a riskless interest-bearing asset? In our view, it is reasonable to employ a speculative motive: Asset holders want to hold money in order to *be able* to buy other assets or goods with zero or very low transaction costs. This of course assumes that there are (implicitly given) transaction costs when fixed-price bonds are turned into money.

The nominal demand for bonds is determined by $f_b(i, r_e^e)$ and the nominal demand for equities by $f_e(i, r_e^e)$, which describe the fractions allocated to these forms of financial wealth. From equation (4.9), we know that actual nominal wealth equals the stocks of financial assets held by the asset holders. We assume, as is usual in portfolio approaches, that the asset holders demand assets of an amount equal in sum to their nominal wealth, as shown in equation (4.9).

In other words, they reallocate their wealth based on new information about the rates of returns on their assets and thus take care of their wealth constraint.

What is left to model in the households sector is the expected rate of return on equities r_e^e, which consists of real dividends per equity ($r^e pK/p_e E$) and expected capital gains π_e, the latter being the expected growth rate of equity prices.

$$r_e^e = \frac{r^e pK}{p_e E} + \pi_e \qquad (4.14)$$

In order to complete the modeling of asset holders' behavior we must describe the evolution of π_e. We assume that there are two types of asset holders, which differ with respect to how they anticipate equity prices. There are *chartists*, who in principle employ adaptive expectations:

$$\dot{\pi}_{ec} = \beta_{\pi_{ec}}(\hat{p}_e - \pi_{ec}), \qquad (4.15)$$

where $\beta_{\pi_{ec}}$ is the adjustment speed toward the actual growth rate of equity prices. The other asset holders, the *fundamentalists*, employ forward-looking expectations:

$$\dot{\pi}_{ef} = \beta_{\pi_{ef}}(\bar{\eta} - \pi_{ef}) \qquad (4.16)$$

where $\bar{\eta}$ is the fundamentalists' expected long-term inflation rate of share prices. Assuming that the aggregate expected inflation rate is a weighted average of the two expected inflation rates, where the weights are determined according to the sizes of the groups, we postulate

$$\pi_e = \alpha_{\pi_{ec}} \pi_{ec} + (1 - \alpha_{\pi_{ec}}) \pi_{ef} \qquad (4.17)$$

Here $\alpha_{\pi_{ec}} \in (0, 1)$ is the ratio of chartists to all asset holders.

4.3.2 Firms

We consider the behavior of firms by means of two submodules. One describes the production framework and firms' investment in business fixed capital; the other introduces the Metzlerian approach of inventory cycles concerning expected sales, actual sales, and the output of firms.

Firms: Production and Investment

$$r^e = (pY^e - wL^d - p\delta K)/(pK) \qquad (4.18)$$

$$Y^p = y^p K \qquad (4.19)$$

$$u = Y/Y^p \qquad (4.20)$$

$$L^d = Y/x \tag{4.21}$$

$$e = L^d/L = Y/(xL) \tag{4.22}$$

$$q = p_e E/(pK) \tag{4.23}$$

$$I = i_q(q-1)K + i_u(u-\bar{u})K + nK = i(\cdot)K \tag{4.24}$$

$$\hat{K} = I/K \tag{4.25}$$

$$p_e \dot{E} = pI + p(\dot{N} - \mathcal{I}) \tag{4.26}$$

Firms are assumed to pay dividends according to expected profits (expected sales net of depreciation and minus the wage sum); see the module of the asset owning households in the previous section. The rate of expected profits r^e is expected real profits per unit of capital as stated in equation (4.18). For producing output, firms utilize a production technology that transforms demanded labor L^d combined with business fixed capital K into output. For convenience we assume that the production takes place by a fixed proportion technology.[7] According to (4.19), potential output Y^p is therefore given at each moment by the fixed coefficient y^p times the existing stock of physical capital. Accordingly, the utilization of productive capacities is shown by the ratio u of actual production Y and the potential output Y^p. The fixed proportions in production also give rise to a constant output-labor coefficient x, with which we can deduce labor demand from out put determined by the goods market as in equation (4.21). The ratio L^d/L thus defines the rate of employment of the model.

The economic behavior of firms also comprises investment decisions into business fixed capital, which is determined independently from households' savings decisions. We here model investment decisions per unit of capital as a function of the deviation of Tobin's q (see Tobin [1969]) from its long-term value 1, and the deviation of actual capacity utilization from a normal rate of capital utilization, and add an exogenous trend term, here given by the natural growth rate n, so that this rate determines the growth path of the economy in the usual way. We employ here Tobin's average q, defined in equation (4.23). It is the ratio of the nominal value of equities and the reproduction costs of the existing stock of capital. Investment in business fixed capital is enforced when q exceeds 1, and is reduced when q is smaller than 1. This influence is represented by the term $i_q(q-1)$ in equation (4.24). The term $i_u(u-\bar{u})$ models the component of investment due to the deviation of the utilization rate of physical capital from its nonaccelerating inflation value $\bar{u}$. The last component, nK, takes account of the natural growth rate n, which is necessary for steady-state analysis if natural growth is considered as exogenously given. Equation (4.26) is the budget constraint of the firms. Investment in business fixed capital and unintended changes in the inventory stock $p(\dot{N} - \mathcal{I})$ must be financed by issuing equities, since they are the only financial instrument of firms in this chapter. Capital stock growth is given by net investment per unit of capital I/K in this demand-determined modeling of the short-term equilibrium position of the economy.

Next we model the inventory dynamics following Metzler (1941) and Franke (1992), very useful approach for describing the goods market disequilibrium dynamics with all of its implications.

Firms Output Adjustment:

$$N^d = \alpha_{n^d} Y^e \qquad (4.27)$$

$$\mathcal{I} = nN^d + \beta_n(N^d - N) \qquad (4.28)$$

$$Y = Y^e + \mathcal{I} \qquad (4.29)$$

$$Y^d = C + I + \delta K + G \qquad (4.30)$$

$$\dot{Y}^e = nY^e + \beta_{y^e}(Y^d - Y^e) \qquad (4.31)$$

$$\dot{N} = Y - Y^d \qquad (4.32)$$

$$S_f = Y - Y^e = \mathcal{I} \qquad (4.33)$$

where $\alpha_{n^d}, \beta_n, \beta_{y^e} \geq 0$.

As shown in equation (4.27), the desired stock of physical inventories is denoted by N^d and is assumed to be a fixed proportion of the expected sales. The planned investments $\mathcal{I}$ in inventories follow a sluggish adjustment process toward the desired stock N^d according to equation (4.28). Taking account of this additional demand for goods, we set the production Y equal to the expected sales of firms plus $\mathcal{I}$ in equation (4.29). For explaining the expectation formation for goods demand, we need the actual total demand for goods, which is given by consumption (of private households and the government) and gross investment by firms (4.30). By knowing the actual demand Y^d, which is always fulfilled, we get the dynamics of expected sales in equation (4.31). These expectations are modeled to be the outcome of an error-correction process, which incorporates the natural growth rate n to take account of the fact that this process operates in a growing economy. The adjustment of sales expectations is driven by the prediction error $(Y^d - Y^e)$, with an adjustment speed given by β_{y^e}. Actual changes in the stock of inventories are given by the deviation of production from goods demanded (4.32). The savings of the firms S_f is, as usual, defined by income minus consumption. Because we assume that firms do not consume anything, their income equals their savings and is given by the excess of production over expected sales, $Y - Y^e$. According to the production account in figure 4.1, the gross accounting profit of firms is $r^e pK + p\mathcal{I} = pC + pI + p\delta K + p\dot{N} + pG$. Using the definition of r^e from equation (4.18), we compute that $pY^e + p\mathcal{I} = pY^d + p\dot{N}$, or equivalently $p(Y - Y^e) = \mathcal{I}$, as equation (4.33) shows.

Uses	Resources
Production Account of Firms:	
Depreciation $p\delta K$	Private consumption pC
Wages wL^d	Gross investment $pI + p\delta K$
Gross accounting profits $\Pi = r^e pK + pI$	Inventory investment $p\dot{N}$
	Public consumption pG
Income Account of Firms:	
Dividends $r^e p_y K$	Gross accounting profits Π
Savings pI	
Accumulation Account of Firms:	
Gross investment $pI + p\delta K$	Depreciation $p\delta K$
Inventory investment $p\dot{N}$	Savings pI
	Financial deficit FD
Financial Account of Firms:	
Financial deficit FD	Equity financing $p_e \dot{E}$

Figure 4.1 Accounting sheets of the firms' sector.

4.3.3 Fiscal and Monetary Authorities

The role of the government in this chapter is to provide the economy with public (unproductive) services within the limits of its budget constraint. Public purchases (and interest payments) are financed through taxes, newly printed money, or newly issued fixed-price bonds ($p_b = 1$). The budget constraint gives rise to some repercussion effects between the public and private sectors.

$$T = \tau_w \omega L^d + T_c \tag{4.34}$$

$$T_c = t_c K + iB/p, \quad t_c = \text{const} \tag{4.35}$$

$$G = gK, \quad g = \text{const} \tag{4.36}$$

$$S_g = T - iB/p - G \tag{4.37}$$

$$\hat{M} = \mu \tag{4.38}$$

$$\dot{B} = pG + iB - pT - \dot{M} \tag{4.39}$$

We model the tax income as consisting of taxes on wage income and capital income T_c. We assume the latter solely for analytical simplicity and make aggregate demand independent of the interest payments of the government.

Doing so simplifies steady-state calculations significantly, as with not including wealth effects on consumption in our model.[8]

For the real purchases of the government in providing government services, we assume, as in Sargent (1987), that they are a fixed proportion g of real capital, which taken together allows us to represent fiscal policy by means of simple parameters on the intensive form level of the model and in the steady-state considerations we discuss later. The real savings of the government (a deficit if it has a negative sign) is defined in equation (4.37) by real taxes minus real interest payments minus real public service expenditures. Again for simplicity, we give the growth rate of money by a constant μ. Equation (4.38) shows the monetary policy rule of the central bank; money is assumed to enter the economy via open market operations of the central bank, which buys short-term bonds from the asset holders when issuing new money. The changes in the short-term bonds supplied by the government are given residually in equation (4.39), which shows the budget constraint of the government sector. This representation of the behavior of the monetary and fiscal authorities clearly shows that the treatment of policy questions does not form a central part of our discussion.

4.3.4 The Wage-Price Spiral

We now turn to one of the modules of our model that can be an important source of instability. We obtain this module by an advanced treatment of wage-price dynamics (compared to the conventional type of PC formulations), picking up the Rose approach (Rose [1990]) of two short-run PCs, the wage PC and the price PC. Adding as in Blanchard and Katz (1999) (see the appendix to chapter 1) a negative influence of the wage share on the growth rate of money wages (and a positive influence on the growth rate of commodity prices) (see Flaschel and Krolzig [2006] for details) would also provide a microfoundation to the wage-price spiral and add a certain amount of self-discipline to this spiral. This has been treated in detail elsewhere (see, e.g., Asada, Chiarella, Flaschel, and Franke [2009]), and we do not consider it here. The wage-price dynamics reads as follows:

$$\hat{w} = \beta_w(e - \bar{e}) + \kappa_w \hat{p} + (1 - \kappa_w)\pi^c \qquad (4.40)$$

$$\hat{p} = \beta_p(u - \bar{u}) + \kappa_p \hat{w} + (1 - \kappa_p)\pi^c \qquad (4.41)$$

$$\dot{\pi}^c = \beta_{\pi^c}(\alpha \hat{p} + (1 - \alpha)(\mu - n) - \pi^c) \qquad (4.42)$$

where $\beta_w, \beta_p, \beta_{\pi^c} \geq 0, 0 \leq \alpha \leq 1$, and $0 \leq \kappa_w, \kappa_p \leq 1$. This approach makes use of the assumption that relative changes in money wages are influenced by demand pressure in the market for labor and by price inflation (as cost-pressure) terms and that price inflation in turn depends on demand pressure in the market for goods and on the growth rate of money wages (as cost-pressure) terms.

Wage inflation is described in equation (4.40), on the one hand by means of a demand pull-term $\beta_w(e - \bar{e})$, which tells us that relative changes in wages depend positively on the gap between actual employment e and its NAIRU value $\bar{e}$. On the other hand, the cost-push elements in wage inflation are the weighted average of short-term (assumed for simplicity as perfectly anticipated) price inflation $\hat{p}$ and a medium-term overall inflation climate π^c, where the weights for these two terms are given by κ_w and $1 - \kappa_w$. The price PC is quite similar; it displays a demand-pull and a cost-push component, too. The demand-pull term is given by the gap between capital utilization and its NAIRU value, $(u - \bar{u})$, and the cost-push element is the κ_p and $1 - \kappa_p$ weighted average of short-term wage inflation $\hat{w}$ (perfectly foreseen) and the medium-term overall inflation climate π^c (see Asada, Chiarella, Flaschel, and Franke [2009] for detailed treatments of the role of this term in a wage-price spiral mechanism). What is left to model is the climate surrounding the current price inflation rate π^c. We postulate in equation (4.42) that changes in the perceived medium-term inflation term are due to an adjustment process toward a weighted average of the current inflation rate and steady-state inflation. Thus we introduce a simple kind of updating mechanism for the inflation climate within which the economy operates, partly based on adaptive expectations, but also partly dependent on fundamental forward-looking expectations. This adjustment process is driven by an adjustment speed β_{π^c}. It is obvious from this description of the wage-price spiral that it is both a very general description of such a cross-over dynamics and one that can be extended meaningfully, for example by an insider-outsider approach that introduces the rate of utilization of the employed workforce into the dynamics of money wages.

The Law of Motion for Real Wages:

The growth rate of real wages is the growth rate of nominal wages minus price inflation:

$$\hat{\omega} = \frac{dw}{dt}/w - \frac{dp}{dt}/p = \hat{w} - \hat{p}$$

Plugging in the laws of motion for nominal wages and prices (and making use of $\kappa = (1 - \kappa_w \kappa_p)^{-1}$):

$$\begin{aligned}\hat{p} &= \beta_p(u - \bar{u}) + \kappa_p \hat{w} + (1 - \kappa_p)\pi^c \\ &= \beta_p(u - \bar{u}) + \kappa_p(\beta_w(e - \bar{e}) + \kappa_w \hat{p} + (1 - \kappa_w)\pi^c) + (1 - \kappa_p)\pi^c \\ &= \beta_p(u - \bar{u}) + \kappa_p \beta_w(e - \bar{e}) + \kappa_p \kappa_w \hat{p} + \kappa_p(1 - \kappa_w)\pi^c + (1 - \kappa_p)\pi^c\end{aligned}$$

that is,

$$\hat{p} = \frac{\beta_p(u - \bar{u}) + \kappa_p \beta_w(e - \bar{e}) + (1 - \kappa_w \kappa_p)\pi^c}{1 - \kappa_w \kappa_p}$$

$$= \kappa(\beta_p(u - \bar{u}) + \kappa_p \beta_w(e - \bar{e})) + \pi^c$$

and

$$\hat{w} = \kappa(\beta_w(e - \bar{e}) + \kappa_w \beta_p(u - \bar{u})) + \pi^c$$

we obtain for the law of motion of the real wage $\omega = w/p$

$$\hat{\omega} = \kappa[(1 - \kappa_p)(\beta_w(e - \bar{e}) - (1 - \kappa_w)\beta_p(u - \bar{u})]$$

The growth rate of real wages thus depends positively on demand pressure in the market for labor and negatively on demand pressure in the market for goods. It is related to economic activity in an ambiguous way; we discuss the implications of this fact later.

This derivation of the law of motion for real wages gives one example for the derivation of the intensive form of the model. This form will, however, be derived only for a modification of it (see section 4.5). In this section, we concentrate on the important partial feedback channels that characterize the working of the dynamics through their interaction.

In a closed two-dimensional framework of the interaction of the real wage with the rate of change of economic activity (assumed to depend positively or negatively on the real wage, called the wage-led and the profit-led case, respectively), we have a clear-cut classification of the dynamic possibilities that may arise, as table 4.1 shows.

Table 4.1 includes wage-led and profit-led entries, showing how economic activity increases with real wages or with real profits. The designations goods-led and labor-market-led show how real wage growth decreases or increases with economic activity (through the wage-price spiral it is subject to). Obviously there are four combinations of these situations, two of which must produce centrifugal forces because of an accelerating feedback mechanism between economic activity

TABLE 4.1. *Four baseline partial real-wage adjustment scenarios.*

	Wage-Led Goods Market	Profit-Led Goods Market
Labor-market-led real-wage adjustment	adverse (divergent)	normal (convergent)
Goods-market-led real-wage adjustment	normal (convergent)	adverse (divergent)

Unleashed Capitalism: The Starting Point for Societal Reform ■ 157

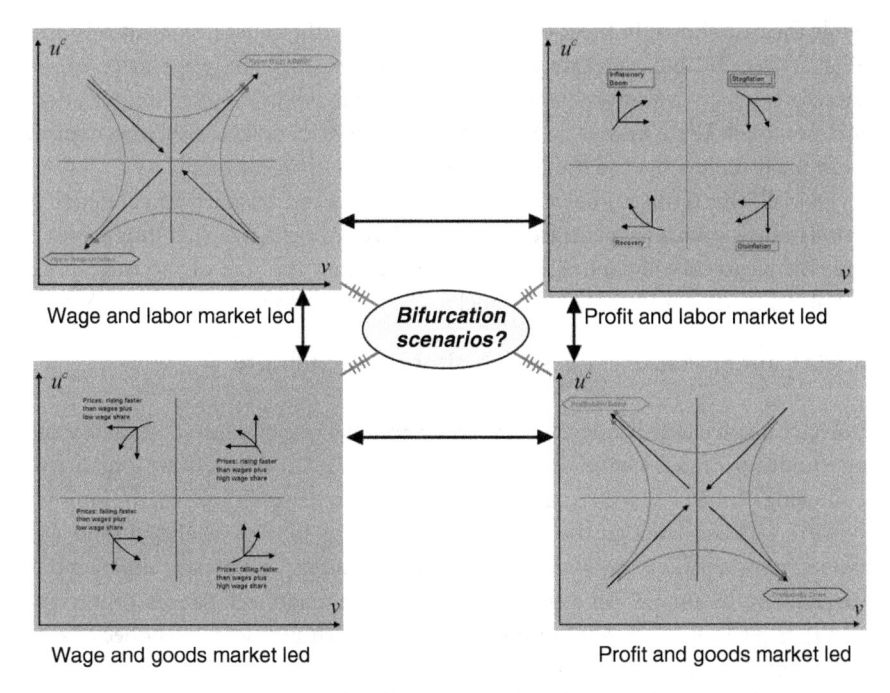

Figure 4.2 Phase portraits of the four types of real-wage channels of Keynesian macrodynamics (u^c: capacity utilization, v: wage share).

and real wages as they are shown in the diagonal of table 4.1. The other two cases combine an expanding relationship with a contracting one, an interaction that produces a stable situation, since the expansion of one state variable is counteracted by the contraction of the other one. The real wage channel, the interaction of the postulated distribution-driven economic activity with real wage changes, thus allows the four possibilities depicted in table 4.1. These possibilities are considered in detail in Proaño, Flaschel, Teuber, and Diallo (2008) and Flaschel, Tavani, Taylor, and Teuber (2007). We summarize the two-dimensional phase portraits of these four possibilities in figure 4.2.

It is intuitively clear that an increasing adjustment speed of money wages is potentially destabilizing if economic activity is wage-led (top left), while the opposite holds for increasing price flexibility (bottom left). By contrast, higher wage flexibility is stabilizing if economic activity depends negatively on the real wage, in particular in depressions, when wages would tend to fall and lead to a recovery in the economy if it is profit-led (top right). Finally, price flexibility is destabilizing in the profit-led case, since it leads to real wage increases in busts and thus strengthens the bust (the opposite occurs in booms). The situation in the top left of the figure may have been typical—as far as the right-hand side is concerned—for the episode that preceded the stagflationary period of the 1970s, while the case shown in the top right may represent the general state after World War II (see the literature we cited earlier for details). The wage-price spiral, therefore, can be explosive under certain conditions, while in other circumstances it is bounded. We consider an accelerating wage-price spiral as the mechanism most likely to endanger the stability of the real part of the economy.

Overall, the result is that wage-price dynamics can become an accelerating spiral in this context (in contrast to what we showed in chapter 3). It thus presents the risk of unleashed capitalism. We briefly discuss the role of the wage-price spiral in the full dynamics of the model in the next section.

4.3.5 Capital Markets: Gross Substitutes and Stability

We have not discussed determination of the nominal rate of interest i and the price of equities p_e and so have not formulated how capital markets are organized. Following Tobin's (1969) portfolio approach (see also Franke and Semmler [1999]), we postulate that the following equilibrium conditions always hold and thus determine the two prices for bonds and equities as statically endogenous variables of the model. All asset supplies are given magnitudes at each moment, and r_e^e is given by $\frac{r^e p K}{p_e E} + \pi_e$ and thus varies at each moment solely because of variations in the share price p_e.

$$M = M^d = f_m(i, r_e^e) W_c^n \qquad (4.43)$$

$$B = B^d = f_b(i, r_e^e) W_c^n \qquad (4.44)$$

$$p_e E = p_e E^d = f_e(i, r_e^e) W_c^n \qquad (4.45)$$

Our model supports the view that the prices or interest rates for the financial assets are determined in the secondary markets, so that these markets are cleared at all times. This implies that the newly issued assets do not significantly affect these prices.

The trade between the asset holders induces a process that makes asset prices fall or rise in order to equilibrate demand and supplies. In the short run (in continuous time), this process gives the structure for the model of the wealth of asset holders, W_c^n, disregarding changes in the share price p_e. This implies that the functions $f_m()$, $f_b()$, and $f_e()$, introduced in equations (4.10)–(4.12), must satisfy the following well-known conditions:

$$f_m(i, r_e^e) + f_b(i, r_e^e) + f_e(i, r_e^e) = 1 \qquad (4.46)$$

$$\frac{\partial f_m(i, r_e^e)}{\partial z} + \frac{\partial f_b(i, r_e^e)}{\partial z} + \frac{\partial f_e(i, r_e^e)}{\partial z} = 0, \quad z \in \{i, r_e^e\} \qquad (4.47)$$

These conditions guarantee that the number of independent equations is equal to the number of statically endogenous variables (i, p_e) that the asset markets are assumed to determine at each moment.

We postulate that the financial assets display the gross substitution property, which means that the demand for all other assets increases whenever the price of another asset rises. For a formal definition, see, for example, MasCollel, Whinston, and Green (1995).

$$\frac{\partial f_b(i, r_e^e)}{\partial i} > 0, \quad \frac{\partial f_m(i, r_e^e)}{\partial i} < 0, \quad \frac{\partial f_e(i, r_e^e)}{\partial i} < 0 \qquad (4.48)$$

$$\frac{\partial f_e(i, r_e^e)}{\partial r_e^e} > 0, \quad \frac{\partial f_m(i, r_e^e)}{\partial r_e^e} < 0, \quad \frac{\partial f_b(i, r_e^e)}{\partial r_e^e} < 0 \qquad (4.49)$$

We add (without proof) that the assumption of gross substitution for the asset demand functions implies a stable ultra-short-term adjustment process for the adjustment of the interest rate i and share prices p_e in the form of a Walrasian tâtonnement process. Such ultra-short-term disequilibrium adjustment processes are assumed as implicitly underlying the considered asset equilibrium determination, but we do not discuss them; we assume they work smoothly behind the equilibrium positions. This Walrasian tâtonnement process ignores the (potentially destabilizing) role of capital gain expectations (instability, however, should not be possible if only fundamentalist expectations are present in such an adjustment process).

4.3.6 Cumulative Processes in Capital Gains Expectations: Chartists' Behavior

Before we consider the potentially destabilizing role of chartist-type capital gains expectations, we discuss the full structure of the Keynes Metzler Goodwin Tobin (KMGT) model as shown in figure 4.3. This figure illustrates the destabilizing role of the wage-price spiral, in which, because of assumed investment behavior, real wages have a positive impact on aggregate demand. As a result, wage flexibility will be destabilizing (if not counteracted by its effects on expected profits and their effect on financial markets and Tobin's q). We have already indicated that financial markets do adjust toward their equilibrium in a stable manner as long as expectations do not really matter. Monetary policy, whether money supply oriented and thus of type $i(M, p)$ or of a Taylor rule type $M(i, \hat{p})$, should—via gross substitution effects—also contribute to the stability of financial markets. Fiscal policy affects the goods and financial markets and may be orthodox or Keynesian. Because of the advanced dynamical structure we face, it is not clear how fiscal policy helps shape the business cycle, a topic we leave for future research. We do discuss self-reference within the asset markets (the closed loop structure at the top of figure 4.3).

**A Keynesian portfolio approach to Ec. growth
(no Keynes- or Mundell-effect channels yet)**

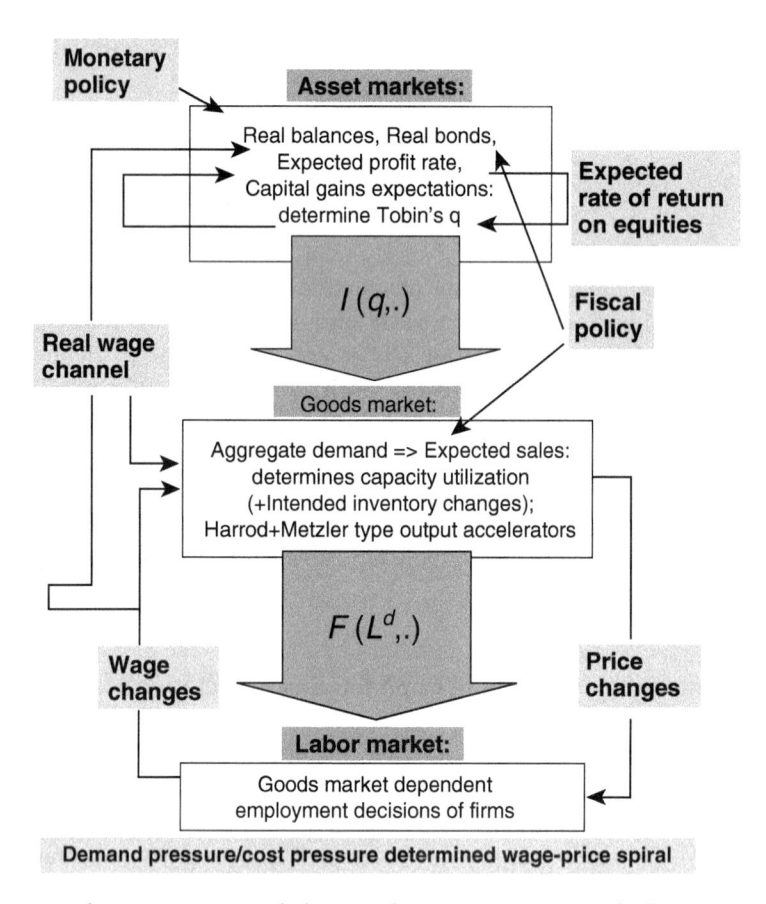

Figure 4.3 The Keynesian causal downward nexus, repercussion feedback structures, supply side dynamics, and policy rules in the KMG portfolio approach.

The laws of motion governing expectations about equity prices are not changed by the intensive form of the model. Thus, they read:

$$\dot{\pi}_{ef} = \beta_{\pi_{ef}}(\bar{\eta} - \pi_{ef}) \tag{4.50}$$

$$\dot{\pi}_{ec} = \beta_{\pi_{ec}}(\hat{p}_e - \pi_{ec}) \tag{4.51}$$

They give rise to the cumulative self-referencing feedback chain, as far as chartists' behavior is concerned, as shown in figure 4.4. We consider an accelerating capital-gain (or -loss) spiral as the mechanism most threatening the stability of the financial part of the economy.

The Share or Equity Market

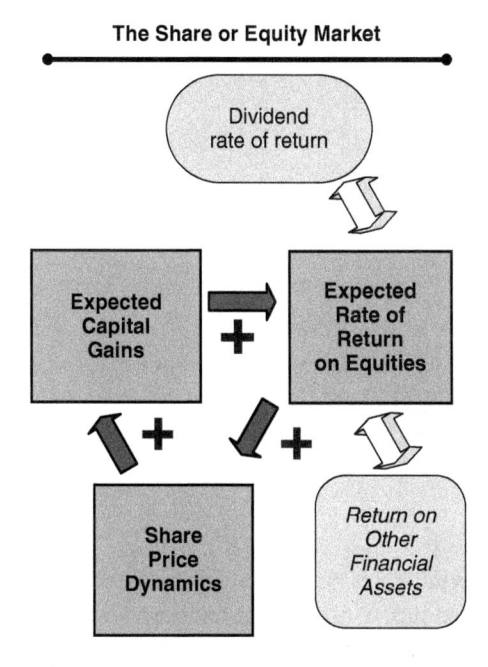

Figure 4.4 The positive-feedback chain on the stock market.

In what follows we need only the value of aggregate capital gains expectations. But to compute it, we need the historic values of the actual appreciation (or depreciation rate) of equity prices $\hat{p}_e$, for which we lack a law of motion, because the general equilibrium approach gives us only the level p_e such that asset markets are in equilibrium. We follow Sargent (1987) by employing an integral representation of the expectation about equity price inflation, which leads us to the following definition of aggregate expectation of equity price inflation:

$$\pi_e(t) = \alpha_{ec}\left[\pi_{ec}(t_0)e^{-\beta_{\pi ec}(t-t_0)} + \beta_{\pi ec}\int_{t_0}^{t} e^{-\beta_{\pi ec}(t-s)}\hat{p}_e(s)ds\right]$$
$$+ (1 - \alpha_{ec})\left[(\pi_{ef}(t_0) - \bar{\eta})e^{-\beta_{\pi ef}t} + \bar{\eta}\right] \quad (4.52)$$

where $\pi_{ec}(t_0)$ and $\pi_{ef}(t_0)$ are the initial values of expectations about the growth rate of equity prices, expected by chartists and fundamentalists at time t_0.

To obtain this equation, we assume that the average expected appreciation rate of equity prices equals the actual inflation rate of equities $\pi_e = \hat{p}_e$. These expectations play an important role in the capital markets because they are one component of the expected rate of return on equities. As one can see in the equation for π_e, the actual overall expectation of equity price inflation is the weighted average of expectations held by fundamentalists and chartists.

From the law of motion for π_{ef} and knowing the initial value of π_{ef} denoted by $\pi_{ef}(t_0)$, we can derive the definite solution

$$\pi_{ef}(t) = (\pi_{ef}(t_0) - \bar{\eta})e^{-\beta_{\pi_{ef}}t} + \bar{\eta}$$

To get the definite solution for the expected equity price inflation held by chartists, from the equation for π_{ec} we can derive the general solution:

$$\pi_{ec}(t) = \beta_{\pi_{ec}} \int_{t_0}^{t} \hat{p}_e(s)e^{-\beta_{\pi_{ec}}(t-s)} ds$$

This representation is equivalent to the exponential lag distribution if $t_0 = -\infty$ (see Gandolfo [1996, chapter 12.4]).

From the general solution, one can easily derive the specific solution:

$$\pi_{ec}(t) = \pi_{ec}(t_0)e^{-\beta_{\pi_{ec}}(t-t_0)} + \beta_{\pi_{ec}} \int_{t_0}^{t} \hat{p}_e(s)e^{-\beta_{\pi_{ec}}(t-s)} ds$$

where $\pi_{ec}(t_0)$ is the initial value of expectations of chartists about the growth rate in equity prices. Building up the weighted sum of the definite solutions according to equation (4.52), we obtain the integral equation.

The derived formula for average capital gains expectations implies that the dynamical system being examined is represented by a combination of seven differential equations with one integral equation, a situation not easy to handle. This is due to the fact that we have in the model's structure a combination of algebraic (equilibrium) equations with differential equations (describing the laws of motion of the economy). A solution to this problem would be to formulate laws of motion for the share prices as well, assuming that the financial variables are driven by stock disequilibria on the asset markets. Such a purely disequilibrium-driven approach to the real *as well as* the financial markets will require more research.

Our framework implies that it is very likely that the full model can be explored only by numerical simulation methods, and that its theoretical stability treatment is possible only if certain special cases of the full model are considered, particularly by abstracting from destabilizing chartists' expectations. We treat added expectations analytically in two steps, first assuming "tranquil" fundamentalists' expectations, and then adding destabilizing chartists' expectations (leading to explosive dynamical outcomes if the speed of the adjustment of their expectations is chosen sufficiently high). We turn next to the stability result one can obtain for the KMG portfolio model.

4.4 ■ A BASELINE-STABILITY SCENARIO

This section formulates a variety of stability propositions, structured hierarchically, by using the so-called cascade of stable matrices approach. It surveys these propositions only intuitively. See Asada et al. (2010a) for details of the model's intensive form, as well as the proofs of the propositions, and for policy applications, which we discuss only briefly. We get the following subdynamics of the full dynamical system by setting the parameters $\beta_p, \beta_w, \beta_n, \beta_{\pi^c}$ in the wage price spiral and the inventory cycle equal to zero.

$$\dot{m} = m(\bar{\mu} - (\pi^c + i(\cdot))), \quad m = \frac{M}{pK} \tag{4.53}$$

$$\dot{b} = \bar{g} - \bar{t}_c^n - \tau_w \omega \frac{y}{x} - \bar{\mu}m - b(\pi^c + i(\cdot)), \quad b = \frac{B}{pK} \tag{4.54}$$

$$\dot{y}^e = \beta_{y^e}\left[c + i(\cdot) + \delta + \bar{g} - y^e\right] + y^e(i(\cdot) - n), \quad y^e = \frac{Y^e}{K} \tag{4.55}$$

As regards stability we can derive the following proposition:

Proposition 1

> The steady state of the system of differential equations (4.53)–(4.55) is locally asymptotically stable if the dynamic multiplier parameter β_{y^e} is sufficiently large, the investment adjustment speed i_u concerning deviations of capital utilization from the normal capital utilization is sufficiently small, and the partial derivatives of desired cash balances with respect to the interest rate $\partial f_m/\partial i$ and the rate of return on equities $\partial f_m/\partial r_e^e$ are sufficiently small. Moreover the stock market must be sufficiently tranquil; that is, the partial derivative $\partial f_e/\partial r_e^e$ must be sufficiently small.

To discuss possible ways economic policy can work to realize these stability conditions, we consider the structure of the asset holders' portfolio choices once again. In the equations that follow, we have added the assumptions that the decision between total money and equities has priority for asset holders and, in regard to equity demand, is made solely in view of the expected rate of return on equities. Decisions in the stock market are therefore independent of the nominal rate of interest, which is only relevant for asset holders' cash management within the money demand $M_3 = M + B$; that is, the money demand for M_3 does not depend on the nominal rate of interest either.[9]

$$p_e E = p_e E^d = f_e(r_e^e)(p_e E + M_3)$$
$$M_3 = M_3^d = f_{be}(r_e^e)(p_e E + M_3), \quad f_e(\cdot) + f_{be}(\cdot) = 1$$
$$B = B^d = f_{bm}(i, M_3), \quad f_{bm}(i) = 1 - f_m(i)$$
$$M = M^d = f_m(i, M_3), \quad M_3 = M + B$$

Equity demand is therefore the crucial part of decisions made in the financial markets, while cash management between money $M = M_1$ and B is a relatively trivial matter, executed, for example, by way of Baumol's well-known financial inventory approach, leading to the textbook formula

$$M = M^d = f_m(i, M+B) = \sqrt{\frac{2\phi(M+B)}{i}}$$

that is,

$$i = \frac{2\phi(M+B)}{M^2}$$

The stability assumptions of proposition 1 concerning the financial markets are therefore fulfilled when the parameter ϕ—which represents the transactions costs of a shift between bonds B and money M—is chosen sufficiently small, and when the stock market is sufficiently tranquil ($\partial f_e / \partial r_e^e$ is sufficiently small). Up to the assumed level of tranquility, this appears not to be a strong assumption in a modern financial system. But note that the structure of the financial markets has been changed here to a certain degree. Thus we assume that this change is irrelevant for the validity of proposition 1, where we would have as corresponding assumptions $\partial f_m / \partial r_e^e = 0$ and $\partial f_m / \partial i$ chosen small without a change in the wealth on which the portfolio choice is based. However, the implication of the last assumption is a strong one, namely that monetary policy is fairly ineffective if the stability assumption, $\partial f_m / \partial i$ small, is made.

The assumption that i_u is small needs examining, because the adjustment of sales expectations to the current state of effective demand can be assumed to be a fast process. We have to assume simply that the government expenditures g now vary anticyclically with economic activity to a sufficient degree so that they can, for example, be expressed as $g = -g_u(u - \bar{u}) + barg$ with the new policy parameter $g_u > 0$. Such a policy may be implemented by a fiscal authority independent from the government and the election cycle on which a political administration depends. We think that the creation of such an authority—parallel to and in cooperation with the already existing monetary authority—represents a desirable institutional change in economic policymaking, but we do not go into the details of such a proposal here. The parameter g_u, characterizing the extent of anticyclical behavior of this fiscal authority, must be chosen such that $i_u - g_u$ fulfills the stability condition just discussed. A countercyclical fiscal policy, therefore, has to be tested to the extent necessary to reduce sufficiently the destabilizing Harrodian investment accelerator effect on the dynamics.

We now expand the system to include the real wage dynamic:

Proposition 2

The interior steady state of the dynamic system extended by

$$\dot{\omega} = \omega \kappa (\kappa_w - 1) \beta_p (\frac{y}{y^p} - \bar{u}) \tag{4.56}$$

is locally asymptotically stable if the conditions in proposition 1 are met and if the parameter β_p is sufficiently small.

The assumption in proposition 2 can be easily modified by supposing instead that the parameter κ_w is sufficiently close to 1. For simplicity we even assume that it is equal to 1, which means that the cost-push term in money wage formation is exactly given by the perfectly foreseen currently established rate of price inflation. We augment this assumption further by positing that the parameter β_w is equal to zero. The economy then exhibits—as far as price inflation is concerned—a scala mobile, namely that wage inflation is always set equal to price inflation. The institutional arrangement for this automatism implies that the social partners, capital and labor, have disciplined their wage setting power accordingly in regard to the wage level—though not wage differentials. Their role is therefore no longer to determine, in an often cumbersome way, how workers are compensated for price level changes, but instead reduced to how wage differentials, working conditions, minimum and maximum real wages, and so on are to be adjusted from a reasonable *microeconomic* perspective. The astonishing macroeconomic result[10] is, however, that a scala mobile, which reduces inflation dynamics to the goods market inflation equation[11]

$$\hat{p} = \frac{1}{1-\kappa_p}\beta_p(u - \bar{u}) + \pi^c, \quad \kappa_p \in (0, 1)$$

makes the economy more stable, by guaranteeing not only the validity of proposition 2 but also that of our next proposition.

In that propositions, we expand the system to include the law of motion for the labor capital ratio:

Proposition 3

The steady state of the dynamic system is locally asymptotically stable if the conditions in proposition 2 are met and if the parameter β_w in the thereby extended dynamics of the real wage is sufficiently small. This extension now includes variations in the labor intensity ratio $l = L/K$:

$$\hat{l} = 1\left[-i_1(q - 1) - i_u\left(\frac{y}{y^p} - \bar{u}\right)\right] \quad (4.57)$$

into the subdynamics.

In another step we add the law of motion of inventories to the laws of motion included so far:

Proposition 4

The steady state of the dynamic system is locally asymptotically stable if the conditions in proposition 3 are met and β_n is sufficiently small, which by its positivity allows the dynamic

$$\dot{v} = y - (c + i(\cdot) + \delta + \bar{g}) - vi(\cdot) \tag{4.58}$$

to feed back into the already considered dynamics.

Concerning the role of the Metzlerian inventory accelerator mechanism, as represented by the parameter β_n, one may argue that closer (numerical) analysis of the model will reveal that the inventory cycle does not represent an important destabilizing mechanism for an empirically relevant range of parameter values and is thus of minor importance for the overall behavior of the economy. The preceding countercyclical fiscal policy rule may, moreover, also be sufficient to tame this short-phase cycle generator. In addition, one may implement a subsidy (or tax) for holding large (small) amounts of inventories, which when properly implemented might exercise a negative influence on the size of the parameter β_n.

Finally let β_{π^c} become positive. We then are back at the full differential equation system (though we still neglect the integral equation of the model and thus the dynamics of capital gains expectations).

Proposition 5

The steady state of the dynamic system is locally asymptotically stable if the conditions in proposition 4 are met and β_{π^c} is changed from zero to a positive value that is chosen sufficiently small, adding the feedbacks of the law of motion for the inflationary climate into the dynamics:

$$\dot{\pi}^c = \alpha\beta_{\pi^c}\kappa[\beta_p(u - \bar{u}) + \kappa_p\beta_w(e - \bar{e})] + (1 - \alpha)\beta_{\pi^c}(\bar{\mu} - n - \pi^c) \tag{4.59}$$

With respect to the scala mobile we discussed, the law of motion for the inflationary climate is reduced to the expression

$$\dot{\pi}^c = \alpha\beta_{\pi^c}\frac{1}{1 - \kappa_p}\beta_p(u - \bar{u}) + (1 - \alpha)\beta_{\pi^c}(\bar{\mu} - n - \pi^c) \tag{4.60}$$

This expression shows that an appropriate monetary and fiscal policy may help to reduce fluctuations in this climate by making excess capacity $u - \bar{u}$ less volatile, by reducing the parameter β_p with which firms move from excess capacity to price inflation, and by finally having a moderating effect on the parameter β_{π^c} when inflation is controlled such that it is generally very small. All these possibilities concern the volatility of the inflationary climate in which the economy is operating. Therefore, they require all agents involved in this process to generally accept that moderate price inflation as desirable, and they agree that monetary and fiscal policy actions that support such a result should be carefully designed and implemented.

A more direct policy choice, however, is available for the issue we have excluded from these stability propositions; namely the control of destabilizing capital gain expectations. For this purpose, we reconsider the chartist process for forming expectations as

$$\dot{\pi}_{ec} = \beta_{\pi_{ec}}((1-\tau_t)\hat{p}_e - \pi_{ec})$$

where τ_t is a Tobinian tax on actual capital gains. The actual capital gains that accrue to equity owners are thereby reduced to $(1-\tau_t)\hat{p}_e$ as the new benchmark value for their revision of capital gain expectations. It is obvious that a 100 percent tax rate would make the model stable, since expectations become irrelevant in this case. The question therefore is how high the Tobin tax must be chosen in order to obtain stability for the full system despite the presence of chartists' capital gain expectations and despite the financial market accelerator they give rise to. Because of the need to employ an integral equation for solving this issue, we leave it for future research. When there is sufficient taxation of capital gains, we may also expect that the stock market is indeed sufficiently tranquil, that is, the partial derivative $\partial f_e/\partial r_e^e$ is sufficiently small.

Summarizing we can observe that this sequence of propositions is founded on the following proof strategy (see Chiarella and Flaschel [2000] for its introduction into the KMG framework).

Summary of the Cascades of Stable Matrices Approach

1. Let some parameters (adjustment speeds) be zero in order to reduce the dimensions of the model to 3. Analyze the Routh-Hurwitz local stability conditions of the resulting (tractable) three-dimensional subsystem.
2. Increase the system by one dimension, assuming a certain parameter to be different from zero. Prove that the determinant of the new enlarged system has the opposite sign of the one of the previous system. The zero eigenvalue corresponding to the previous but already enlarged situation must then become negative (in addition to the three negative eigenvalues already shown to exist in the previous system).
3. Increase the system by one dimension by assuming that another parameter becomes positive and is thus different from zero. Prove that the determinant of the thereby enlarged system has the opposite sign of the one of the previous system, so that a zero eigenvalue must again change to a negative one (in addition to the ones already existing). Continue in the same way by increasing the system by another dimension again, and so on.

4. The employed choice of the parameter sequence should be based on identification of the stabilizing feedback channels of the model, such as the Keynes effect, and also on knowledge of the destabilizing ones, such as the Mundell-Tobin effect, which must be kept sufficiently small.

The KMG portfolio approach therefore exploits intuitively the many feedback chains that exist in such a fully developed Keynesian dynamics of monetary growth.

4.5 ■ LIKELY OUTCOMES OF UNLEASHED CAPITALISM: LOCAL INSTABILITY AND REGIME-SWITCH-INDUCED VIABILITY

We have briefly described when we can expect the steady state of the dynamics to be attracting. Such local stability can be proved in the way described (see Köper [2003] and Asada, Chiarella, Flaschel, and Franke [2009] for further details) if the wage-price spiral is operating in a sufficiently sluggish way (i.e., the parameters $\beta_p, \beta_w, \beta_{\pi^c}$ are chosen sufficiently small), if the Metzlerian inventory adjustment process is sufficiently slow (the parameter β_n is sufficiently small) but the dynamic multiplier β_{y^e} sufficiently fast, if the Harrodian capacity effect as measured by the parameter i_u is weak, if money demand is responding to interest rate changes and to rate of return on equities changes in a sufficiently weak fashion, *and* if the stock market reactions to expected rate of return changes are moderate. In the next section we reconsider this proposition from the perspective of two risk-bearing assets rather than one, providing a detailed reformulation of these assertions for the case in which short-term bonds are replaced by long-term ones.

These results are intuitively very appealing, since they basically indicate that the wage-price spiral must be fairly damped, the Keynesian dynamic multiplier must be stable and not distorted too much by Metzlerian inventory cycles, and the Harrodian knife-edge growth accelerator must be weak and money demand fairly irresponsive to rate-of-return changes on financial assets (and chartists and the stock market tamed by a Tobin tax). Such assumptions represent fairly plausible conditions from a Keynesian perspective, though they may not often apply in reality. Yet we have shown how policy can help to establish stability of the steady state should the private sector not provide it. The stability conditions become more complicated if long-term bonds are used instead of the risk-free fixed-price bonds so far considered (see section 4.6).

In this section we provide some examples of the emergence of business fluctuations and local instabilities, involving damped oscillations, loss of stability via Hopf bifurcation, the generation of limit cycles as business cycle fluctuations from the global perspective by adding downward money wage rigidity to the money wage PC, and finally—through this kinked wage PC—the generation of complex dynamics if increases in certain adjustment speeds make the steady state strongly repelling. See Chiarella, Flaschel, Proaño, and Semmler (2009) for more detailed studies of the implications of such kinked money wage PCs.

The simulations in the top left of figure 4.5 show damped oscillations when the parameter choices of our stability conclusions are applied (see section 4.5 for their detailed representation in the case of two risky assets). In the remaining three eigenvalue diagrams, we plot the maximum real part of eigenvalues against crucial parameters of the dynamical system, with the expected results that increasing speeds of adjustments in the movements of the inflationary climate and in capital gain expectations of chartists will be destabilizing, while price flexibility is stabilizing (and, correspondingly, wage flexibility is destabilizing, but tamed in figure 4.6 through the exclusion of wage deflation). However, the graphs in the top and bottom right of figure 4.6 show that there is a weak but persistent negative trend in real balances per unit of capital and thus, on average, a persistent dominance of inflation over real and monetary growth. We conjecture that this is caused by the asymmetry in the wage PC whose existence affects nominal inflation, but not the real cycle (shown in two projections on the left-hand side of figure 4.6).

Figure 4.7 illustrates how the KMGT system can generate complex dynamics if the destabilizing feedback channels (here the degree of wage flexibility or a fast adjustment of chartists' expectations) make the steady state strongly repelling. Here, as in many other simulations performed for various models of KMG growth, the kinked wage PC with its downwardly rigid money wage assumption appears to be a powerful tool that stops the explosiveness existing around the steady state and turns the economy into a viable one, exhibiting bounded fluctuations even over very long time horizons.

Yet here too, we have a weak tendency toward excessive inflation, thus a downward trend in real money balance per unit of capital as shown in the phase plots in the middle of figure 4.7 and in the time series presentations of the variable m in the bottom right. These time series representations also show that there is decreasing volatility (damped oscillations as time evolves) and thus a tendency to converge toward an inflationary trend term in the very, very long run (60,000 years in the plot shown in the bottom right).

In figure 4.8, we show an example for a period (cycle) doubling route to complex dynamics, but not chaos, from the economic point of view, since the cycles that are generated are fairly similar to each other. We increase the speed of adjustment of money wages from $\beta_w = 1.4$ to $\beta_w = 2.0$ and then to $\beta_w = 2.82$ and to $\beta_w = 3.0$. The dynamics remain viable over such a broad range of adjustment speeds for money wages, because of the kink in the money wage PC and despite a strong local instability around the steady state described earlier. To the right of the attractors, the trajectories are of a fairly smooth type, yet in the top left they are going through some turbulence, which makes the attractor more and more complex with the increasing adjustment speed of money wages.

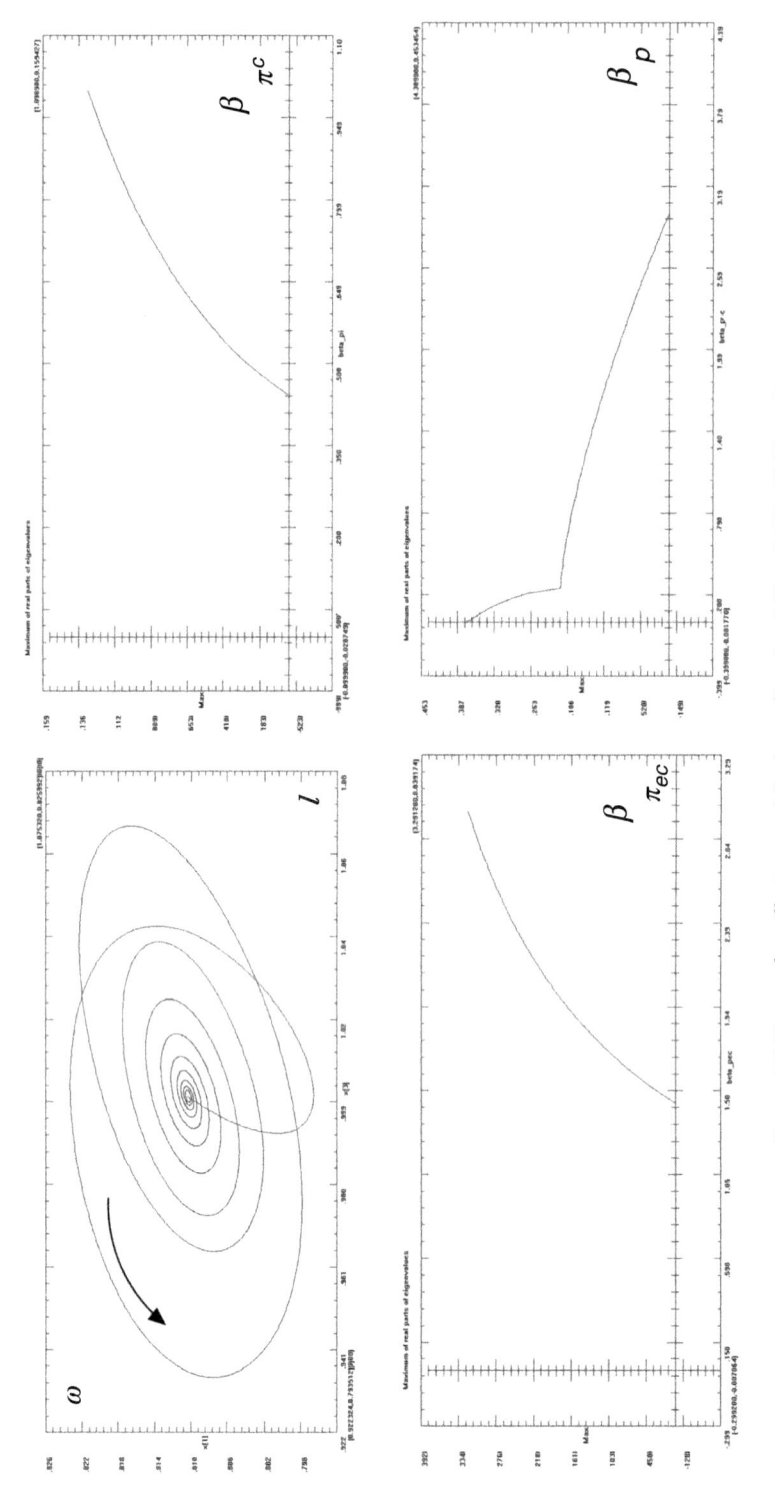

Figure 4.5 Damped oscillations and the loss of local stability via Hopf bifurcations.

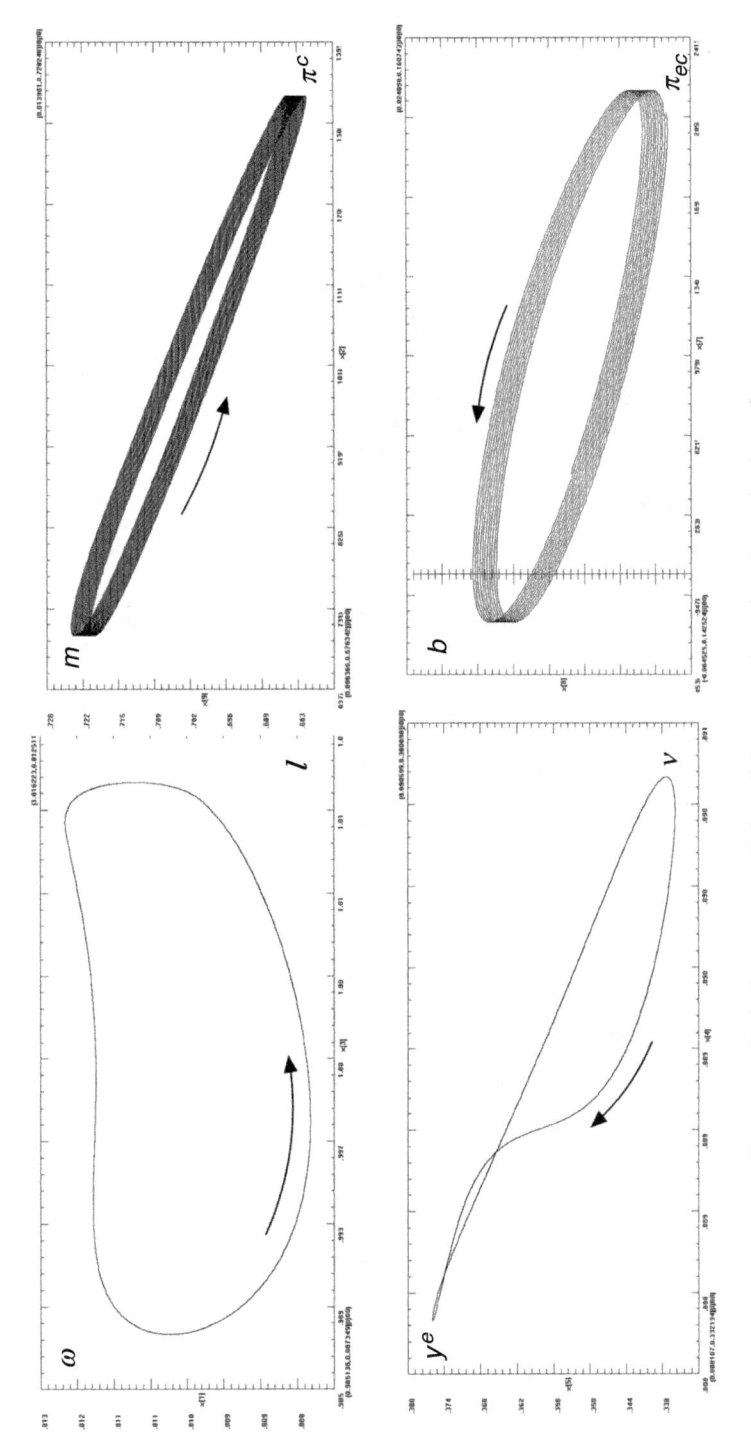

Figure 4.6 Kinked money wage PCs and the generation of persistent business fluctuations.

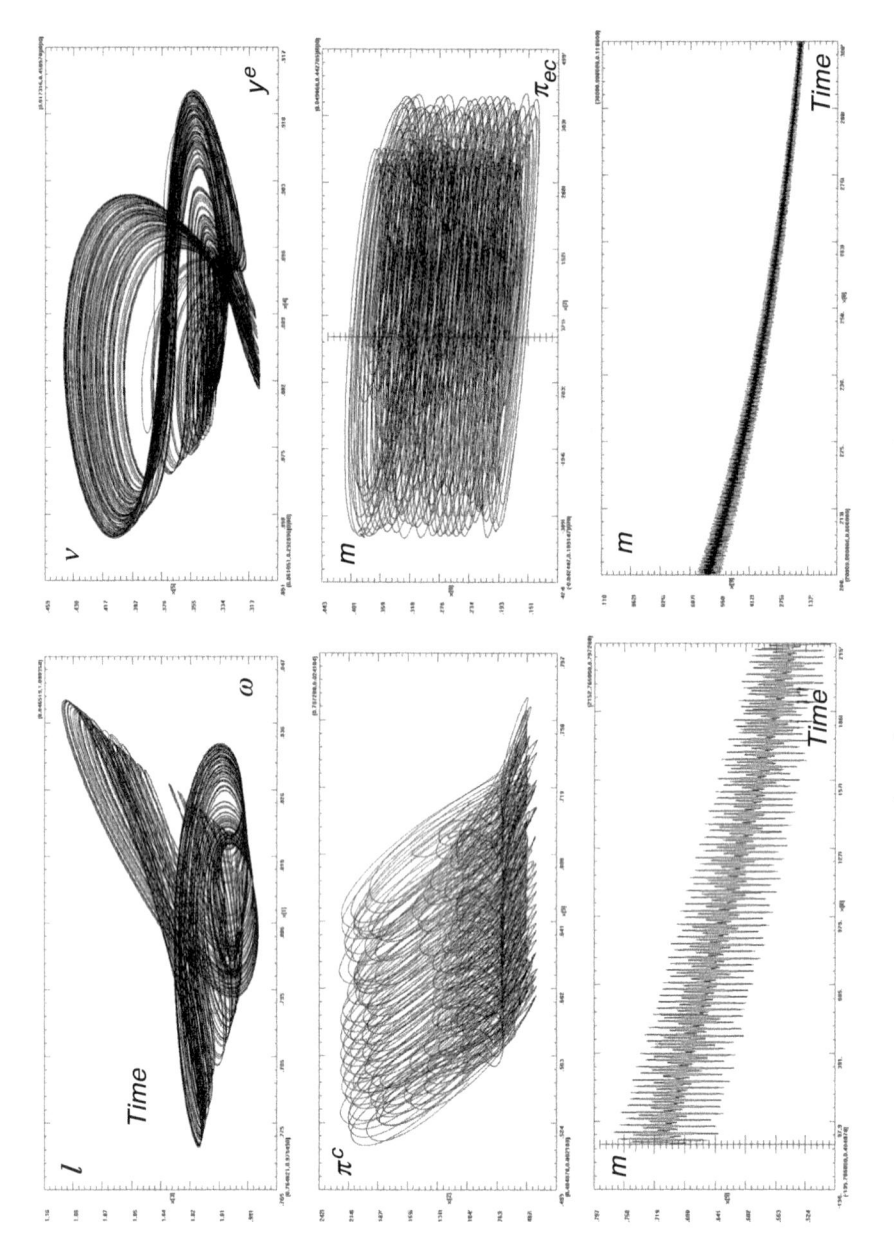

Figure 4.7 Complex real attractors and asymmetric inflation dynamics.

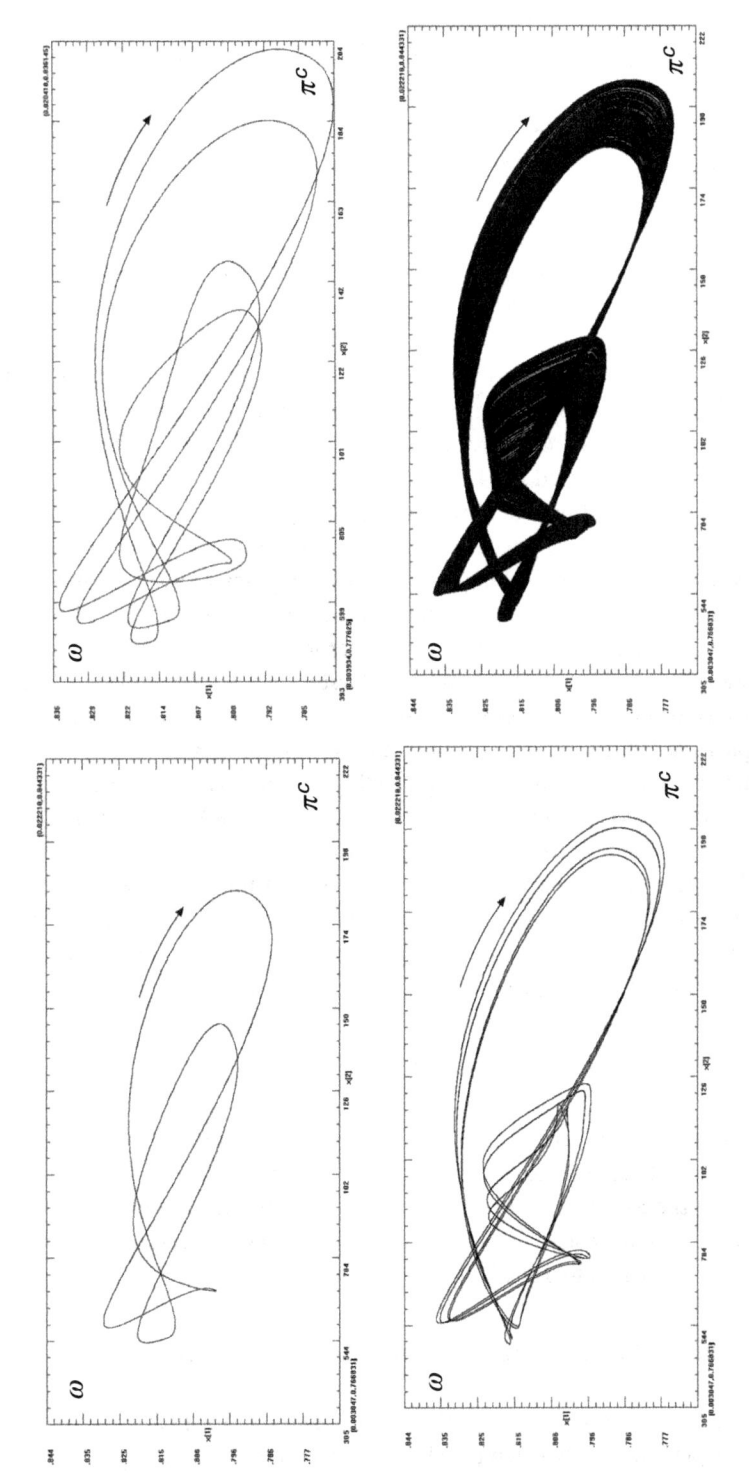

Figure 4.8 A period-doubling route to complex dynamics.

We do not go into the details of these simulations here any further, but only present them as evidence that this model is capable of producing various dynamic outcomes and is thus a very open one with respect to possible implications (it needs empirical estimation of its parameter values for more specific results). Chiarella, Flaschel, Proaño, and Semmler (2009) provide detailed numerical studies of this KMGT model.

4.6 ■ A FURTHER RISK-BEARING ASSET: LONG-TERM BONDS

In the basic KMGT model so far considered, money, short-term bonds, and equities formed the set of existing financial assets. We chose these assets because our primary goal was to explicate the way in which the financial part of the economy with equilibrated markets is embedded in the real part of the economy with inherent disequilibrium. Nevertheless, there are good reasons to vary this restricted set in order to account for long-term bonds, because it is often claimed that the market for long-term bonds competes more directly with the equity markets. They are more comparable with respect to the time horizon of investment. Thus it seems natural to consider long-term bonds in the financial asset analysis. But instead of enlarging the system, we simply replace the short-term bonds with long-term bonds. We do so because we want to keep the analysis as simple as possible when we show that the concept of long-term bonds fits well in a framework similar to that of the preceding sections. Moreover, there are now two risky assets and the capital gains they provide in the KMGT approach, which brings it closer to the situation in actual economies.[12]

In this section, we deal with an alternative set of financial assets: money M, long-term bonds B^l, and equities E. We assume long-term bonds to be perpetuities valued at any time with price p_b. A long-term bond pays out one unit of money in every period and displays an expected rate of return, r_b^e:

$$r_b^e = 1/p_b + \pi_b \qquad (4.61)$$

This expected rate of return per period on long-term bonds is the sum of the inverse price, which denotes the interest rate, and the expected capital gain, where the latter is the expected growth rate in prices of long-term bonds π_b. As with equities, we now have a positive feedback chain involving capital gains on long-term bonds, shown in figure 4.9.

4.6.1 Households, Government, and Financial Markets

To model the new situation, we exploit the modeling of the preceding and give a detailed explanation only when the changes affect the structural equations.

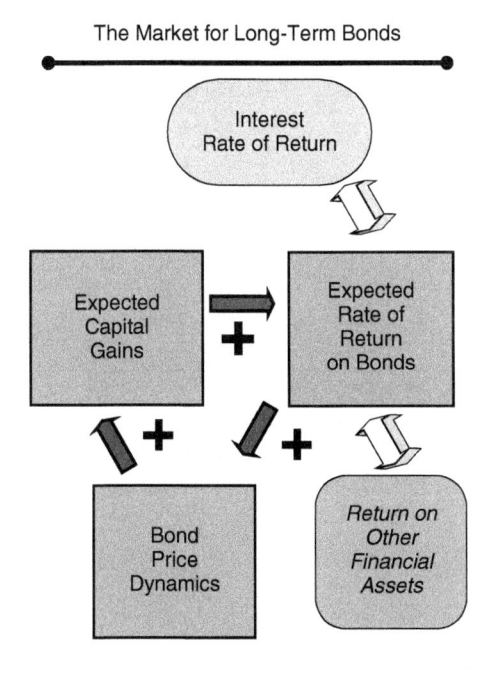

Unleashed Capitalism: The Starting Point for Societal Reform ■ 175

Figure 4.9 The positive-feedback chain on the market for long-term bonds.

Private Households

The worker households are not affected at all, because they are assumed to consume all their income and save nothing; they are not involved in asset markets. But the other type of households, the asset holders experience some changes. We start with the equations for income, consumption, and saving:

$$C_c = (1 - s_c)[r^e K + B^l - T_c] \qquad (4.62)$$

$$S_c = s_c[r^e K + B^l - T_c] \qquad (4.63)$$

$$= (\dot{M} + p_b \dot{B}^l + p_e \dot{E})/p \qquad (4.64)$$

$$W_c = (M + p_b B^l + p_e E)/p, \quad W_c^n = pW_c \qquad (4.65)$$

The sources of income consist of dividend payments of firms to asset holders, $r_e K$, and interest payments for the long-term bonds, B^l. The income is diminished by a tax T_c. Thus the saving propensity s_c of asset holders, according to equations (4.62) and (4.63), gives consumption and saving.

As we have seen, the saving of assets creates financial wealth. The desired nominal amounts of the financial assets are determined by means of demand functions that depend on the rates of return of the assets and wealth according to the following:

$$M^d = f_m(r_b^e, r_e^e)W_c^n \qquad (4.66)$$

$$p_b B^{ld} = f_{b^l}(r_b^e, r_e^e)W_c^n \qquad (4.67)$$

$$p_e E^d = f_e(r_b^e, r_e^e)W_c^n \qquad (4.68)$$

$$W_c^n = M^d + p_b B^{ld} + p_e E^d \qquad (4.69)$$

Government

With respect to the government, the taxation of asset holders changes, and hence the equations for government saving and budget must be adjusted.

$$T = \tau_w \omega L^d + T_c \qquad (4.70)$$

$$T_c = t_c K + B^l/p, \quad \text{with } t_c = \text{const} \qquad (4.71)$$

$$G = gK, \quad g = \text{const} \qquad (4.72)$$

$$S_g = T - B^l/p - G \qquad (4.73)$$

$$\hat{M} = \mu \qquad (4.74)$$

$$\dot{M} + p_b \dot{B}^l = pG + B^l - pT \qquad (4.75)$$

The real tax levied on asset holders consists now of a fixed proportion on total capital $t_c K$ and of the stock of bonds. This is a useful trick to avoid interest payments in the consumption function of asset holders and, as we will see, plays a role in the government budget constraint. The saving of the government is then given by the income $T = \tau_w w L^d + T_c$ minus the government purchases for interest payments and provision of government services. From this we can derive the government budget equation as shown in equation (4.75). All purchases minus income must be financed by issuing money or long-term bonds.

Financial Markets

As we have seen in the modeling of the asset holders, the demands for financial assets depend crucially on the rates of return on long-term bonds and equities. Thus, in order to reach an equilibrium at every moment in money, bond, and equity markets, the rates of return have to adjust to their equilibrium values instantaneously.

Naturally the demand functions of the asset holders in the capital markets fulfill the adding up constraints

$$f_m + f_{b^l} + f_e = 1 \qquad (4.76)$$

and

$$\frac{\partial f_m}{\partial z} + \frac{\partial f_{b^l}}{\partial z} + \frac{\partial f_e}{\partial z} = 0, \quad \forall \ z \in \{r_b^e, r_e^e\} \tag{4.77}$$

Again we assume that the gross substitution property of the demand function is met.

4.6.2 Intensive Form

Shifting the new model into capital intensive form, we must explicitly derive the law of motion for the intensive form of long-term bonds B^l/pK. Therefore we solve equation (4.75) with respect to $\dot{B}^l$ giving

$$\dot{B}^l = \frac{1}{P_b}(pG + B^l - pT - \dot{M}) \tag{4.78}$$

Inserting this relation into

$$\dot{b}^l = \frac{\partial \frac{B^l}{pK}}{\partial t} = \frac{\dot{B}^l}{pK} - b^l(\hat{p} + I/K)$$

we get

$$\begin{aligned}\dot{b}^l &= \frac{\frac{1}{P_b}(pG + B^l - pT - \dot{M})}{pK} - b^l(\hat{p} + I/K) \\ &= \frac{1}{P_b}(g - t_c - \tau_w \omega l^d - \mu m) - b^l(\hat{p} + I/K)\end{aligned} \tag{4.79}$$

Note that b^l here is not the nominal value of long-term bonds per unit of capital. As we have to account explicitly for the price of the long-term bonds, we do not aggregate their price and number. Using the law of motion of goods prices, we see that the law of motion of long-term bonds is

$$\dot{b}^l = \frac{1}{P_b}(g - t_c - \tau_w \omega l^d - \mu m) - b^l(\kappa[\beta_p(u - \bar{u}) + \kappa_p \beta_w(e - \bar{e})] + \pi^c + i(\cdot))$$

178 ■ FLEXICURITY CAPITALISM

With these preliminary considerations in place, the entire model can be set up. First we start with the statically endogenous variables needed later in the differential equations.

$$y = (1 + \alpha_{n^d}(n + \beta_n))y^e - \beta_n v \tag{4.80}$$

$$l^d = y/x \tag{4.81}$$

$$c = (1 - \tau_w)\omega l^d + (1 - s_c)(y^e - \delta - \omega l^d - t_c) \tag{4.82}$$

$$i(\cdot) = i_q(q - 1) + i_u(u - \bar{u}) + n \tag{4.83}$$

$$y^d = c + i(\cdot) + \delta + g \tag{4.84}$$

$$r_e^e = \frac{r^e}{q} + \pi_e \tag{4.85}$$

$$r_b^e = \frac{1}{p_b} + \pi_b \tag{4.86}$$

$$\pi_e = \alpha_{\pi_e}\pi_{ec} + (1 - \alpha_{\pi_e})\pi_{ef} \tag{4.87}$$

$$\pi_b = \alpha_{\pi_b}\pi_{bc} + (1 - \alpha_{\pi_b})\pi_{bf} \tag{4.88}$$

$$e = l^d/l \tag{4.89}$$

$$u = y/y^p \tag{4.90}$$

$$r^e = y^e - \delta - \omega l^d \tag{4.91}$$

Tobin's q and the price for long-term bonds p_b are responsible for the equilibrium in the financial markets for money, long-term bonds, and equities at every moment. The intensive form of the demand functions reads

$$m^d = f_m(r_b^e, r_e^e)(m + p_b b^l + q) \tag{4.92}$$

$$p_b b^{ld} = f_{b^l}(r_b^e, r_e^e)(m + p_b b^l + q) \tag{4.93}$$

$$q = f_e(r_b^e, r_e^e)(m + p_b b^l + q) \tag{4.94}$$

Thus the solution of the following two equilibrium conditions gives a combination of q and p_b that equilibrates the money market and the bond market:[13]

$$f_m(\frac{1}{p_b} + \pi_b, \frac{r^e}{q} + \pi_e)(m + p_b b^l + q) - m = 0 \tag{4.95}$$

$$f_{b^l}(\frac{1}{p_b} + \pi_b, \frac{r^e}{q} + \pi_e)(m + p_b b^l + q) - b = 0 \tag{4.96}$$

The growth rates of wages and prices are given by

$$\hat{w} = \kappa\left(\beta_w(e - \bar{e}) + \kappa_w\beta_p(u - \bar{u})\right) + \pi^c \quad (4.97)$$

and

$$\hat{p} = \kappa\left(\beta_p(u - \bar{u}) + \kappa_p\beta_w(e - \bar{e})\right) + \pi^c \quad (4.98)$$

with $\kappa = (1 - \kappa_w\kappa_p)^{-1}$. From those equations we can derive the growth rate of real wages.

Now the differential equations, the core of the model, can be expressed:

$$\hat{\omega} = \kappa[(1 - \kappa_p)\beta_w(e - \bar{e}) + (\kappa_w - 1)\beta_p(u - \bar{u})], \quad (4.99)$$

$$\dot{\pi}^c = \alpha\beta_{\pi^c}\kappa[\beta_p(u - \bar{u}) + \kappa_p\beta_w(e - \bar{e})] + (1 - \alpha)\beta_{\pi^c}(\mu - n - \pi^c), \quad (4.100)$$

$$\hat{l} = n - i(\cdot) = -i_q(q - 1) - i_u(u - \bar{u}), \quad (4.101)$$

$$\dot{y}^e = \beta_{y^e}(y^d - y^e) + (n - i(\cdot))y^e, \quad (4.102)$$

$$\dot{\nu} = y - y^d - i(\cdot)\nu, \quad (4.103)$$

$$\dot{\pi}^c_{bf} = \beta_{\pi_{bf}}(\bar{\eta}_b - \pi_{bf}), \quad (4.104)$$

$$\dot{\pi}_{bc} = \beta_{\pi_{bc}}(\hat{p}_b - \pi_{bc}) \quad (4.105)$$

$$\dot{\pi}_{ef} = \beta_{\pi_{ef}}(\bar{\eta}_e - \pi_{ef}), \quad (4.106)$$

$$\dot{\pi}_{ec} = \beta_{\pi_{ec}}(\hat{p}_e - \pi_{ec}) \quad (4.107)$$

$$\dot{b}^l = \frac{1}{p_b}(g - t_c - \tau_w\omega l^d - \mu m)$$
$$- b\left(\kappa[\beta_p(u - \bar{u}) + \kappa_p\beta_w(e - \bar{e})] + \pi^c + i(\cdot)\right), \quad (4.108)$$

$$\dot{m} = m\mu - m(\kappa[\beta_p(u - \bar{u}) + \kappa_p\beta_w(e - \bar{e})] + \pi^c + i(\cdot)). \quad (4.109)$$

4.6.3 Steady State

Proposition 6

Assume that

1. The saving propensity of the asset holders s_c is sufficiently large
2. The government runs a primary deficit
3. The long-term expectations for equity price inflation of the fundamentalists equal the steady-state inflation rate of the prices of goods

4. The demand functions for financial assets are such that

$$\lim_{r_b^e \to 0} (f_m(r_b^e, r^e + \pi_e) + f_b(r_b^e, r^e + \pi_e)) < \bar{\phi}$$

and

$$\lim_{r_b^e \to \infty} (f_m(r_b^e, r^e + \pi_e) + f_b(r_b^e, r^e + \pi_e)) > \bar{\phi}$$

with $\bar{\phi} = \frac{g - t_c - \tau_w \omega l^d}{g - t_c - \tau_w \omega l^d + \mu}$; then the dynamic system built up by equations (4.99) to (4.109) displays a unique interior steady state with $\omega^o, l^o, y^{eo}, v^o, b^o, m^o > 0$.

Proof: The evaluation of the steady state is analogous to the computation of the steady state in the case of short-term bonds. Thus we simply restate the steady-state relation of the previous part, which is the same as in the case of perpetuities:

$$e^o = \bar{e}, \quad u^o = \bar{u} \qquad (4.110)$$

and

$$\hat{p}^o = \pi^{co}, \quad \pi^{co} = \mu - n, \quad q^o = 1, \quad y^o = \bar{u} y^p, \quad l^o = \frac{l^{do}}{\bar{e}} = \frac{y^o}{\bar{e}x}$$

$$v^o = \alpha_{nd} y^e$$

and

$$y^{eo} = \frac{y^o}{1 + \alpha_{nd}}$$

$$\omega^o = \frac{y^{eo} - n - \delta - g - (1 - s_c)(y^{eo} - \delta - t_c)}{(s_c - \tau_w) l^{do}} \qquad (4.111)$$

The proof of the previous statements for the nonfinancial part of the economy is exactly the same as in the proof for the corresponding proposition in the preceding section. Now we consider the financial part. What are the steady-state values of m, p_b, r_e^e, r_b^e? With the rate of return on long-term bonds defined in equation (4.61), we need a constant price for the bonds p_b. Thus in steady state $\hat{p}_b = 0$. The government budget equation reads

$$\dot{m} + p_b \dot{b}^l = (g - t_c - \tau_w \omega l^d) + (m + p_b b^l)(\hat{p} + i(\cdot)) \qquad (4.112)$$

In the steady state, the derivatives with respect to time equal zero; for the supply of money and long-term bonds, we can write

$$m + p_b b^l = (g - t_c - \tau_w \omega l^d)/\mu \qquad (4.113)$$

Unleashed Capitalism: The Starting Point for Societal Reform ▪ 181

This together with $q^o = 1$ in the steady state means that the aggregated demands for money and long-term bonds must equal the aggregated supply, which we can write

$$\left(f_m(r_b^e, r_e^e) + f_{b^l}(r_b^e, r_e^e)\right)(m + p_b b^l + 1) = (g - t_c - \tau_w \omega l^d)/\mu \qquad (4.114)$$

This leads to the equation

$$m + p_b b^l = [f_m(r_b^e, r_e^e) + f_{b^l}(r_b^e, r_e^e)](m + p_b b^l + 1) \qquad (4.115)$$

Or equivalently we know that in the steady state the following equation must hold:

$$[f_m(r_b^e, r_e^e) + f_{b^l}(r_b^e, r_e^e)](m + p_b b^l + 1) = \bar{\phi} \qquad (4.116)$$

with $\bar{\phi} = (g - t_c - \tau_w \omega l^d)/\mu$.

We now show that the left-hand side of the latter equation is a strictly monotonic increasing function in p_b, which means that there can be at most one value that fulfills equation (4.116), because the right-hand side is a constant. For this we derive the demands with respect to p_b:

$$\frac{\partial(m^d + p_b b^{ld})}{\partial p_b} = \frac{\partial(m^d + p_b b^{ld})}{\partial r_b^e} \frac{\partial r_b^e}{\partial p_b}$$

We consider the right side: the first term of the product is positive, which is a consequence of the adding-up constraint (4.77) and the signs of the derivatives of the demands with respect to r_b^e (gross substitution property). The second derivative is negative, which can be proved from the definition of r_b^e in equation (4.61). Hence, the sum of nominal money demand and nominal bond demand is a monotonically decreasing function in p_b. Thus there cannot be more than one p_b that leads to a steady state. Now we have to ensure that there is a bond price that fulfills the equation. It may be possible that the demand will never reach the value $\bar{\phi}$. But the proposition assures, first, that with a sufficiently small p_b, the money and long-term bond demand is lower than $\bar{\phi}$, and, second, that with a sufficiently large p_b, the same demand exceeds $\bar{\phi}$. Thus by continuity and monotonicity there must be exactly one p_b that allows for equilibrium in the asset markets.

4.6.4 Comparative Statics

We have shown that under certain conditions stated in proposition 6, there is a unique steady state in the macroeconomic model. We have not specified

182 ■ FLEXICURITY CAPITALISM

the demand functions for the financial assets. We specify the demands in a neighborhood of the interior steady state in the following:

$$f_m(r_b^e, r_e^e) = \alpha_{m0} - \alpha_{m1} r_b^e - \alpha_{m2}(\frac{r^e}{q} + \pi_e)(m + p_b b^l + q) \qquad (4.117)$$

$$f_{b^l}(r_b^e, r_e^e) = \alpha_{b^l 0} - \alpha_{b^l 1} r_b^e - \alpha_{b^l 2}(\frac{r^e}{q} + \pi_e)(m + p_b b^l + q) \qquad (4.118)$$

$$f_e(r_b^e, r_e^e) = \alpha_{e0} - \alpha_{e1} r_b^e - \alpha_{e2}(\frac{r^e}{q} + \pi_e)(m + p_b b^l + q) \qquad (4.119)$$

Denoting the excess demand for cash balances by F_1 and the excess demand for long-term bonds with F_2, we can define the excess demands as

$$F_1(p_b, q; \pi_b, r^e, \pi_e, b^l, m)$$
$$= \left[\alpha_{m0} - \alpha_{m1}\left(\frac{1}{p_b} + \pi_b\right) - \alpha_{m2}\left(\frac{r^e}{q} + \pi_e\right)\right](m + p_b b^l + q) - m$$

$$F_2(p_b, q; \pi_b, r^e, \pi_e, b^l, m)$$
$$= \left[\alpha_{b^l 0} + \alpha_{b^l 1}\left(\frac{1}{p_b} + \pi_b\right) - \alpha_{b^l 2}\left(\frac{r^e}{q} + \pi_e\right)\right](m + p_b b^l + q) - p_b b^l$$

At equilibrium $F_1 = 0$ and $F_2 = 0$, and we can apply the implicit function theorem in its general form:

$$\begin{pmatrix} \frac{\partial p_b}{\partial m} \\ \frac{\partial q}{\partial m} \end{pmatrix} = -\begin{pmatrix} \frac{\partial F_1}{\partial p_b} & \frac{\partial F_1}{\partial q} \\ \frac{\partial F_2}{\partial p_b} & \frac{\partial F_2}{\partial q} \end{pmatrix}^{-1} \begin{pmatrix} \frac{\partial F_1}{\partial m} \\ \frac{\partial F_2}{\partial m} \end{pmatrix}$$

or equivalently

$$\begin{pmatrix} \frac{\partial p_b}{\partial m} \\ \frac{\partial q}{\partial m} \end{pmatrix} = -\begin{vmatrix} \frac{\partial F_1}{\partial p_b} & \frac{\partial F_1}{\partial q} \\ \frac{\partial F_2}{\partial p_b} & \frac{\partial F_2}{\partial q} \end{vmatrix}^{-1} \begin{pmatrix} \frac{\partial F_2}{\partial q} & -\frac{\partial F_1}{\partial q} \\ -\frac{\partial F_2}{\partial p_b} & \frac{\partial F_1}{\partial p_b} \end{pmatrix} \begin{pmatrix} \frac{\partial F_1}{\partial m} \\ \frac{\partial F_2}{\partial m} \end{pmatrix}$$

In our case we denote the determinant of the denominator Δ, for which we compute:

$$\Delta = \begin{vmatrix} \frac{\partial F_1}{\partial p_b} & \frac{\partial F_1}{\partial q} \\ \frac{\partial F_2}{\partial p_b} & \frac{\partial F_2}{\partial q} \end{vmatrix}$$

$$= \left(\alpha_{m1} \frac{1}{p_b^2}(m + p_b b^l + q) + \frac{m b^l}{m + p_b b^l + q}\right)$$

$$\times \left(\alpha_{b!2} \frac{r^e}{q^2} (m + p_b b^l + q) + \frac{p_b b^l}{m + p_b b^l + q} \right)$$

$$- \left(-\alpha_{b!1} \frac{1}{p_b^2} (m + p_b b^l + q) + (\frac{p_b b^l}{m + p_b b^l + q} - 1) b^l \right)$$

$$\times \left(\alpha_{m2} \frac{r^e}{q^2} (m + p_b b^l + q) + \frac{m}{m + p_b b^l + q} \right)$$

$$= \alpha_{m1} \alpha_{b!2} \frac{1}{p_b^2} \frac{r^e}{q^2} (m + p_b b^l + q)^2 + \alpha_{m1} \frac{1}{p_b^2} p_b b^l + \alpha_{b!2} \frac{r^e}{q^2} m b^l$$

$$+ \frac{m b^l p_b b^l}{(m + p_b b^l + q)^2} + \alpha_{b!1} \alpha_{m2} \frac{1}{p_b^2} \frac{r^e}{q^2} (m + p_b b^l + q)^2 + \alpha_{b!1} \frac{1}{p_b^2} m$$

$$+ \alpha_{m2} \frac{r^e}{q^2} (m + q) b^l + \frac{(m + q) m b^l}{(m + p_b b^l + q)^2}$$

$$= (\alpha_{m1} \alpha_{b!2} + \alpha_{b!1} \alpha_{m2}) \frac{1}{p_b^2} \frac{r^e}{q^2} (m + p_b b^l + q)^2 + \alpha_{m1} \frac{1}{p_b^2} p_b b^l + \alpha_{b!2} \frac{r^e}{q^2} m b^l$$

$$+ \alpha_{b!1} \frac{1}{p_b^2} m + \alpha_{m2} \frac{r^e}{q^2} (m + q) b^l + \frac{m b^l}{m + p_b b^l + q} \quad (4.120)$$

From the latter, we can easily conclude that

$$\Delta > 0$$

because all terms of the sum are positive. In the following we make extensive use of the positive sign of the determinant. To check the qualitative influence of the exogenous variables on the price for long-term bonds, we only have to evaluate the sign of the term

$$\frac{1}{\Delta} \left(\frac{\partial F_1}{\partial q} \frac{\partial F_2}{\partial z} - \frac{\partial F_2}{\partial q} \frac{\partial F_1}{\partial z} \right) \quad \forall \ z \in \{\pi_e, \pi_b, r^e, m, b^l\}$$

and for qualitative reactions on Tobin's q, that of

$$\frac{1}{\Delta} \left(\frac{\partial F_2}{\partial p_b} \frac{\partial F_1}{\partial z} - \frac{\partial F_1}{\partial p_b} \frac{\partial F_2}{\partial z} \right) \quad \forall \ z \in \{\pi_e, \pi_b, r^e, m, b^l\}$$

We now evaluate the comparative statics of the dynamic system in the neighborhood of the steady state.

Effect of Money Supply on the Price of Bonds

$$\frac{\partial p_b}{\partial m} = \frac{1}{\Delta}\left(\frac{\partial F_1}{\partial q}\frac{\partial F_2}{\partial m} - \frac{\partial F_2}{\partial q}\frac{\partial F_1}{\partial m}\right)$$

$$= \frac{1}{\Delta}\left(\alpha_{m2}\frac{r^e}{q^2}(m+p_b b^l+q) + \frac{m}{m+p_b b^l+q}\right)\frac{p_b b^l}{m+p_b b^l+q}$$

$$- \frac{1}{\Delta}\left(\alpha_{b l 2}\frac{r^e}{q^2}(m+p_b b^l+q) + \frac{p_b b^l}{m+p_b b^l+q}\right)\left(\frac{m}{m+p_b b^l+q} - 1\right)$$

$$= \frac{1}{\Delta}\left(\alpha_{m2}\frac{r^e}{q^2}p_b b^l + \frac{m p_b b^l}{(m+p_b b^l+q)^2} + \alpha_{b l 2}\frac{r^e}{q^2}(p_b b^l+q) - \frac{p_b b^l(-p_b b^l - q)}{(m+p_b b^l+q)^2}\right)$$

$$= \frac{1}{\Delta}\left(\alpha_{m2}\frac{r^e}{q^2}p_b b^l + \alpha_{b l 2}\frac{r^e}{q^2}(p_b b^l+q) + \frac{p_b b^l}{m+p_b b^l+q}\right)$$

which is positive since there are no negative terms in the sum. Thus, a rise (fall) in money stock leads to rising (falling) p_b.

Effect of Bond Supply on the Bond Price

$$\frac{\partial p_b}{\partial b^l} = \frac{1}{\Delta}\left(\frac{\partial F_1}{\partial q}\frac{\partial F_2}{\partial b^l} - \frac{\partial F_2}{\partial q}\frac{\partial F_1}{\partial b^l}\right)$$

$$= \frac{1}{\Delta}\left(\alpha_{m2}\frac{r^e}{q^2}(m+p_b b^l+q) + \frac{m}{m+p_b b^l+q}\right)\left(\frac{p_b b^l}{m+p_b b^l+q} - 1\right)p_b$$

$$- \frac{1}{\Delta}\left(\alpha_{b l 2}\frac{r^e}{q^2}(m+p_b b^l+q) + \frac{p_b b^l}{m+p_b b^l+q}\right)\frac{m}{m+p_b b^l+q}p_b$$

$$= \frac{1}{\Delta}\left(\alpha_{m2}\frac{r^e}{q^2}p_b(-m-q) + \frac{p_b m(-m-q)}{(m+p_b b^l+q)^2} - \alpha_{b l 2}\frac{r^e}{q^2}p_b m - \frac{p_b b^l p_b m}{(m+p_b b^l+q)^2}\right)$$

$$= \frac{1}{\Delta}\left(\alpha_{m2}\frac{r^e}{q^2}p_b(-m-q) - \alpha_{b l 2}\frac{r^e}{q^2}p_b m - \frac{p_b m}{m+p_b b^l+q}\right)$$

$$= \frac{p_b}{\Delta}\left(-\alpha_{m2}\frac{r^e}{q^2}(m+q) - \alpha_{b l 2}\frac{r^e}{q^2}m - \frac{m}{m+p_b b^l+q}\right) < 0$$

A rise in the supply of long-term bonds lowers the price of the bonds.

Effect of Money Supply on Tobin's q

$$\frac{\partial q}{\partial m} = \frac{1}{\Delta}\left(\frac{\partial F_2}{\partial p_b}\frac{\partial F_1}{\partial m} - \frac{\partial F_1}{\partial p_b}\frac{\partial F_2}{\partial m}\right)$$

$$= \frac{1}{\Delta}\left(-\alpha_{b^l1}\frac{1}{p_b^2}(m+p_b b^l+q)+(\frac{p_b b^l}{m+p_b b^l+q}-1)b^l\right)\left(\frac{m}{m+p_b b^l+q}-1\right)$$

$$-\frac{1}{\Delta}\left(\alpha_{m1}\frac{1}{p_b^2}(m+p_b b^l+q)+\frac{m}{m+p_b b^l+q}b^l\right)\frac{p_b b^l}{m+p_b b^l+q}$$

$$= \frac{1}{\Delta}\left(\alpha_{b^l1}\frac{1}{p_b^2}(p_b b^l+q)+\frac{(m+q)b^l(p_b b^l+q)}{(m+p_b b^l+q)^2}-\alpha_{m1}\frac{1}{p_b^2}p_b b^l-\frac{mb^l p_b b^l}{(m+p_b b^l+q)^2}\right)$$

$$= \frac{1}{\Delta}\left(\alpha_{b^l1}\frac{1}{p_b^2}(p_b b^l+q)-\alpha_{m1}\frac{1}{p_b^2}(p_b b^l)+\frac{b^l q}{m+p_b b^l+q}\right)$$

$$= \frac{1}{\Delta}\left((\alpha_{b^l1}-\alpha_{m1})\frac{1}{p_b^2}p_b b^l+\alpha_{b^l1}\frac{1}{p_b^2}q+\frac{b^l q}{m+p_b b^l+q}\right)$$

which is positive because the gross substitution property gives $(\alpha_{b^l1} - \alpha_{m1}) > 0$, and we can conclude that

$$\frac{\partial q}{\partial m} > 0$$

Effect of Bond Supply on Tobin's q

$$\frac{\partial q}{\partial b^l} = \frac{1}{\Delta}\left(\frac{\partial F_2}{\partial p_b}\frac{\partial F_1}{\partial b^l}-\frac{\partial F_1}{\partial p_b}\frac{\partial F_2}{\partial b^l}\right)$$

$$= \frac{1}{\Delta}\left(-\alpha_{b^l1}\frac{1}{p_b^2}(m+p_b b^l+q)+(\frac{p_b b^l}{m+p_b b^l+q}-1)b^l\right)\left(\frac{m}{m+p_b b^l+q}p_b\right)$$

$$-\frac{1}{\Delta}\left(\alpha_{m1}\frac{1}{p_b^2}(m+p_b b^l+q)+\frac{m}{m+p_b b^l+q}b^l\right)\left(\frac{p_b b^l}{m+p_b b^l+q}-1\right)p_b$$

$$= \frac{1}{\Delta}\left(-\alpha_{b^l1}\frac{1}{p_b}m+\alpha_{m1}\frac{1}{p_b}(m+q)\right)$$

thus

$$\frac{\partial q}{\partial b^l} \begin{array}{c}<\\=\\>\end{array} 0 \quad \text{if} \quad \alpha_{m1} \begin{array}{c}<\\=\\>\end{array} \alpha_{b^l1}\frac{m}{m+q}$$

We note that capital gain expectations can have ambiguous effects on the variables considered here.

For some later considerations the following proposition is useful.

Proposition 7

The following inequality holds:

$$\frac{\partial q}{\partial m} > \frac{1}{p_b}\frac{\partial q}{\partial b^l}$$

Proof:

$$(\alpha_{b^l 1} - \alpha_{m1})\frac{1}{p_b^2} p_b b^l + \alpha_{b^l 1}\frac{1}{p_b^2} q + \frac{b^l q}{m + p_b b^l + q} > (\alpha_{m1} - \alpha_{b^l 1})\frac{1}{p_b^2} m + \alpha_{m1}\frac{1}{p_b^2} q$$

$$(\alpha_{b^l 1} - \alpha_{m1})\frac{1}{p_b^2}(m + p_b b^l + q) + \frac{b^l q}{m + p_b b^l + q} > 0$$

We know that $(\alpha_{b^l 1} - \alpha_{m1}) > 0$ and all other variables are positive in steady state. □

4.6.5 Stability

In line with the basic model treated in the preceding section, we focus on the local stability properties of the dynamic system. We will only derive a stability result for the three-dimensional system, since the cascade of stable matrices approach of the preceding chapter can be repeated here without much change (see Köper [2003, chapter 7] for details).

The Three-Dimensional System

Proposition 8

Assume that the values of ω, ν, π^c, π_{ec}, π_{ef}, π_{bc}, and π_{bf} are all at their steady state values. Setting the parameters β_p, β_w, β_{π^c}, β_n, $\beta_{\pi_{ec}}$, $\beta_{\pi_{ef}}$, $\beta_{\pi_{bc}}$, $\beta_{\pi_{bf}} = 0$, i.e., ω, ν, π^c, π_{ec}, π_{ef}, π_{bc}, and π_{bf} will all remain at their steady-state values. Further, assume that the conditions for the existence of a steady state in proposition 6 are fulfilled. Then the dynamic system

$$\dot{m} = m\mu - m(\pi^c + i(\cdot))$$
$$\dot{b}^l = \frac{1}{p_b}(g - t_c - \tau_w \omega l^d - \mu m) - b^l(\pi^c + i(\cdot)) \qquad (4.121)$$
$$\dot{y}^e = \beta_{y^e}(y^d - y^e) + (n - i(\cdot))y^e$$

exhibits a locally asymptotically steady state, if the following is true: β_{y^e} is sufficiently large, i_u is sufficiently small, and the partial derivative $\frac{\partial q}{\partial b^l}$ [14] and α_{m2}, $\alpha_{b^l 2}$ are sufficiently small.

These conditions are more demanding than the ones we listed for the case of short-term bonds in place of long-term bonds. Nevertheless, they also suggest that the wage-price spiral should be weak, the multiplier not plagued by a Metzlerian inventory dynamics and Harrodian growth accelerator, and the capital gains expectations switched off in the financial markets. Moreover, the conditions α_{m2}, $\alpha_{b^l 2}$ as small imply that α_{e2} is also small (and of opposite sign), that is, the stock market is again assumed as being in a relatively tranquil state.

Proof:
The Jacobian of the system (4.121) is

$$J^o = \begin{pmatrix} -m\frac{\partial i(\cdot)}{\partial m} & -m\frac{\partial i(\cdot)}{\partial b^l} & -m\frac{\partial i(\cdot)}{\partial y^e} \\ \frac{\partial p_b}{\partial m}(\cdot) - \frac{\mu}{p_b} - b^l\frac{\partial i(\cdot)}{\partial m} & \frac{\partial p_b}{\partial b^l}(\cdot) - \mu - b^l\frac{\partial i(\cdot)}{\partial b^l} & -\frac{1}{p_b}\tau_w\omega\frac{1}{x}\frac{\partial y}{\partial y^e} - b^l\frac{\partial i(\cdot)}{\partial y^e} \\ (\beta_{y^e} - y^e)\frac{\partial i(\cdot)}{\partial m} & (\beta_{y^e} - y^e)\frac{\partial i(\cdot)}{\partial b^l} & \beta_{y^e}(\frac{\partial c}{\partial y^e} - 1) + (\beta_{y^e} - y^e)\frac{\partial i(\cdot)}{dy^e} \end{pmatrix}$$

with $i(\cdot) = -\frac{1}{p_b^2}(g - t_c - \tau_w\omega l^d - \mu m)$ at the steady state. In the steady state, we can therefore conclude from the law of motion of b^l that

$$i(\cdot) = -\frac{1}{p_b}b^l\mu$$

We are going to prove the local asymptotic stability by means of the necessary and sufficient Routh–Hurwitz conditions for a dynamic system with three differential equations.

$$\text{trace } J^o < 0 \quad (4.122)$$

$$\det J^o < 0 \quad (4.123)$$

$$|J_1^o| + |J_2^o| + |J_3^o| > 0 \quad (4.124)$$

$$\text{ta}(J^o)(J_1^o + J_2^o + J_3^o) - \det J^o < 0 \quad (4.125)$$

with J_i being the second order principal minor of the matrix entry J_{ii}^o. To prove the first Routh–Hurwitz condition, we must calculate the trace of J^o:

$$\text{tr } J^o = -m\frac{\partial i(\cdot)}{\partial m} + \frac{\partial p_b}{\partial b^l}(\cdot) - \mu - b^l\frac{\partial i(\cdot)}{\partial b^l} + \beta_{y^e}(\frac{\partial c}{\partial y^e} - 1) + (\beta_{y^e} - y^e)\frac{\partial i(\cdot)}{\partial y^e}$$

or equivalently

$$\text{tr } J^o = -mi_q\frac{\partial q}{\partial m} - b^l i_q\frac{\partial q}{\partial b^l} - \frac{\partial p_b}{\partial b^l}\frac{1}{p_b}b^l\mu - \mu + \beta_{y^e}\left(\frac{\partial c}{\partial y^e} + \frac{\partial i(\cdot)}{\partial y^e} - 1\right) - y^e\frac{\partial i(\cdot)}{\partial y^e}$$

The first two terms of the sum can be recalculated as

$$-mi_q \frac{\partial q}{\partial m} - b^l i_q \frac{\partial q}{\partial b^l}$$

$$= -\frac{1}{\Delta} i_q (\alpha_{bl1} \frac{1}{p_b^2} m(p_b b^l + q) - \alpha_{m1} \frac{1}{p_b^2} mp_b b^l + \frac{mb^l q}{m + p_b b^l + q}$$

$$+ \alpha_{bl1} \frac{1}{p_b^2} mp_b b^l + \alpha_{m1} \frac{1}{p_b^2} (m+q) p_b b^l)$$

$$= -\frac{1}{\Delta} i_q (\alpha_{bl1} \frac{1}{p_b^2} mq + \alpha_{m1} \frac{1}{p_b^2} p_b b^l q + \frac{mb^l q}{m + p_b b^l + q})$$

We have seen in section 4.6.4 that Δ is positive, hence $-mi_q \frac{\partial q}{\partial m} - b^l i_q \frac{\partial q}{\partial b^l} < 0$.

The next two parts of the sum in the trace equation are $-\frac{\partial p_b}{\partial b^l} \frac{1}{p_b} b^l \mu - \mu$, which we can prove to have a negative sign by

$$-\frac{\partial p_b}{\partial b^l} (1/p_b \mu b^l) - \mu < 0$$

$$-\frac{\partial p_b}{\partial b^l} (1/p_b b^l) - 1 < 0$$

$$\frac{1}{\Delta} \left(\alpha_{m2} \frac{r^e}{q^2} b^l (m+q) + \alpha_{bl2} \frac{r^e}{q^2} b^l m + \frac{mb^l}{m + p_b b^l + q} \right) < 1$$

The positive denominator exceeds the positive numerator, as one can see by means of equation (4.120), and the inequality is true.

Analogously to the model with short-term bonds, one can show that the term $\beta_{y^e}(\frac{\partial c}{\partial y^e} - 1)$ is negative. Adding $\beta_{y^e} \frac{\partial i(\cdot)}{\partial y^e}$ we get $\beta_{y^e}(\frac{\partial c}{\partial y^e} + \frac{\partial i(\cdot)}{\partial y^e} - 1)$. To determine the sign of $\frac{\partial i(\cdot)}{\partial y^e}$, we calculate:

$$\frac{\partial i(\cdot)}{\partial y^e} \qquad (4.126)$$

$$= i_q \frac{\partial q}{\partial y^e} + i_u \frac{1}{x} \frac{\partial y}{\partial y^e} \qquad (4.127)$$

$$= i_q \frac{\partial q}{\partial r^e} \frac{\partial r^e}{\partial y^e} + i_u \frac{1}{x} \frac{\partial y}{\partial y^e} \qquad (4.128)$$

We know already from section 4.6.4 that $\frac{\partial q}{\partial r^e} > 0$. The other partial derivatives are also positive, which is easy to verify by using the definitions of y and r^e. To guarantee a negative trace, although the adjustment speed β_{y^e} may be very large, the term $\frac{\partial c}{\partial y^e} - \frac{\partial i(\cdot)}{\partial y^e} - 1$ must stay negative. The condition i_u as sufficiently small limits the influence of the second part of the sum in (4.128), and α_{bl2} and α_{m2} as sufficiently small make the first part of the sum in (4.128) sufficiently small.[15] The only positive entry then is $y^e \frac{\partial i(\cdot)}{\partial y^e}$. For every value of this last element of the sum, we know that there are sufficiently large values for β_{y^e} that preserve the negative sign of the trace. Hence a sufficiently large speed of adjustment of actual production to expected demand assures that the first Routh–Hurwitz condition is met.

The second Routh–Hurwitz condition concerns the sum of the secondary principal minors denoted by $|J_1^o|$, $|J_2^o|$, $|J_3^o|$ of the Jacobian J^o.

$$|J_1^o| = \begin{vmatrix} -\frac{\partial p_b}{\partial b^l}\frac{1}{p_b}b^l\mu - \mu - b^l i_q \frac{\partial q}{\partial b^l} & -\frac{1}{p_b}\tau_w \omega \frac{1}{x}\frac{\partial y}{\partial y^e} - b^l \frac{\partial i(\cdot)}{\partial y^e} \\ (\beta_{y^e} - y^e) i_q \frac{\partial q}{\partial b^l} & \beta_{y^e}(\frac{\partial c}{\partial y^e} - 1) + (\beta_{y^e} - y^e)\frac{\partial i(\cdot)}{\partial y^e} \end{vmatrix}$$

What assumptions do we have to make to guarantee that this determinant is positive? We know $-\frac{\partial p_b}{\partial b^l}\frac{1}{p_b}b^l\mu - \mu$ is negative, as shown in the proof of the negative sign of the trace.

We know that $0 < \frac{\partial p_b}{\partial b^l}\frac{1}{p_b}b^l < 1$. Hence, a sufficient condition to let $|J_1^o| > 0$ is $\frac{\partial q}{\partial b^l} > 0$.

$$|J_2^o| = \begin{vmatrix} -m i_q \frac{\partial q}{\partial m} & -m \frac{\partial i(\cdot)}{\partial y^e} \\ (\beta_{y^e} - y^e) i_q \frac{\partial q}{\partial m} & \beta_{y^e}(\frac{\partial c}{\partial y^e} - 1) + (\beta_{y^e} - y^e)\frac{\partial i(\cdot)}{\partial y^e} \end{vmatrix}$$

$$= \begin{vmatrix} -m i_q \frac{\partial q}{\partial m} & -m \frac{\partial i(\cdot)}{\partial y^e} \\ 0 & \beta_{y^e}(\frac{\partial c}{\partial y^e} - 1) \end{vmatrix}.$$

This determinant is positive because $\frac{\partial q}{\partial m} > 0$ holds true. We consider next:

$$|J_3^o| = \begin{vmatrix} -m i_q \frac{\partial q}{\partial m} & -m i_q \frac{\partial q}{\partial b^l} \\ \frac{\partial p_b}{\partial m}(\cdot) - \frac{1}{p_b}\mu - b^l i_q \frac{\partial q}{\partial m} & \frac{\partial p_b}{\partial b^l}(\cdot) - \mu - b^l i_q \frac{\partial q}{\partial b^l} \end{vmatrix}$$

$$= \begin{vmatrix} -m i_q \frac{\partial q}{\partial m} & -m i_q \frac{\partial q}{\partial b^l} \\ \frac{\partial p_b}{\partial m}(\cdot) - \frac{1}{p_b}\mu & \frac{\partial p_b}{\partial b^l}(\cdot) - \mu \end{vmatrix}$$

The last principal minor in this calculation is positive when considering sufficiently small but positive values of the expression $\frac{\partial q}{\partial b^l} > 0$. With all three principal minors positive, we know that the sum must also be positive.

$$|J_1^o| + |J_2^o| + |J_3^o| > 0$$

The third Routh–Hurwitz condition (4.123) reads

$$\begin{vmatrix} -mi_q\frac{\partial q}{\partial m} & -mi_q\frac{\partial q}{\partial b^l} & -m\frac{\partial i(\cdot)}{\partial y^e} \\ \frac{\partial p_b}{\partial m}(\cdot)-\frac{\mu}{p_b}-b^l i_q\frac{\partial q}{\partial m} & \frac{\partial p_b}{\partial b^l}(\cdot)-\mu-b^l i_q\frac{\partial q}{\partial b^l} & -\frac{1}{p_b}\tau_w\omega\frac{1}{x}\frac{\partial y}{\partial y^e}-b^l\frac{\partial i(\cdot)}{\partial y^e} \\ (\beta_{y^e}-y^e)i_q\frac{\partial q}{\partial m} & (\beta_{y^e}-y^e)i_q\frac{\partial q}{\partial b^l} & \beta_{y^e}(\frac{\partial c}{\partial y^e}-1)+(\beta_{y^e}-y^e)\frac{\partial i(\cdot)}{dy^e} \end{vmatrix}$$

$$= \begin{vmatrix} -mi_q\frac{\partial q}{\partial m} & -mi_q\frac{\partial q}{\partial b^l} & -m\frac{\partial i(\cdot)}{\partial y^e} \\ \frac{\partial p_b}{\partial m}(\cdot)-\frac{1}{p_b}\mu-b^l i_q\frac{\partial q}{\partial m} & \frac{\partial p_b}{\partial b^l}(\cdot)-\mu-b^l i_q\frac{\partial q}{\partial b^l} & -\frac{1}{p_b}\tau_w\omega\frac{1}{x}\frac{\partial y}{\partial y^e}-b^l\frac{\partial i(\cdot)}{\partial y^e} \\ 0 & 0 & \beta_{y^e}(\frac{\partial c}{\partial y^e}-1) \end{vmatrix}$$

$$= \beta_{y^e}\left(\frac{\partial c}{\partial y^e}-1\right)|J_3^o|$$

where $|J_3^o|$ is the second order principal minor, which we have shown to be positive if $\frac{\partial q}{\partial b^l} > 0$ holds true. We know that $\beta_{y^e}(\frac{\partial c}{\partial y^e}-1)$ is negative, hence the determinant is also negative.

The last Routh–Hurwitz condition in equation (4.125)

$$\mathrm{tr}J^o(J_1^o + J_2^o + J_3^o) - \det J^o < 0$$

is fulfilled, when considering sufficiently large values of β_{y^e}, because β_{y^e} is quadratic with a positive sign in the first term of the sum, and only linear in the second term. □

This proposition (when adding the same cascade of stable matrices as in the preceding section) characterizes the domain of the parameter space in which we can expect the dynamics to converge to its steady-state position. This is a good starting point for further analysis of the KMGT model with two risk-bearing assets, as well as numerical analysis of the size of the basin of attraction of the steady state and the domains in parameter space where a certain stability scenario will prevail. Moreover, the assumptions made in order to obtain this proposition indicate which policy brings the economy closer to convergence to a point attractor (the balanced growth path).

Such policies primarily concern a countercyclical fiscal policy (to tame the Harrodian accelerator process in the investment behavior of firms), a wage-management policy that controls the wage-price spiral of the model, and a capital gain taxation policy that at least reduces the financial market accelerating effects in the interaction of capital gains with capital gain expectations. More may be needed to obtain damped oscillations around the balanced growth path than just reductions in the volatility of the implied business cycle.

In the case of financial markets, we intend in future research to provide a flow approach for determining actual asset price appreciations. This approach is required in discussing open economies, because of the need to consider the balance of payments in such a framework. This framework is based on stock disequilibria and their resulting, somewhat delayed stock adjustment principles.

This makes asset prices dynamically endogenous variables (when we remove the integral equation from the model, as in the next section) and allows policy to further reduce these stock adjustment speeds, by way of some sort of "Tobin taxation" in the stock market and in the market for long-term bonds. Moreover, in regard to the wage-price spiral, one has to make use of the lessons in chapters 1–3 for reforming labor institutions and managing the dynamical processes that regulate the goods markets.

4.6.6 Summary

This section on the KMGT approach considers an alternative set of financial assets available to asset holders. Instead of interest-bearing short-term bonds, we have introduced long-term bonds that also bear interest, but which allow for capital gains or losses through changes in the market price of these bonds. The KMGT structure, however, needed only marginal adjustments, thanks to our modular system approach. We have preserved the findings of the preceding section, and thus do not depend on the simple features of short-term bonds (which are, in fact, equivalent to saving deposits). More complex assets can therefore be implemented without losing analytical tractability. The lack of proof for results with chartists' expectation behavior, however, is a result of the lack of an explicit law of motion for the actual appreciation rate of the assets. But partial models face the same problem in this respect. A way out of this problem may be the formulation of adjustment processes for bonds and equity prices, a possibility that remains for future research.

4.7 ■ INTEREST-RATE POLICY IN THE KMG PORTFOLIO APPROACH

In this section we return to the KMGT model we considered in detail in section 4.3. Our modification of it here takes into account the theory of the short-term rate. Keynes noted:

> Where, however, (as in the United States, 1933–1934) open-market operations have been limited to the purchase of very short-dated securities, the effect may, of course, be mainly confined to the very short-term rate of interest and have but little reaction on the much more important long-term rates of interest.
>
> Keynes (1936, p. 197)

An extension to the dynamic model of this section (with its second risky asset) would be highly desirable, but we leave it for future research. As monetary policy, we employ a conventional Taylor interest rate rule, assumed to be given by the following two-stage procedure:

$$i^* = i_o - \bar{\pi} + \hat{p} + \alpha_p(\hat{p} - \bar{\pi}) + \alpha_u(u - \bar{u}) \qquad (4.129)$$

$$\dot{i} = \alpha_i(i^* - i) \qquad (4.130)$$

The first equation describes the interest rate target i^* of the central bank and the second the actual setting of the short-term interest rate by way of interest rate smoothing. The target rate of the central bank i^* is made dependent on the steady-state real rate of interest, augmented by actual inflation back to a specific nominal rate of interest, and is as usual dependent on the inflation gap with respect to the target inflation rate $\bar{\pi}$ and the capacity utilization gap (as a measure of the output gap). With respect to this interest rate target, interest rate smoothing occurs with strength α_i.

Inserting i^* and rearranging terms, we derive from this latter expression the following reduced form of a Taylor interest rate rule

$$\dot{i} = -\gamma_i(i - i_o) + \gamma_p(\hat{p} - \bar{\pi}) + \gamma_u(u - \bar{u})$$

where we have $\gamma_i = \alpha_i$, $\gamma_p = \alpha_i(1 + \alpha_p)$, i.e., $\alpha_p = \gamma_p/\alpha_i - 1$ and $\gamma_u = \alpha_i\alpha_u$.

The establishment of such a rule assumes that money supply is now endogenous and is adjusted instantaneously, such that the interest rate i is established by the asset markets. Following Tobin's portfolio approach as reformulated in section 4.3, we again postulate that the following equilibrium conditions always hold and now determine the endogenous static variables M, p_e of the model, since the short-term interest rate is fixed by the central bank. Hence, not all asset supplies are given magnitudes at each moment. The value of r_e^e is given by $\frac{r^e pK}{p_e E} + \pi_e$ and thus varies at each moment solely because of variations in the share price p_e.

$$M = M^d = f_m(i, r_e^e)W_c^n, \quad i \text{ given} \qquad (4.131)$$

$$B = B^d = f_b(i, r_e^e)W_c^n, \quad W_c^n = M + B + p_e E \qquad (4.132)$$

$$p_e E = p_e E^d = f_e(i, r_e^e)W_c^n, \quad r_e^e = \frac{r^e pK}{p_e E} + \pi_e \qquad (4.133)$$

The trade between the asset holders induces again a process that makes equity prices and the stock demand for money rise or fall so that demands and supplies are equilibrated for bonds and equities (while money supply is always adjusted to money demand). The functions $f_m()$, $f_b()$, and $f_e()$, introduced in equations (4.10) to (4.12), must satisfy the following conditions:

$$f_m(i, r_e^e) + f_b(i, r_e^e) + f_e(i, r_e^e) = 1 \qquad (4.134)$$

$$\frac{\partial f_m(i, r_e^e)}{\partial z} + \frac{\partial f_b(i, r_e^e)}{\partial z} + \frac{\partial f_e(i, r_e^e)}{\partial z} = 0, \quad \forall z \in \{i, r_e^e\} \qquad (4.135)$$

These conditions guarantee that the number of independent equations is equal to the number of endogenous static variables (now M, p_e), so that the asset markets can be assumed to be in equilibrium at each moment.

We postulate that the financial assets display the gross substitution property, which means that the demand for all other assets increases whenever the price of another asset rises.

$$\frac{\partial f_b(i, r_e^e)}{\partial i} > 0, \quad \frac{\partial f_m(i, r_e^e)}{\partial i} < 0, \quad \frac{\partial f_e(i, r_e^e)}{\partial i} < 0 \quad (4.136)$$

$$\frac{\partial f_e(i, r_e^e)}{\partial r_e^e} > 0, \quad \frac{\partial f_m(i, r_e^e)}{\partial r_e^e} < 0, \quad \frac{\partial f_b(i, r_e^e)}{\partial r_e^e} < 0 \quad (4.137)$$

We assume that such an equilibrium exists in the gross substitute case, and note that the markets now have to solve for an interdependent money supply and the prices of stocks. This task is as difficult as the one where the money supply was a given magnitude, and thus shows that the simple LM view of the working of the Taylor rule often associated with its existence is not sufficient to understand what is going on in the financial markets.

We add, again without proof, that the assumption of gross substitution for the asset demand functions implies a stable ultra-short-term adjustment process for the share prices p_e in the form of a Walrasian tâtonnement process (where the money supply always accommodates money demand in the definition of the nominal wealth of asset holders). We assume that such disequilibrium adjustment processes implicitly underlie the asset equilibrium determination we consider, but we do not explicitly examine them; we assume they work smoothly behind the equilibrium positions we consider. This Walrasian tâtonnement process ignores the (potentially destabilizing) role of capital gain expectations.

The laws of motion governing the expectations about the equity prices read again as follows:

$$\dot{\pi}_{ef} = \beta_{\pi_{ef}}(\bar{\eta} - \pi_{ef}) \quad (4.138)$$

$$\dot{\pi}_{ec} = \beta_{\pi_{ec}}(\hat{p}_e - \pi_{ec}) \quad (4.139)$$

Only the value of aggregate capital gains expectations is needed for the model. But to compute it, we need the historic values of the actual inflation of equity prices $\hat{p}_e$, for which we lack a law of motion, because the general equilibrium approach yields only the level p_e, such that asset markets are in equilibrium. We follow Sargent (1987) by employing an integral representation of the expectation about equity price inflation, which leads us to the following definition of aggregate expectation of equity price inflation:

$$\pi_e(t) = \alpha_{ec}\left[\pi_{ec}(t_0)e^{-\beta_{\pi ec}(t-t_0)} + \beta_{\pi ec}\int_{t_0}^{t} e^{-\beta_{\pi ec}(t-s)}\hat{p}_e(s)ds\right]$$
$$+ (1-\alpha_{ec})\left[(\pi_{ef}(t_0) - \bar{\eta})e^{-\beta_{\pi ef}t} + \bar{\eta}\right] \qquad (4.140)$$

where $\pi_{ec}(t_0)$ and $\pi_{ef}(t_0)$ are the initial values of the expectations about the growth rate of equity prices, performed by the chartists and the fundamentalists at time t_0.

These are the modifications of the model in sections 4.3 and 4.4, when we assume a Taylor interest rate policy represents monetary policy. We assert, but cannot prove, that the stability theorems and their proofs can be generalized to this situation so that stability prevails again if the adjustment processes in the economy are of a sufficiently sluggish nature.

We thus have introduced three prototypes of the KMGT approach to Keynesian monetary growth dynamics, two with short-term bonds and either exogenous money supply or a given nominal interest rate in each moment and one with a conventional LM-curve, but two risk-bearing assets, equities and long-term bonds. We close by assuming now—as a fourth case—a Taylor interest rate policy in the KMG macrodynamics of the latter, more advanced portfolio. Such a policy appears not to be possible, since there is no short-term interest rate in the case including money and two risk-bearing assets. Interpreting the money supply as being of M_3 type, including interest-bearing saving deposits, implies the equations

$$M = M(i)$$
$$\dot{i} = -\gamma_i(i - i_o) + \gamma_p(\hat{p} - \bar{\pi}) + \gamma_u(u - \bar{u})$$

for the evolution of this money supply, since it is endogenously determined in the case of a temporarily given nominal rate of interest (through the cash management processes of the households with this enlarged concept of money supply). This fourth type of KMG portfolio dynamics therefore adds the law of motion of the interest rate to the other laws of motion, against a background in which the rate of interest now works through financial market's adjustment processes for equities and long-term bonds in relation to stock and long-term bond prices, before it can reach the real sector through its impact on Tobin's q, and from there on the investment behavior of firms. The route that monetary policy has to take is therefore a long and complicated one (particularly through the impacts it may have on capital gains expectations), as summarized in figure 4.10.

Money supply accommodates to money demand in this monetary regime, which is determined endogenously together with stock and bond prices reacting to the interest rate signal given by the central bank. The outcome of how prices for the two risky assets will in fact change may therefore be very uncertain, particularly in situations in which there is money hoarding.

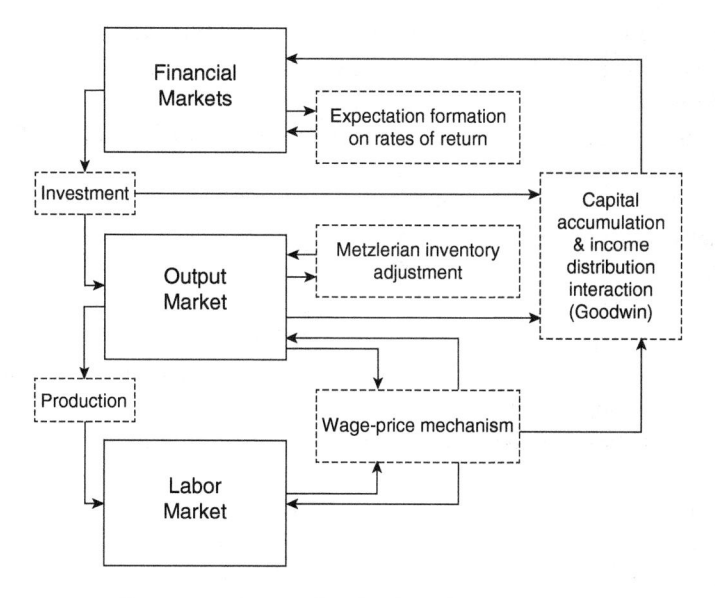

Figure 4.10 Financial and real markets interaction.

4.8 ■ CONCLUSION

In this chapter, we have extended the KMG baseline model of Chiarella and Flaschel (2000) and Chiarella, Flaschel, and Franke (2005) toward an explicit treatment of financial markets in various ways. We have shown that this framework is flexible enough to allow for model types that integrate further important—or new—aspects of the real-financial markets interaction. In particular, the use of risky long-term bonds—besides equities—rather than risk-free short-term bonds is an important modification of the baseline framework, since it provides the modeling of the rarely considered (at least in macrodynamics) situation in which two risky assets coexist in the interaction of the real and the financial markets.

As the model has been formulated it exhibits three potentially centrifugal mechanisms: the Harrodian investment-sales accelerator, the wage-price spiral in its interaction with aggregate demand, and two financial market accelerator mechanisms that can also lead to explosive spirals in the adjustment between expected and actual capital gains. The positive feedback between the investment behavior and capacity utilization rate of firms can be weakened or even fully controlled (depending on the strength of the chosen policy) if the government implements a strictly countercyclical expenditure policy rule (which, in the simplest addition to the KMGT model, we assume to be a tax financed out of capital income). The positive (under certain conditions) feedback channel between real wages and economic activity needs coordinated effort by unions, firms, and the government in order to implement basically moderate deviations from a scala mobile type wage inflation adjustment mechanism. The cumulative capital-gains expectation processes can be controlled by way of a Tobin tax on such gains (and, in addition, by a money supply rule that acts in a countercyclical way on the stock market, which we have not considered).

These three spirals, two in the real sector of the economy and one in the financial sector of our model, mirror (without any control through fiscal and monetary policy) in a basic way the unleashed forces of current capitalism. They must be further examined from the perspectives of this chapter and the institutional perspective of chapter 3 to show how they can be tamed to such a degree that they start working for the advantage of the economy and not for its destabilization, or even breakdown. In chapter 3 we considered a simplified form of the wage-price dynamics of this chapter and showed that the resulting dynamics would not only be always asymptotically stable but could also be made monotonically convergent if the employment adjustment policy of firms in view of the over- or underemployment of its current workforce worked with sufficient speed. Moreover, we showed the introduction of credit creates, on the one hand, (unwanted) Keynesian demand fluctuations, depending on the investment policy of firms, but implies, on the other hand, still damped business cycle fluctuations, a situation with which an employer of first resort can cope.

We demonstrated that unleashed nine-dimensional KMG portfolio capitalism is capable of producing a variety of outcomes with sometimes complex attractors, not only for plausible parameter values but also for larger variations in some of them. The essential move to get at least these stability results was to assume a behavioral nonlinearity in the money wage PC, based on the fact that money wages can be flexible in an upward direction, but are, at least to a certain degree, inflexible in the downward direction. This feature of actual labor market institutions appears to be responsible for the fact that the worst result, namely economic breakdown, could mostly be avoided in actual capitalist economies. But this nonlinearity in adjustment processes for the money wage represents only a minimal scenario that keeps capitalism functions, as Keynes noted:

> To suppose that a flexible wage policy is a right and proper adjunct of a system which on the whole is one of *laissez-faire,* is the opposite of the truth.
>
> Keynes (1936, p. 269)

We have argued in many ways that we must go far beyond such instinctive behavioral reactions of workers to obtain a social structure of capital accumulation that is compatible with the institutions of a democratic society in the long run.

5 Conclusions

The starting point of this book was the work by Marx, Kalecki, Keynes, and Schumpeter. Our goal was to demonstrate that neither the Marx reserve-army mechanism nor mass unemployment as a disciplining device, as in Kalecki's work, is necessary for the functioning of a capitalistic system. We could show in a dynamic framework that the introduction of minimum and maximum real wages can attenuate the negative consequences of booms and recessions in market economies. But we emphasize that a prerequisite for this outcome is that markets, including the labor market, are sufficiently flexible, implying that employers must not be constrained in their hiring and firing decisions. Furthermore, lower and upper bounds for real wages can be one ingredient of a flexicurity economy that overcomes the conflict between capital and labor. Thus, flexicurity capitalism can be considered a Western type of competitive socialism, as envisaged by Schumpeter, that successfully solves not only the coordination problem but also the incentive problem in the principal-agent scenario of an economy.

The concept of flexicurity economies, or more generally flexicurity societies, is a subject of debate. Chapter 3 showed that such a society must be built on three pillars that keep it socially intact and on a path to further socioeconomic progress: reform of labor market institutions as suggested in our model; reform of the educational sector, resulting in a comprehensive schooling system based on equal opportunity principles on the primary and secondary school levels; and a process to form leading elected executive persons (in short: elites) who must make decisions in a democratic society in an efficient, socially acceptable, and innovative way, both on the economic and political levels of such a society.

These three pillars of a modern democratic society have to be integrated and treated in depth in the model of real-financial market interaction we have discussed in its own right in chapter 4. They should be implemented in ways that significantly moderate the external conflict between capital and labor, described in chapter 1, over the wage-price spiral and the profit- and wage-squeeze mechanisms that shape its dynamics, and they must overcome the internal conflict between capital and labor, described in chapter 2, over the enforcement of work discipline (and also the adoption of new technologies). The flexicurity concept we discussed in chapter 3 may thus lead to implementation of active labor market policies that combine flexibility in production with income and employment security, by solving market coordination as well as agent incentive problems in ways compatible not only with the capitalist principles of the conduct of small, medium, and large firms but also with social and democratic principles for the provision of living standards for all members of the society, concerning base income, employment security for adults and adequate educational systems for children and young adults.

■ MATHEMATICAL APPENDIX: STABILITY THEOREMS

LOCAL AND GLOBAL STABILITY ISSUES

1. Local and Global Stability in a System of Differential Equations

Let $\dot{x} \equiv \frac{dx}{dt} = f(x)$, $x \in R^n$ be a system of n-dimensional differential equations that has an equilibrium point x^o such that $f(x^o) = 0$, where t is interpreted as "time". The equilibrium point of this system is said to be *locally asymptotically stable*, if every trajectory starting sufficiently near the equilibrium point converges to it as $t \to +\infty$. If stability is independent of the distance of the initial state from the equilibrium point, the equilibrium point is said to be *globally asymptotically stable*, or *asymptotically stable in the large* (see Gandolfo [1996, p. 333]).

2. Theorems on Stability of a System of Linear Differential Equations and on Local Stability of a System of Nonlinear Differential Equations

Theorem A.1 (Local stability / instability theorem; see Gandolfo [1996, pp. 360–362])

Let $\dot{x}_i = f_i(x), x = [x_1, x_2, \cdots, x_n] \in R^n \mid (i = 1, 2, \cdots, n)$ be an n-dimensional system of differential equations that has an equilibrium point $x^o = [x_1^o, x_2^o, \cdots, x_n^o]$ such that $f(x^o) = 0$. Suppose that the functions f_i have continuous first-order partial derivatives, and consider the Jacobian matrix evaluated *at the equilibrium point* x^o

$$J = \begin{bmatrix} f_{11} & f_{12} & \cdots & f_{1n} \\ f_{21} & f_{22} & \cdots & f_{2n} \\ \vdots & \vdots & \ddots & \vdots \\ f_{n1} & f_{n2} & \cdots & f_{nn} \end{bmatrix}$$

where $f_{ij} = \partial f_i / \partial x_j$ $(i, j = 1, 2, \cdots, n)$ are evaluated at the equilibrium point.

(i) The equilibrium point of this system is locally asymptotically stable if all the roots of the characteristic equation $|\lambda I - J| = 0$ have negative real parts.

(ii) The equilibrium point of this system is unstable if at least one root of the characteristic equation $|\lambda I - J| = 0$ has a positive real part.

(iii) The stability of the equilibrium point cannot be determined from the properties of the Jacobian matrix if all the roots of the characteristic equation $|\lambda I - J| = 0$ have nonpositive real parts but at least one root has zero real part.

Theorem A.2 (See Murata (1977, pp. 14–16)

Let A be an (n × n) matrix such that

$$A = \begin{bmatrix} a_{11} & a_{12} & \cdots & a_{1n} \\ a_{21} & a_{22} & \cdots & a_{2n} \\ \vdots & \vdots & \ddots & \vdots \\ a_{n1} & a_{n2} & \cdots & a_{nn} \end{bmatrix}$$

(i) We can express the characteristic equation $|\lambda I - A| = 0$ as

$$|\lambda I - A| = \lambda^n + a_1 \lambda^{n-1} + a_2 \lambda^{n-2} + \cdots + a_r \lambda^{n-r} + \cdots + a_{n-1} \lambda + a_n = 0, \quad (5.1)$$

where

$$a_1 = -\text{trace } A = -\sum_{i=1}^{n} a_{ii}, \quad a_2 = (-1)^2 \sum_{i<j} \begin{vmatrix} a_{ii} & a_{ij} \\ a_{ji} & a_{jj} \end{vmatrix}, \cdots,$$

$$a_r = (-1)^r \sum_{i<j<\cdots<k} \underbrace{\begin{vmatrix} a_{ii} & a_{ij} & \cdots & a_{ik} \\ a_{ji} & a_{jj} & \cdots & a_{jk} \\ \vdots & \vdots & \ddots & \vdots \\ a_{ki} & a_{kj} & \cdots & a_{kk} \end{vmatrix}}_{(r)}, \cdots, \quad a_n = (-1)^n \det A.$$

(ii) Let λ_i ($i = 1, 2, \cdots, n$) be the roots of the characteristic equation (5.1). Then we have

$$\text{trace } J = \sum_{i=1}^{n} a_{ii} = \sum_{i=1}^{n} \lambda_i, \quad \det A = \prod_{i=1}^{n} \lambda_i$$

Routh-Hurwitz conditions

Theorem A.3 (Routh-Hurwitz conditions for stable roots in an n-dimensional system; cf. Murata [1977, p. 92] and Gandolfo [1996, pp. 221–222])[1]

All of the roots of the characteristic equation (5.1) have negative real parts *if and only if* the following set of inequalities is satisfied:

$$\Delta_1 = a_1 > 0, \quad \Delta_2 = \begin{vmatrix} a_1 & a_3 \\ 1 & a_2 \end{vmatrix} > 0, \quad \Delta_3 = \begin{vmatrix} a_1 & a_3 & a_5 \\ 1 & a_2 & a_4 \\ 0 & a_1 & a_3 \end{vmatrix} > 0, \cdots,$$

$$\Delta_n = \begin{vmatrix} a_1 & a_3 & a_5 & a_7 & \cdots & 0 \\ 1 & a_2 & a_4 & a_6 & \cdots & 0 \\ 0 & a_1 & a_3 & a_5 & \cdots & 0 \\ 0 & 1 & a_2 & a_4 & \cdots & 0 \\ 0 & 0 & a_1 & a_3 & \cdots & 0 \\ \vdots & \vdots & \vdots & \vdots & \ddots & \vdots \\ 0 & 0 & 0 & 0 & \cdots & a_n \end{vmatrix} > 0$$

The following theorems A.4–A.6 are corollaries of theorem A.3.

Theorem A.4 (Routh-Hurwitz conditions for a two-dimensional system)

All of the roots of the characteristic equation

$$\lambda^2 + a_1 \lambda + a_2 = 0$$

have negative real parts if and only if the set of inequalities

$$a_1 > 0, \quad a_2 > 0$$

is satisfied.

Theorem A.5 (Routh-Hurwitz conditions for a three-dimensional system)

All of the roots of the characteristic equation

$$\lambda^3 + a_1 \lambda^2 + a_2 \lambda + a_3 = 0$$

have negative real parts if and only if the set of inequalities

$$a_1 > 0, \quad a_3 > 0, \quad a_1 a_2 - a_3 > 0 \tag{5.2}$$

is satisfied.

<u>Remark on theorem A.5:</u>

The inequality $a_2 > 0$ is always satisfied if the set of inequalities (5.2) is satisfied.

Theorem A.6 (Routh-Hurwitz conditions for a four-dimensional system)

All roots of the characteristic equation

$$\lambda^4 + a_1 \lambda^3 + a_2 \lambda^2 + a_3 \lambda + a_4 = 0,$$

have negative real parts if and only if the set of inequalities

$$a_1 > 0, \quad a_3 > 0, \quad a_4 > 0, \quad \Phi \equiv a_1 a_2 a_3 - a_1^2 a_4 - a_3^2 > 0, \tag{5.3}$$

is satisfied.

Remark on theorem A.6:

The inequality $a_2 > 0$ is always satisfied if the set of inequalities (5.3) is satisfied.

3. Theorems on Global Stability of a System of Nonlinear Differential Equations

Liapunov's theorem and Olech's theorem

Theorem A.7 (Liapunov's theorem; cf. Gandolfo [1996, p. 410])

Let $\dot{x} = f(x)$, $x = [x_1, x_2, \cdots, x_n] \in R^n$ be an n-dimensional system of differential equations that has the unique equilibrium point $x^o = [x_1^o, x_2^o, \cdots, x_n^o]$ such that $f(x^o) = 0$. Suppose that there exists a scalar function $V = V(x - x^o)$ with continuous first derivatives and with the following properties (1)–(5):

1. $V \geq 0$,
2. $V = 0$ if and only if $x_i - x_i^o = 0$ for all $i \in \{1, 2, \cdots n\}$,
3. $V \to +\infty$ as $\|x - x^o\| \to +\infty$,
4. $\dot{V} = \sum_{i=1}^{n} \frac{\partial V}{\partial(x_i - x_i^o)} \dot{x}_i \leq 0$,
5. $\dot{V} = 0$ if and only if $x_i - x_i* = 0$ for all $i \in \{1, 2, \cdots, n\}$.

Then the equilibrium point x^o of this system is globally asymptotically stable.

Remark on theorem A.7:

The function $V = V(x - x^o)$ is called the "Liapunov function".

Theorem A.8 (Olech's theorem; cf. Olech [1963] and Gandolfo [1996, pp. 354–355])

Let $\dot{x}_i = f_i(x_1, x_2)(i = 1, 2)$ be a two-dimensional system of differential equations that has the unique equilibrium point (x_1^o, x_2^o) such that $f_i(x_1^o, x_2^o) = 0$ ($i = 1, 2$). Suppose that the functions f_i have continuous first-order partial derivatives. Furthermore, suppose that the following properties (1)–(3) are satisfied:

1. $\frac{\partial f_1}{\partial x_1} + \frac{\partial f_2}{\partial x_2} < 0$ everywhere,
2. $(\frac{\partial f_1}{\partial x_1})(\frac{\partial f_2}{\partial x_2}) - (\frac{\partial f_1}{\partial x_2})(\frac{\partial f_2}{\partial x_1}) > 0$ everywhere,
3. $(\frac{\partial f_1}{\partial x_1})(\frac{\partial f_2}{\partial x_2}) \neq 0$ everywhere, or alternatively, $(\frac{\partial f_1}{\partial x_2})(\frac{\partial f_2}{\partial x_1}) \neq 0$ everywhere.

Then the equilibrium point of the above system is globally asymptotically stable.

4. Theorems That Are Useful to Establish the Existence of Closed Orbits in a System of Nonlinear Differential Equations

Poincaré-Bendixson theorem and Hopf-bifurcation theorem

Theorem A.9 (Poincaré-Bendixson theorem; cf. Hirsch and Smale [1974, chapter 11])

Let $\dot{x}_i = f_i(x_1, x_2)(i = 1, 2)$ be a two-dimensional system of differential equations with the functions f_i continuous. A nonempty compact limit set of the trajectory of this system, which contains no equilibrium point, is a closed orbit.

Theorem A.10 (Hopf bifurcation theorem for an n-dimensional system; cf. Guckenheimer and Holmes [1983, pp. 151–152], Lorenz [1993, p. 96], and Gandolfo [1996, p. 477])[2]

Let $\dot{x} = f(x; \varepsilon), x \in R^n, \varepsilon \in R$ be an n-dimensional system of differential equations depending upon a parameter ε. Suppose that the following conditions (1)–(3) are satisfied:

(1) The system has a smooth curve of equilibria given by $f(x^o(\varepsilon); \varepsilon) = 0$,

(2) The characteristic equation $|\lambda I - Df(x^o(\varepsilon_0); \varepsilon_0)| = 0$ has a pair of purely imaginary roots $\lambda(\varepsilon_0), \bar{\lambda}(\varepsilon_0)$ and no other roots with zero real parts, where $Df(x^o(\varepsilon_0); \varepsilon_0)$ is the Jacobian matrix of this system at $(x^o(\varepsilon_0), \varepsilon_0)$ with the parameter value ε_0,

(3) $\left. \frac{d\{Re\lambda(\varepsilon)\}}{d\varepsilon} \right|_{\varepsilon=\varepsilon_0} \neq 0$, where $Re\lambda(\varepsilon)$ is the real part of $\lambda(\varepsilon)$.

Then, there exists a continuous function $\varepsilon(\gamma)$ with $\varepsilon(0) = \varepsilon_0$, and for all sufficiently small values of $\gamma \neq 0$ there exists a continuous family of nonconstant periodic solution $x(t, \gamma)$ for this dynamical system, which collapses to the equilibrium point $x^o(\varepsilon_0)$ as $\gamma \to 0$. The period of the cycle is close to $2\pi/Im\lambda(\varepsilon_0)$, where $Im\lambda(\varepsilon_0)$ is the imaginary part of $\lambda(\varepsilon_0)$.

Remark on theorem A.10:

We can replace condition (3) in theorem A.10 by the following weaker condition (3a) (cf. Alexander and York [1978]):

(3a) For all ε which are near but not equal to ε_0, no characteristic root has zero real part.

The following theorem by Liu (1994) provides a convenient criterion for the occurrence of the so called simple Hopf bifurcation in an n-dimensional system. The "simple" Hopf bifurcation is defined as the Hopf bifurcation in which all the characteristic roots *except* a pair of purely imaginary ones have negative real parts.

Theorem A.11 (Liu's theorem; see Liu [1994])

Consider the following characteristic equation with $n \geq 3$:

$$\lambda^n + a_1\lambda^{n-1} + a_2\lambda^{n-2} + \cdots + a_{n-1}\lambda + a_n = 0$$

This characteristic equation has a pair of purely imaginary roots and (n − 2) roots with negative real parts *if and only if* the following set of conditions is satisfied:

$$\Delta_i > 0 \text{ for all } i \in \{1, 2, \cdots, n-2\}, \quad \Delta_{n-1} = 0, \quad a_n > 0$$

where $\Delta_i (i = 1, 2, \cdots, n-1)$ are Routh-Hurwitz terms defined as

$$\Delta_1 = a_1, \quad \Delta_2 = \begin{vmatrix} a_1 & a_3 \\ 1 & a_2 \end{vmatrix}, \quad \Delta_3 = \begin{vmatrix} a_1 & a_3 & a_5 \\ 1 & a_2 & a_4 \\ 0 & a_1 & a_3 \end{vmatrix}, \cdots,$$

$$\Delta_{n-1} = \begin{vmatrix} a_1 & a_3 & a_5 & a_7 & \cdots & 0 & 0 \\ 1 & a_2 & a_4 & a_6 & \cdots & 0 & 0 \\ 0 & a_1 & a_3 & a_5 & \cdots & 0 & 0 \\ 0 & 1 & a_2 & a_4 & \cdots & 0 & 0 \\ 0 & 0 & a_1 & a_3 & \cdots & 0 & 0 \\ \vdots & \vdots & \vdots & \vdots & \ddots & \vdots & \vdots \\ 0 & 0 & 0 & 0 & \cdots & a_n & 0 \\ 0 & 0 & 0 & 0 & \cdots & a_{n-1} & 0 \\ 0 & 0 & 0 & 0 & \cdots & a_{n-2} & a_n \\ 0 & 0 & 0 & 0 & \cdots & a_{n-3} & a_{n-1} \end{vmatrix}$$

The following theorems A.12–A.14 provide us with some convenient criteria for two-dimensional, three-dimensional, and four-dimensional Hopf bifurcations respectively. It is worth noting that these criteria provide us with useful information on the "nonsimple" as well as the "simple" Hopf bifurcations.

Theorem A.12

The characteristic equation

$$\lambda^2 + a_1 \lambda + a_2 = 0$$

has a pair of purely imaginary roots *if and only if* the set of conditions

$$a_1 = 0, \quad a_2 > 0$$

is satisfied. In this case, we have the explicit solution $\lambda = \pm i \sqrt{a_2}$, where $i = \sqrt{-1}$.

Proof Obvious, because we have the solution $\lambda = (-a_1 \pm \sqrt{a_1^2 - 4a_2})/2$.

Theorem A.13 (cf. Asada (1995) and Asada and Semmler [1995])

The characteristic equation

$$\lambda^3 + a_1\lambda^2 + a_2\lambda + a_3 = 0$$

has a pair of purely imaginary roots *if and only if* the set of conditions

$$a_2 > 0, \quad a_1 a_2 - a_3 = 0$$

is satisfied. In this case, we have the explicit solution $\lambda = -a_1, \pm i\sqrt{a_2}$, where $i = \sqrt{-1}$.

Theorem A.14 (cf. Yoshida and Asada [2001], and Asada and Yoshida [2003])

Consider the characteristic equation

$$\lambda^4 + a_1\lambda^3 + a_2\lambda^2 + a_3\lambda + a_4 = 0 \tag{5.4}$$

(i) The characteristic equation (5.4) has a pair of purely imaginary roots and two roots with nonzero real parts *if and only if* either of the following set of conditions (A) or (B) is satisfied:

(A) $a_1 a_3 > 0$, $a_4 \neq 0$, $\Phi \equiv a_1 a_2 a_3 - a_1^2 a_4 - a_3^2 = 0$.
(B) $a_1 = a_3 = 0$, $a_4 < 0$.

(ii) The characteristic equation (5.4) has a pair of purely imaginary roots and two roots with negative real parts *if and only if* the following set of conditions (C) is satisfied:

(C) $a_1 > 0$, $a_3 > 0$, $a_4 > 0$, $\Phi \equiv a_1 a_2 a_3 - a_1^2 a_4 - a_3^2 = 0$.

Remarks on theorem A.14:

(1) The condition $\Phi = 0$ is always satisfied if the set of conditions (B) is satisfied.

(2) The inequality $a_2 > 0$ is always satisfied if the set of conditions (C) is satisfied.

(3) We can derive theorem A.14 (ii) from theorem A.11 as a special case with $n = 4$, although we cannot derive theorem A.14 (i) from theorem A.11.

▎ NOTES

▎ Introduction

1. See the appendix in Flaschel (2009, chapter 10) for details of his characterization of the MKS system.

2. See chapter 1 for details.

3. We emphasize here, in addition, that we consider only closed economies in this book and, therefore, do not allow for international migration of capital and labor.

▎ 1. Marx: Socially Acceptable Capitalism?

1. This chapter is an expanded version of our article Flaschel and Greiner (2009).

2. Or monopolistic competition, which does not modify the qualitative structure of the model in essential ways.

3. Of a simple type; see the appendix of this chapter for a microfounded extension of these wage-price dynamics.

4. We caution that this illustration may contain many more interactions of economic variables in its background than in the variant of the Goodwin model considered in this chapter.

5. An econometric analysis of the separation of the business cycle from the long-phased distributive cycle for the US economy after World War II is provided in Kauermann, Teuber, and Flaschel (2009).

6. To our knowledge, the first study of an unemployment benefit system in the context of the Goodwin growth cycle model was provided by Glombowski and Krüger (1984). They discuss various benefit systems and their implications for stability in the context of Goodwinian fluctuating growth.

7. We abstract here from errors in the anticipation of the price inflation rate that—when added—do not alter the qualitative dynamics of the model very much (as long as they are moderate).

8. Or the real wage $\omega = w/p$ divided by labor productivity $z = Y/L$.

9. The graph of the function H indicates that nonlinear behavioral equations can also be treated in this way, since we require solely that the graph of the function H exhibit a single, global sink and thus need not be strictly convex in particular; see Flaschel (2008, chapter 4) for details.

10. In fact, a proper sink.

11. Note that we abstract from increases in productivity. Otherwise, the total would be the inflation rate plus the increase in productivity, times n.

12. The abstract one-good model of this chapter, therefore, now allows the use of this good not only for consumption and investment, but also for benefit payments out of an accumulated stock of unemployment funds.

13. Since there are no financial assets present in the model. Note that one assumes here that the parameter τ is chosen so that these stocks are not exhausted in the course of the growth fluctuations considered. If they were to be exhausted, however, it would not change the implied dynamics—because of the assumption of full capacity growth—but simply represents a situation in which the model temporarily returns to the Goodwin case with no unemployment benefits.

14. Note that a minimum wage restriction still allows the wage share to approach its limit value 1. Should that happen, a maximum wage restriction—as considered later—would be needed in addition.

15. In terms of the Blanchard and Katz (1999) model in the appendix of this chapter, the adjustment parameter β_{wv} is given in their notation by $1 - \theta\lambda$, and thus is strictly positive if labor productivity plays a role in the formulation of their reservation wages as well as of the real wages that are targeted by unions in their wage negotiations.

16. See Wörgötter (1986) for details on this point.

17. In this section, lowercase letters (including w and p) indicate logarithms and we denote the rate of unemployment by $U = 1 - e$.

18. Note that the parameter in front of U_{t-1} cannot be interpreted as a speed of adjustment coefficient anymore.

2. Kalecki: Full Employment Welfare Capitalism?

1. This chapter is based on Flaschel, Franke, and Semmler (2008). Permission from Routledge Publishing House to reuse the material from this chapter is gratefully acknowledged.

2. See, for example, Flaschel and Skott (2006) and Asada, Flaschel, and Skott (2006) for related models of capital accumulation.

3. Flaschel and Skott (2006) and Asada, Flaschel, and Skott (2006) consider a similar model of Steindlian accumulation dynamics.

4. An alternative assumption about investment behavior is given by

$$I/K = i_o(y - \bar{y}) + i_{\rho^m}(\rho^m - \rho_o^m) - i_e(e - \bar{e}_f) + \bar{a}, \quad \rho^m = (1 - \omega/x)\bar{y} \qquad (2.28)$$

which separates short-term business cycle utilization rate effects from normal utilization profitability effects ρ^m caused by changing income distribution. Note also that we do not discuss the financing of investment explicitly. A justification for this is that all profits are paid out as dividends and all investment is financed by the issue of new equities, the value of which is not yet feeding back into the investment decision of firms.

5. $\kappa = 1/(1 - \kappa_w \kappa_p)$.

6. See also the concluding section of the chapter.

7. We add to this consideration that the investment function when estimated for the US economy shows a significant negative influence of the rate of employment on the rate of capital accumulation I/K which indicates that this economy may not be of the type just considered (at least partially).

8. We also assume again that the β_e-terms are the dominant ones in our formulation of the dynamics of the employment rate.

9. We assume now that only the β_{eu}-term is dominant in our formulation of the dynamics of the employment rate (but that the role of $\beta_{e\omega}$ is negligible).

10. We note with respect to this parameter set that the parameter $\bar{a} = \rho_o$ may be considered as much too high from the empirical point of view, though it also represents a profit share of 30 percent. Yet, since this rate also represents the growth rate of the economy it is of course of exceptional size. The model therefore needs reformulation, by adding deductions from profits that drive a sufficient wedge between its rate of profit and the resulting rate of growth.

11. A similar expression applies to the reduced-form wage level inflation rate, but need not be discussed explicitly unless wage policy is taken into account in addition to monetary and fiscal policy.

12. We expect the steady state to be locally unique, since its defining 5 equations should imply a Jacobian with non-zero determinant, but cannot say anything on global uniqueness for the moment.

3. Schumpeter: Capitalism, Flexicurity, and Democracy?

1. In discussing the first pillar, we also take account of pension funds as well as health care (organized by the public sector), which in turn and together with reformed labor market institutions provide the supports underlying the labor market component of the flexicurity approach.

2. This chapter is based on Flaschel, Greiner, and Luchtenberg (2009).

3. See Kauermann, Teuber, and Flaschel (2009) for a description of this decomposition methodology.

4. See United Nations (1998, article 23): Universal Declaration of Human Rights, 1948 (http://www.un.org/Overview/rights.html).

5. See http://www.eurofound.europa.eu/areas/industrialrelations/dictionary/definitions/flexicurity.htm.

6. See note 5.

7. An important issue in Tcherneva and Wray (2005), moreover, is whether full employment is compatible with price "stability" (a target rate of 2 percent, for example). To treat this issue in the context of our flexicurity model requires an integration of the Keynesian business cycle (see Flaschel et al. [2008] for such an extension). In this context, one then has to introduce countercyclical fiscal as well as monetary policy rules and show that such rules can control the business cycle and inflation to such a degree that the concept of an employer of first resort, described in this chapter, remains viable.

8. Of course, there is simple work to be done within firms, but this is part of the job of skilled and highly skilled workers.

9. The term S_1 is equal to $\delta_r R + \dot{R}$.

10. Note that we also assume that all persons work in this economy after schooling and before retirement, both women and men (with child-raising obligations left in the background of the model).

11. We discuss later the determination of this ratio.

12. Even if we assume wage income taxation here too, since these taxes do not leave the public sector, they can thus be omitted from its representation.

13. See Flaschel et al. (2008) for details of the derivation of this real wage $\omega_{1a} = w_{1a}/p$ PC; note that this curve implicitly assumes that the steady state value of the real wage describes the situation where capital stock growth is equal to the natural growth rate n of the labor force.

14. Moreover, any fluctuations away from the steady-state ratio $l_o = \bar{l}$ are also ignored in the remainder of this chapter, which allows us to save one law of motion in the subsequent stability analysis (see Flaschel et al. [2008] for an explanation of this decision). We emphasize, however, the need to treat this issue explicitly when considering skill formation and heterogeneous skills.

15. Moreover, we also ignore the originally considered $-\hat{K}$ in the following first law of motion without a loss of generality.

16. Refer to figure 3.3, where the postwar period up to the 1960s seemed to suggest that the working of the reserve-army mechanism had been overcome, a suggestion disproved in subsequent years in a striking way.

17. With respect to concrete numbers, one therefore could assume, for example, $t_c = 6$, $t_s = 12$, $t_u = 5$, $t_b = 47$, $t_a = 42$, $t_r = 15$. We stress here that the considered age structure is still a very stylized one in light of figure 3.3.

18. Source: http://www.edu.fi/english/SubPage.asp?path=500,4699.

19. The ratio $\frac{L_1^d}{t_a L_0}$ compares employment in the first sector (of highly skilled workers) with the common core employment of all workers.

20. Source: http://www.edu.fi/english/SubPage.asp?path=500,4699.

21. Standard Keynesian assumptions will again ensure that $y^o > 0$ holds true.

22. See Vis (2007) on such matters.

23. Based on Alchian (1950) and Krause and Nesemann (1999).

24. See Flaschel, Franke, and Veneziani (2009) for the details of such an approach to labor values and its implications.

4. Unleashed Capitalism: The Starting Point for Societal Reform

1. The analytical part of this chapter, in section 4.6, has been taken from Köper (2003, chapter 7); see also Köper and Flaschel (2000) for an initial approach in such a direction. We thank Carsten Köper for allowing us to reuse this material from his PhD thesis. The analysis of this chapter—including a much more detailed discussion of stabilizing fiscal and monetary policies—is pursued further in Asada et al. (2010a, b).

2. See also the literature to which these authors refer.

3. See, however, Chiarella, Flaschel, Groh, Köper, and Semmler (1999) for extensions of this approach in this latter direction.

4. See Chiarella, Flaschel, Groh, Köper, and Semmler (1999) for extensions of this approach with respect to workers' consumption and savings behavior.

5. See also Chiarella and Flaschel (1996, 1998, 1999, 2006), the last two books also for the treatment of open economies in the KMG framework.

6. See Chiarella, Flaschel, Groh, and Semmler (2000) for the inclusion of workers' savings in a KMG framework.

7. See Chiarella, Flaschel, Groh, and Semmler (2000) for the treatment of neoclassical smooth factor substitution.

8. See Sargent (1987) for another application of this assumption.

9. Note that we assume that the stock B is considered as a substitute for (or representation of) interest-bearing savings deposits.

10. Note, however, that this scala mobile needs some reformulation in the case of a positive growth rate of labor productivity and that it may create difficulties when the economy is an open one and subjected to significant import price inflation.

11. This equation also shows that it may be better for firms not to react to current wage inflation immediately, but to put significant weight on the medium-term evolution of the inflationary climate π^c.

12. This section is taken from Köper (2003, chapter 7). We thank Carsten Köper for allowing us to reuse this material. A detailed reconsideration of the model type of this section is provided in Asada et al. (2010b), where alternative proofs to those in this section are provided and where detailed policy applications are formulated and proved, by discussing scenarios in which the stability of the private sector of the economy can be established or improved.

13. A solution will automatically equilibrate the equity market by means of Walras's law.

14. This condition can be shown to hold true if the parameter α_{m2} is chosen sufficiently large; see Köper (2003, chapter 7) for details.

15. Alternatively to the condition of a small $\alpha_{b!2}$ and α_{m2}, one can also consider sufficiently small i_q.

■ Mathematical Appendix: Stability Theorems

1. See also Gantmacher (1954) for many details that can be associated with these conditions and Brock and Malliaris (1989) for a compact representation of them.

2. See also Strogatz (1994) and Wiggins (1990) in this regard.

REFERENCES

Alchian, A.A. (1950). *Uncertainty, evolution, and economic theory*. Journal of Political Economy, 58, 211–221.

Alexander, J.C. and J.A. York (1978). *Global bifurcation of periodic orbits*. American Journal of Mathematics, 100, 263–292.

Andersen, T.M. and M. Svarer (2007). Flexicurity – labor market performance in Denmark. Munich: CESifo working paper 2108.

Asada, T. (1995). *Kaldorian dynamics in an open economy*. Journal of Economics, 2, 1–16.

Asada, T. and W. Semmler (1995). *Growth and finance: An intertemporal model*. Journal of Macroeconomics, 17, 623–649.

Asada, T., C. Chiarella, P. Flaschel, T. Mouakil, C. Proaño and W. Semmler (2010a). Stabilizing an Unstable Economy: On the Choice of Proper Policy Measures. Bielefeld University: CEMM working paper.

Asada, T., P. Flaschel, C. Köper and W. Semmler (2010b). Stabilizing an Unstable Economy: Policy Rules to Safeguard Real and Financial Market Stability. CEMM working paper.

Asada, T., C. Chiarella, P. Flaschel and R. Franke (2003). *Open Economy Macrodynamics*. Heidelberg: Springer.

Asada, T. and H. Yoshida (2003). *Coefficient criterion for four-dimensional Hopf-bifurcations: A complete mathematical characterization and applications to economic dynamics*. Chaos, Solitons & Fractals, 18, 421–423.

Asada, T., P. Flaschel and P. Skott (2006). *Prosperity and Stagnation in Capitalist Economies*. In: C. Chiarella, P. Flaschel, R. Franke and W. Semmler (eds.): *Quantitative and Empirical Analysis of Nonlinear Dynamic Macromodels*. Contributions to Economic Analysis (Series Editors: B. Baltagi, E. Sadka and D. Wildasin), Elsevier, Amsterdam, 413–448.

Asada, T., P. Chen, C. Chiarella and P. Flaschel (2006). *AD-AS and the Phillips curve. A baseline disequilibrium approach*. In: C. Chiarella, P. Flaschel, R. Franke and W. Semmler (eds.): *Quantitative and Empirical Analysis of Nonlinear Dynamic Macromodels*. Contributions to Economic Analysis (Series Editors: B. Baltagi, E. Sadka and D. Wildasin), Elsevier, Amsterdam, 173–227.

Asada, T., C. Chiarella, P. Flaschel and R. Franke (2009). *Manetary Macrodynamics*. New York: Routledge.

Barbosa-Filho, N. and L. Taylor (2006). *Distributive and Demand Cycles in the US Economy – A Structuralist Goodwin Model*. Metroeconomica, 57 issue 3, pp. 389–411.

Blanchard, O.J. and L. Katz (1999). *Wage dynamics: Reconciling theory and evidence*. American Economic Review. Papers and Proceedings, 89, 69–74.

Bowles, S., D. Gordon and T.E. Weisskopf (1983). *Beyond the Waste Land*. New York: Anchor Press.

Brock, W.A. and A.G. Malliaris (1989). *Differential Equations, Stability and Chaos in Dynamic Economics*. Amsterdam: North Holland.

Center for Strategic and International Studies (2006). *Future Watch, October 2006: Flexicurity-Denmark-Style.* Washington, D.C.

Chen, P., C. Chiarella, P. Flaschel and W. Semmler (2006). *Keynesian Macrodynamics and the Phillips Curve. An estimated baseline macro-model for the U.S. economy.* In: C. Chiarella, P. Flaschel, R. Franke and W. Semmler (eds.): *Quantitative and Empirical Analysis of Nonlinear Dynamic Macromodels.* Contributions to Economic Analysis. Elsevier, Amsterdam, 229–284.

Chiarella, C. and P. Flaschel (1996). *An Itegrative Approach to Prototype 2D-Macromodels of Growth, Price and Inventory Dynamics.* Chaos, Solitons & Fractals.

Chiarella, C. and P. Flaschel (1998). *Dynamics of Natural Rates of Growth and Employment.* Macroeconomic Dynamics.

Chiarella, C. and P. Flaschel (1999). *Keynesian monetary growth in open economies.* Annals of Operations Research.

Chiarella, C. and P. Flaschel (2000a). *The Dynamics of Keynesian Monetary Growth. Macrofoundations.* Cambridge, UK: Cambridge University Press.

Chiarella, C. and P. Flaschel (2000b). *High Order Disequilibrium Growth Dynamics: Theoretical Aspects and Numerical Features.* Journal of Economic Dynamics and Control, 24, 935–963.

Chiarella, C., P. Flaschel and R. Franke (2005). *Foundations for a Disequilibrium Theory of the Business Cycle. Qualitative Analysis and Quantitative Assessment.* Cambridge, UK: Cambridge University Press.

Chiarella, C., P. Flaschel, G. Groh, C. Köper and W. Semmler (1999). *Towards Applied Disequilibrium Growth Theory: VI. Substituion, Money Holdings, Wealth-Effects and Further Extensions.* UTS Sydney, Discussion paper.

Chiarella, C., P. Flaschel, H. Hung and W. Semmler (2006). *Portfolio Choice, Asset Accumulation and Macroeconomic Activity. A Tobinian Stock-Flow Approach.* University of Technology, Sydney: Book manuscript.

Chiarella, C., P. Flaschel and W. Semmler (2000). *Modern Macroeconometric Model Building. Theory, Numerical Analysis and Applications.* Book manuscript.

COUNCIL (2002). *Council resolution of 27 June 2002 on lifelong learning.* In: Official Journal of the European Communities C 163/1 (http://europa.eu/eur-lex/pri/en/oj/dat/2002/c_163/c_16320020709en00010003.pdf (read 11-18-2007).

Docherty, P. (2005). *Money And Employment: A Study of the Theoretical Implications of Endogenous Money.* Aldershot, UK: Edward Elgar.

Duncan K.F. and L. Taylor (2006). *A Heterodox Growth and Distribution Model.* In: N. Salvadori (ed.): *Economic Growth and Distribution: On the Nature and Causes of the Wealth of Nations.* Cheltenham, UK and Northampton, MA, USA: Edward Elgar.

Esping-Anderson, G. (1990). *The Three Worlds of Welfare Capitalism.* Cambridge, UK: Cambridge University Press.

European Commission (2007). *Towards Common Principles of Flexicurity: More and Better Jobs Through Flexibility and Security.* Brussels, 27-06-2007, COM(2007)359final.

Flaschel, P. (2008). *The Macrodynamics of Capitalism. Elements for a Synthesis of Marx, Keynes and Schumpeter.* Heidelberg: Springer Verlag, forthcoming.

Flaschel, P. (2009). *Macrodynamics. Elements for a Synthesis of Marx, Keynes and Schumpeter.* Heidelberg: Springer.

Flaschel, P., R. Franke and W. Semmler (1997). *Dynamic Macroeconomics: Instability, Fluctuations and Grwoth in Monetary Economies.* Cambridge, MA: MIT Press.

Flaschel, P., R. Franke and W. Semmler (2008). Kaleckian investment and employment cycles in postwar industrialized economies. In: P. Flaschel and M. Landesmann (eds.): *Mathematical Economics and the Dynamics of Capitalism*. London: Routledge, 35–65.

Flaschel, P., R. Franke and R. Veneziani (2009). *Labor Productivity and the Law of Falling Labor Content*. Bielefeld University: Unpublished manuscript.

Flaschel, P., A. Greiner, S. Luchtenberg and E. Nell (2008). *Varieties of capitalism. The flexicurity model*. In: P. Flaschel and M. Landesmann (eds.): *Mathematical Economics and the Dynamics of Capitalism*, London: Routledge, 76–104.

Flaschel, P. and A. Greiner (2009). *Employment Cycles and Minimum Wages. A Macro View. Structural Change and Economic Dynamics*, forthcoming.

Flaschel, P., A. Greiner and S. Luchtenberg (2009). Labor Market Institutions, Education and Elites in Flexicurity Societies. Bielefeld University: CEMM Working paper no. 150.

Flaschel, P., A. Greiner, C. Logeay and C. Proaño (2010). Employment Cycles, Low Income Work and the Dynamic Impact of Minimum Wages. A Macro Perspective. Bielefeld University: CEMM Working paper.

Flaschel, P. and H.-M. Krolzig (2006). *Wage-price Phillips curves and macroeconomic stability: Basic structural form, estimation and analysis*. In: C. Chiarella, P. Flaschel, R. Franke and W. Semmler (eds.): *Quantitative and Empirical Analysis of Nonlinear Dynamic Macromodels*. Contributions to Economic Analysis (Series Editors: B. Baltagi, E. Sadka and D. Wildasin). Amsterdam: Elsevier.

Flaschel, P. and P. Skott (2006). *Steindl models of growth and stagnation*. Metroeconomica, 57, 305–340.

Flaschel, P., D. Tavani, L. Taylor, and T. Teuber (2007). *A structuralist model of the wage-price spiral with non-linear demand pressure terms*. Bielefeld University: CEMM Working paper no. 155.

Franke, R. (1992). *A Metzlerian Model of Inventory Growth Cycles*. Discussion paper, Bielefel University.

Friedman, M. (1968). *The role of monetary policy*. American Economic Review, 58, 1–17.

Funk, L. (2008). *European Flexicurity Policies. A Critical Assessment*. The International Journal of Comparative Labour Law and Industrial Relations, 24, 349–384.

Gandolfo, G. (1996). *Economic Dynamics* (Third Edition). Berlin: Springer.

Gantmacher, F.R. (1954). *Theory of Matrices*. New York: Interscience Publishers.

Glombowski, J. and M. Krüger (1984). *Unemployment insurance and cyclical growth*. In: R. Goodwin, M. Krüger, and A. Vercelli (eds.): *Nonlinear Models of Fluctuating Growth*. Heidelberg: Springer, 25–46.

Godley, W. (1999). Money and Credit in a Keynesian Model of Income Determination. *Cambridge Journal of Economics*, 23, 393–411.

Godley, W. and M. Lavoie (2007). *Monetary Economics: An Integrated Approach to Credit, Money, Income, Production and Wealth*. Basingstoke and New York: Macmillan.

Goodwin, R. (1967). *A growth cycle*. In: C.H. Feinstein (ed.): Socialism, Capitalism and Economic Growth, Cambridge, UK: Cambridge University Press, 54–58.

Goodwin, R. M. (1972). *A Growth Cycle*. In E.K. Hunt and J.G. Schwartz (eds.): A Critique of Economic Theory. Harmondsworth: Penguin Books, 442–449.

Greiner, A. and P. Flaschel (2009a). Economic growth and the employer of last resort: A simple model of flexicurity capitalism. *Research in Economics*, 63, 102–113.

Greiner, A. and P. Flaschel (2009b). Economic policy in a growth model with human capital, heterogenous agents and unemployment. *Computational Economics*, 33, 175–192.

Greiner, A. and P. Flaschel (2010). Public debt and public investment in an endogenous growth model with real wage rigidities. *Scottish Journal of Political Economy*, 57, 68–84.

Groth, C. and J.B. Madsen (2007). *Medium-term fluctuations and the "Great Ratios" of economic growth*. University of Copenhagen: Working paper.

Guckenheimer, J. and P. Holmes (1983). *Nonlinear Oscillations, Dynamical Systems, and Bifurcations of Vector Fields*. Heidelberg: Springer.

Hanusch, H. and A. Pyka (2007a). *The Elgar Companion to Neo-Schumpeterian Economics*. Aldershot: Edward Elgar.

Hanusch, H. and A. Pyka (2007b). Principles of Neo-Schumpeterian Economics. *Cambridge Journal of Economics*, 31, 275–289.

Hartmann, M. (2007). *The Sociology of Elites*. London: Routledge.

Higley, J. (2006). *Elite theory in political sociology*. University of Texas. http://theoriesofsocialchange.files.wordpress.com/2010/02/higley_elite_theory_ipsa_2008.pdf

Hirsch, M. and S. Smale (1974). *Differential Equations, Dynamical Systems and Linear Algebra*. London: Academic Press.

Kalecki, M. (1943). *Political aspects of full employment*. Reprinted in M. Kalecki, Selected Essays on the Dynamics of the Capitalist Economy, Cambridge, UK: Cambridge University Press, 1971.

Kaldor, N. (1940). *A model of the trade cycle*. Economic Journal, 50, 78–92.

Kauermann, G., T. Teuber and P. Flaschel (2009). *Estimating loops and cycles using penalized splines*. Bielefeld: CEM working paper.

Keynes, J.M. (1936). *The General Theory of Employment, Interest and Money*. New York: Macmillan.

Klesse, H.-J. and O. Voss (2007). *Fremder Leute Geld*. Wirtschaftswoche, 51, 78–85.

Köper, C. (2003). *Real-Financial Interaction in Contemporary Models of AS-AD Growth*. Bern: Peter Lang.

Köper, C. and P. Flaschel (2000). Towards an advanced model of the real – financial interaction: A KMG portfolio approach, rev. ed. 2003. Bielefeld University: Working paper.

Krause, U. and T. Nesemann (1999). *Differenzengleichungen und diskrete dynamische Systeme*. Stuttgart: Teubner.

Liu, W.M. (1994). *Criterion of Hopf bifurcations without using eigenvalues*. Journal of Mathematical Analysis and Applications, 1982, 250–256.

Lorenz, H.-W. (1993). *Nonlinear dynamical economics and chaotic motion*, 2nd ed. Heidelberg: Springer.

Marx, K. (1954). *Capital*, Volume I-III. London: Lawrence and Wishart.

Metzler, L.A. (1941). *The Nature and Stability of Inventory Cycles*. Review of Economic Statistics.

Ministry of Education and Science of Sweden (2004). *Equity in education. Thematic review. Country analytical report*. Sweden. http://www.oecd.org/dataoecd/30/22/38697408.pdf (read 11-18-2007).

Minsry, H.P (1982). *Stabilizing an Unstable Economy*. New York: McGraw Hill.

Mills, C.W. (1959). *The Power Elite*. New York: Oxford University Press.

Mises, Ludwig von (1951). *Socialism. An Economic and Sociological Analysis*. New Haven: Yale University Press.

Murata, Y. (1977). *Mathematics for Stability and Optimization of Economic Systems*. New York: Academic Press.

OECD (2007). *Education at a Glance 2007*. http://www.oecd.org/document/30/ 0,3343,en_2649_39263294_39251550_1_1_1_1,00.html (read 11-18-2007).
Olech, A.M. (1963). *On the global stability of an autonomous system in the plane*. In: P. Lasalle and P. Díaz (eds.): Contributions to Differential Equations, 1, 389–400.
Okun, A.M. (1970). *The Political Economy of Prosperity*. Washington, D.C.: The Brookings Institution.
Pareto, V. (1935). *The Mind and Society*. New York: Harcourt Brace.
Pareto, V. (1968). *The Rise and Fall of Elites: An Application of Theoretical Sociology*. Totowa: Bedminster Press.
Proaño, C., P. Flaschel, M.B. Diallo, and T. Teuber (2007). Distributive cycles, business fluctuations and the wage-led/profit-led debate. Bielefeld University: CEMM Working paper no. 154
Quirk, V. et al. (2006). The job guarantee in practice. The University of Newcastle, Australia: Center of Full Employment and Equity, Working paper no. 06-15.
Report of the special rapporteur on education, Vernor Muñoz, on his mission to Germany (13-21 February 2006) http://www.netzwerk-bildungsfreiheit.de/pdf/ Munoz_Mission_on_Germany.pdf (read 11-18-2007).
Roemer, J. (1994). *A Future for Socialism*. Cambridge, MA: Harvard University Press.
Rose, H. (1967). *On the non-linear theory of the employment cycle*. Review of Economic Studies, 34, 153–173.
Rose, H. (1990). *Macroeconomic Dynamics. A Marshallian Synthesis*. Cambridge, MA: Basil Blackwell.
Rothkopf, D. (2009). *Superclass: The Global Power Elite and the World They Are Making*. New York: Farrar, Strauss & Giroux.
Sargent, T.J. (1987). *Macroeconomic Theory*. New York: Academic Press.
Schumpeter, J. (1912). *The Theory of Economic Development*. London: Oxford University Press.
Schumpeter, J. (1939). *Business Cycles*, Vol. I, II. Philadelphia: Porcupine Press.
Schumpeter, J. (1942). *Capitalism, Socialism and Democracy*. New York: Harper & Row.
Scott, J. (1990). *The Sociology of Elites*, Volume I–III. Aldershot: Edward Elgar.
Sinn, H.-W. (2007). *Minimum wages stop the curse of history*. Press Release of CESifo Institute for Economic Research, 29 October, 2007.
Solow, R. (1956). *A contribution to the theory of economic growth*. Quarterly Journal of Economics, 70, 65–94.
Sraffa, P. (1970). *The Works and Correspondence of David Ricardo*. Vol. I: *On the Principles of Political Economy and Taxation*. Cambridge, UK: Cambridge University Press.
Strogatz, S.H. (1994). *Nonlinear Dynamics and Chaos*. New York: Addison-Wesley.
Swedberg, R. (1991). *Schumpeter. A Biography*. Princeton: Princeton University Press.
Tchernova, P. and L.R. Wray (2005). Can basic income and job guarantees deliver on their premises. University of Missouri-Kansas City: Center for Full Employment and Price Stability, Working paper no. 42.
Tobin, J. (1969). *A General Equilibrium Approach to Monetary Theory*. Journal of Money, Credit, and Banking, 1:1, 15–29.
Viebrock, E. and J. Clasen (2009). *Flexicurity and Welfare Reform: A Review*. Socio-Economic Review, 7, 305–331.
Vis, B. (2007). *States of welfare or states of workfare? Welfare state restructuring in 16 capitalist democracies, 1985-2002*. Policy & Politics, 35, 105–122.

Wiggins, S. (1990). *Introduction to applied nonlinear dynamical systems and chaos*. Heidelberg: Springer.

Wilthagen, T. (1998). 'Flexicurity: A New Paradigm for Labour Market Policy Reform?', Berlin: WZB Discussion paper FS I, 98–202.

Wilthagen, T. and F. Tros (2004). The concept of 'flexicurity': a new approach to regulating employment and labour markets. *Transfer*, 2, 166–186.

Wörgötter, A. (1986). *Who's who in Goodwin's growth cycle*. Jahrbuch für Nationalökonomie und Statistik, 201, 222–228.

Yunker, J.A. (1995). Post-Lange market socialism: An evaluation of profit-oriented proposals. *Journal of Economic Issues*, 29. Republished in: Yunker, J.A. (2001): On the Political Economy of Market Socialism Essays and Analyses. London: Ashgate.

Yoshida, H. and Asada, T. (2007). *Dynamic analysis of policy lag in a Keynes-Goodwin model: Stability, instability, cycles and chaos*. Journal of Economic Behavior & Organization, 62, 441–469.

INDEX

aggregate supply, 32
Alchian, A.A., 130, 136
Alexander, J.C., 203
Andersen, T.M., 75
Asada, T.
    full employment welfare capitalism, 33–34, 36, 43–44, 63
    stability theorem, 204–205
    unleashed capitalism, 146, 154–155, 163, 168
asset holders, 163, 175–176, 191, 192–193
    households, 148–150
asset prices, 158–159
Australia, 75

balanced growth, 39–41, 49–54
balanced reproduction, 82–86, 140–142
Barbosa-Filho, N., 20
basic income, 16–22
basic income guarantee (BIG), 75
Beyond the Waste Land (Bowles, Gordon and Weisskopf), 16
Blanchard, O.J., 26, 33, 69, 145, 154
Blanchard and Katz error correction
    automatic stabilizers, 23–24
    flexicurity capitalism, 69, 82, 92, 108–109
    full employment welfare capitalism, 30, 32, 39, 40, 50, 53, 60
    stability of balanced reproduction, 140
bond price, 184
bond supply, 184–185
Bourdieu, Pierre, 129
Bowles, S., 16
Brandt, Willy, 62
business administration elites, 120

capacity utilization, 104
Capital, vol. 1 (Marx), 1, 2, 110
Capital, vol. 2 (Marx), 74
capital accumulation, 7, 38–39
capital and labor, conflict between, 1–3

capital gains
    expectations, 159–162, 195–196
    spirals, 144
capital markets, gross substitutes and stability, 158–159
capitalism
    decomposition of, 70, 112
    future of, 114–116
Capitalism, Socialism, and Democracy (Schumpeter), 3, 66, 72, 74, 113
career advancement of elites, 124–125
cascade of stable matrices approach, 162–168, 186, 190
central bank, 59, 119, 154
chartist asset holders, 150, 159–162, 191
Chen, P., 31–32, 33, 36
Chiarella, C.
    full employment welfare capitalism, 33, 36, 43, 61
    unleashed capitalism, 145–148, 154–155, 167–169, 174, 195
children, education of, 98–100, 122–123
citizenship education, 101
Clasen, J., 75
closed orbits in system of nonlinear differential equations, 203–205
Cobb-Douglas average, 26
combined wages, 21–22
commercial banks, failure of, 127
comparative statics, 181–186
competition in schools, 99–100
competitive socialism. *See* socialism
Comprehensive Neo-Schumpterian Economics (CNSE), 5
conflict-driven economies, 49–50, 64
consensus-based economies, 15, 48–49, 64
consumption, 77–82
corporate bonds, 104–107
countercyclical fiscal policy, 164, 166, 190
creative destruction, 110–114, 115, 137
credit, 86–88, 90–92, 111

credit management, 6
cultural elites, 121

DAD, 37–38, 41
damped oscillations, 168–170
DAS, 38–39, 41
debt financing, 90–91, 108–109
demand, laws of motion, 37
demand driven output levels, 134–136
democracy, 67, 72
　education, 101
　social cohesion, 76
Denmark, 73
depressions, economic, 2, 5, 19, 62–64, 104, 143, 157
deregulation, labor market, 72–73
disequilibrium aggregate demand (DAD), 37–38, 41
disequilibrium aggregate supply (DAS), 38–39, 41
dissent-driven economy, 15
dynamic multiplier instability, 54

economic development, definitions of, 110
economic elites, 120
educational system, 4, 25, 93–104
　elites, 121–123, 138–139
　in flexicurity capitalism, 67, 69, 115–116
eigenvalues, 56–57, 169
elites, 4, 117–130, 138
　decision making, 117–120
　failures of, 126–127
　preferences, 125–126
　selection of, 67, 75, 118
employer of first resort (EFR), 68, 75, 85, 138
employer of last resort (ELR), 69, 75
employment cycles, 58–63
employment dynamics, 37–38
employment rate, 30, 33–38, 41–44, 51, 60, 64
entrepreneurs, 110–111, 113
equal opportunities in education, 97–102, 122–123
equity demand, 163
equity prices, 193
Erhard, Ludwid, 72
European Union
　educational system, 101
　flexicurity system, 4, 6, 28, 67, 74, 115

feedback channels, 43–49
financial crisis
　United States, 143
　worldwide, 125, 127, 128
financial markets, 176–177, 190–191, 195
　reform of, 67
Finland, educational system, 93–94, 102–104
firms
　investment, 150–152
　output adjustment, 152–153
　price-setting, 130
　production, 150–152
　property rights, 119–120
fiscal authorities, 153–154
fiscal policy, 61–63, 119, 166–167
Flaschel, P.
　dynamic multiplier process, 34
　flexicurity system, 25, 69, 73, 77, 84–85, 108–109
　full employment, 63
　Goodwin growth cycle, 12, 15
　kinked wage PC, 169
　KMG model, 145–148, 167, 195
　KMGS model, 43–45
　KMGT model, 174
　minimum and maximum wages, 20
　MKS system, 116
　monetary policy, 61
　real wage error-correction, 33
　reserve-army mechanism, 8
　stability of balanced reproduction, 82, 140
　steady state, 168
　wage-price spiral, 36, 154–155
flexibility, economic, 68, 76, 137, 138
flexicurity capitalism, 4–5
　arguments for, 114–116, 197–198
　basic principles, 74–77, 137–140
　benefits of, 92
　defined, 67, 74
　demand problems, 109
　economic growth, 77–82
　elites, renumeration of, 127–128
　elites, role in, 128–130
　macrodynamic framework, 68–74
　social aspects, 113
France, 92, 97

Franke, R.
    full employment welfare capitalism, 43
    unleashed capitalism, 145–146,
        154–155, 158, 168, 195
Friedman, Milton, 27–28
full employment
    economic aspects, 29–32
    in flexicurity system, 67, 74–75
    Kalecki, M., 3, 27
    opposition of industrial leaders, 61, 63
    political aspects, 29–32, 58, 63, 72
fundamentalist asset holders, 150, 161
Funk, L., 75

Gandolfo, G., 162, 199–200, 202–203
"General Law of Capitalist Accumulation"
    (Marx), 1, 2
General Theory (Keynes), 114
Germany, 62, 92, 97, 125
    minimum wages, 9–10
Glombowski, J., 206n6
goods market inflation, 165
Goodwin, R., 1, 29–30, 42, 45, 129, 147
    M(arx)K(eynes)S(chumpeter)
        system, 116
Goodwin closed orbits, 19–20
Goodwin growth cycle
    classical, 10–15
    minimum wages, 17–18, 22, 24–25
    problems of, 68–69, 77
    profit-led economy, 51
Goodwin reserve-army growth cycle, 8
Goodwin reserve-army mechanism, 65
Goodwin wage share/employment rate
    cycle, 70
Goodwin-Rose growth-cycle dynamics, 36
Goodwin-Rose type reserve-army
    mechanism, 44
Goodwin-type lower turning points, 54
Goodwin-type upper turning points, 51–53
Gordon, D., 16
government
    budget, 176
    expenditure, 61–63
    sector, 78–82, 119
    services, 153–154
Great Britain, 97
Great Depression, 143
Greiner, A., 8, 69
Groh, G., 145, 147

gross substitution, 158–159, 193
Groth, C., 11
Guckenheimer, J., 203

Hanusch, H., 5, 111
Harrodian accelerator
    mechanism, 43–44
Harrodian investment-sales
    accelerator, 195
Harrod-type investment accelerator
    mechanism, 43–44
Hartmann, M., 118, 125, 129
health care, 208n1
highly skilled workers, 78–81, 83, 93
    education of, 100
    growth rate of, 140
Hirsch, M., 14, 203
Holmes, P., 203
Hopf bifurcation, 168, 170
    theorem, 203–204
households, 147–150
human rights, 10, 123
    equal opportunity in education, 97, 101
    right to work, 12, 16, 70
    United Nations' *Universal Declaration
        of Human Rights*, 16, 73
Hung, H., 61

incentives for elites, 117, 125–126
income distribution, 12–15
income guarantee, 138
industrial sector, 77–82, 85
inflation, 132–134, 154–155, 169, 172
innovation-management processes, 6
instability, 49–54, 168–174
    See also stability
intensive form of long-term bonds,
    177–179
interest-rate policy, 61, 191–194
investment, 77–82, 87, 90–92
    political aspects, 58–63

Jacobian matrix, 47, 187, 189
    J, 50, 52, 53, 54
    steady state, 42–43, 49, 92
job guarantee (JG) principles, 75

Kaldor, N., 43
Kaldorian approach, 146

Kalecki: full employment welfare
    capitalism, 27–65
  aggregate supply, 32
  balanced growth, 39–41, 49–54
  capital accumulation, 38–39
  central bank, 59
  conflict-driven economies, 49–50, 64
  consensus-based
    economies, 48–49, 64
  demand, laws of motion, 37
  disequilibrium aggregate demand
    (DAD), 37–38, 41
  disequilibrium aggregate supply (DAS),
    38–39, 41
  dynamic multiplier instability, 54
  eigenvalue diagrams, 56–57
  employment cycles, 58–63
  employment dynamics, 37–38
  employment rate, 30, 33–38, 41–44, 51,
    60, 64
  feedback channels, 43–49
  fiscal policy, 61–63
  full employment, 27, 58, 61, 63
    economic and political aspects, 29–32
  government expenditure, 61–63
  instability, 49–54
  interest-rate policy, 61
  investment, political aspects, 58–63
  labor market, external, 30
  laws of motion, 36–39
  lower turning points
    Goodwin-type, 54
    Rose-type, 53
  market economies, types of, 65
  monetary policy, 59–61
  multiplier dynamics, 37–38
  price inflation, 58
  profit-led economy, 52, 54
  real wages, 31, 36, 45–48, 50, 53
    dynamics, 38–39
  reduced-form three-dimensional
    dynamics, 41–43
  reserve-army mechanism, 28, 43–51
    Kalecki, 45–48, 50–51, 54, 65
    Kalecki-Steindl, 43–44
  stability, 47–48
  steady state, 32, 39–43, 48–50,
    56–58, 60
  supply, laws of motion, 37

unemployment
    disciplinary aspects, 27–28
    mass, 35, 65
  upper turning points
    Goodwin-type, 51–53
    Kalecki-type, 50–51
  wage adjustment speeds, 55
  wage-led economy, 49–50
  wage-price dynamics, 32–36
  wage-price spiral, 36
  welfare state, 65
    economic growth and, 28–29
  workforce utilization, 30
Kalecki, M., 1, 3, 197
  capital-labor relationship, 29
  full employment, employer
    opinions of, 35
  policy, economic, 53
  Political Aspects of Full Employment
    (Kalecki), 27–28, 72
  political aspects of full employment
    welfare capitalism, 58, 63
Kaleckian dynamics, 109
Kaleckian markup pricing process, 139
Kalecki-Goodwin-Rose (KGR)
    accumulation and employment
    dynamics, 42
Kalecki-Goodwin-type economy, 28
Kalecki-type upper turning points, 50–51
Katz, L., 26, 33, 69, 154
Keynes, J.M., 3, 197
  capital development as a casino, 138
  compared to flexicurity system, 73
  financial market objectives, 143
  flexible wage policy, 196
  general theory, 74
  General Theory (Keynes), 114
  short-term rate of interest, 191
Keynes effects, 43–45, 60, 168
Keynes Goodwin Rose (KGR)
    model, 43, 45
Keynes Metzler Goodwin Steindl (KMGS)
    model, 43–45
Keynesian aggregate demand, 37–38, 46,
    51–52, 136
Keynesian business fluctuations, 104–109
Keynesian demand, 85–86, 116
Keynesian dynamic multiplier, 139

Keynesian dynamics, 143–145, 147, 159–160
Keynesian IS-equilibrium determination, 106–107
Keynesian price-quantity dynamics, 136
Keynesianism, 27–28
Keynes-Kalecki goods market and employment dynamics, 36
Keynes/Kalecki-Goodwin/Rose model, 63
Keynes-Metzler-Goodwin (KMG) model, 43, 145–150, 160, 162, 167–169, 195–196
KGR (Kalecki-Goodwin-Rose) accumulation and employment dynamics, 42
KGR dynamics, 54
  numerical examples, 54–58
KGR (Keynes Goodwin Rose) model, 43, 45
Klesse, H.-J., 9
KMG (Keynes-Metzler-Goodwin) model, 43, 145–150, 160, 162, 167–169, 195–196
KMGS (Keynes Metzler Goodwin Steindl) model, 43–45
KMGT model, 159, 169, 174, 190–191, 195
Köper, C., 168, 186, 209n1
Krause, U., 132–133
Krolzig, H.-M., 108–109, 145, 154
Krüger, M., 206n6

labor market, external, 30
labor market deregulation, 72–73
labor market reform, 67, 139
laissez-faire capitalism, 73
law of natural wages, 7–8
law of value, 110
laws of motion, 36–39
  demand, 37
  inflationary climate, 166
  inventories, 165
  labor capital ratio, 165
  real wages, 155–158
  supply, 37
Liapunov function
  classical growth dynamics, 13–14
  minimum wages, 19–20, 23
  stability of balanced reproduction, 83–84, 140–141
Liapunov's theorem, 202

lifelong learning, 100–101
Liu, W.M., 203
Logeay, C., 8
long-term bonds, 168–174, 174–191, 195
Lorenz, H.-W., 203
lower turning points, 53–54
Luchtenberg, S., 69

macrodynamics, 145–146
Madsen, J.B., 11
Malthusian theory, 7–8
market economies, types of, 65
markup pricing, 130–136
Marx, K., 4, 197
  Capital, vol. 1 (Marx), 1, 2, 110
  Capital, vol. 2 (Marx), 74
  capital and labor, interaction of, 7–8
  general law of accumulation, 73, 113–114
  "General Law of Capitalist Accumulation" (Marx), 1–2
  law of value, 110
  mass unemployment, 70
  reproduction schemes, 74, 116
  See also reserve-army mechanism
Marx: socially acceptable capitalism, 7–26
  basic income, 16–22
  capital accumulation, dynamics of, 7
  combined wages, 21–22
  consensus economy, 15
  dissent-driven economy, 15
  educational system, 25
  growth dynamics, classical, 12–15
  human rights, 10, 12, 16
  income distribution, 12–15
  law of natural wages, 7–8
  maximum wages, 10, 19–20, 22–23, 25
  minimum wages, 8–12, 16–23, 24–25
  negotiations between capital and labor, 22–24
  price inflation, 22
  reserve-army mechanism, 8–9, 16, 25
  right to work, 16
  steady state, 22–24
  unemployment, 12–15
    benefits, 17–22
    mass, 10, 25
  wage inflation, 22–23
  wages, regulation of, 7–10

M(arx)K(eynes)S(chumpeter) system (MKS), 1, 4, 116, 129
maximum wages, 10, 19–20, 22–23, 25
Metzler, L.A., 147
Metzlerian inventory accelerator mechanism, 166
Metzlerian inventory cycles, 150
Metzlerian inventory dynamics, 43–45
Meztlerian inventory adjustment processes, 107
minimum wages, 8–12, 16–23, 24–25
Minsky, Hyman, 143–144
MKS system, 1, 4, 116, 129
monetary authorities, 153–154
monetary policy, 59–61, 166–167
money supply, 184, 192–194
money wages, 196
multiplier dynamics, 37–38
Mundell effects, 43–45, 60
Mundell-Tobin effect, 168
Murata, Y., 200

NAIRU
  classical growth dynamics, 12, 15
  full employment welfare capitalism, 39, 55, 57, 59, 61
  minimum wages, 19, 22
  unleashed capitalism, 155
National Board of Education, Finland, 93
negotiations between capital and labor, 22–24
Nell, E., 69
Neo-Schumpterian Corridor, 5
Nesemann, 132–133
"no child left behind," 122–123
nonlinear differential equations, 199–205
Nordic countries, 65, 76, 112, 115

Okun, A.M., 46
Okun's law
  flexicurity capitalism, 83–84, 90, 109
  full employment welfare capitalism, 30, 45, 50, 64
  stability of balanced reproduction, 140
Olech, A.M., 202
Olech's theorem, 202

Organization for Economic Co-operation and Development (OECD), 96, 100
outcomes, 168–174

pension funds, 84–91, 141–142, 208n1
period (cycle) doubling route to complex dynamics, 169, 173
Perron theorem, 132
Phillips curve (PC)
  kinked money wage, 168–169, 171
  money-wage, 26, 168–169
  nominal-wage, 12
  price, 30, 39–40, 60, 109
  real-wage, 82, 140
  short-run (wage and price), 154
  wage, 20, 23–24, 33, 39–40, 60, 69, 108
Poincaré-Bendixson theorem, 203
Political Aspects of Full Employment (Kalecki), 27–28, 72
political elites, 119, 120
political learning, 101
price inflation, 22, 58, 108–109, 165–167
price-quantity dynamics, 139
price-setting rules, 130–136
primary labor market, 77–82
Proaño, C., 8, 169, 174
profit
  maximization, 130
  profit-led economy, 52, 54
  profit-led goods market, 156–157
  rates, 133–134
public services, 153–154
Pyka, A., 5, 111

Quesnay, 75
Quirk, V., 75

Rasmussen, Poul Nyrup, 74
real markets, 195
real wages
  dynamics, 38–39
  and employment rate, 45–48
  growth rate, 82–83
  labor market led, 31
  law of motion, 155–158
  real wage dynamic, 164–165
  Rose real-wage effect, 50, 53
  steady state value of, 90
  and wage-price spiral, 36

real-financial market interaction, 144–147
recessions, 2, 63, 104, 197
reduced-form three-dimensional
    dynamics, 41–43
regime-switch induced viability, 168–174
reserve-army mechanism
    abolishment of, 139
    in capitalism, 5, 16, 114
    Goodwin type, 44–46, 65
    Kaleckian, 47–51, 54, 65
    Kalecki-Steindl, 43–44
    Marxian, 1–2, 8–9, 25, 68, 116
Ricardo, David, 7
right to work, 16
    See also human rights
Roemer, John, 66, 116, 129–130
Rose, H., 29, 33, 45, 154
Rose effect, 53
Rose real-wage channel, 50
Rose-type lower turning points, 53
Routh-Hurwitz conditions
    full employment welfare capitalism,
        46–49, 50–53
    stability theorem, 200–201, 204
    unleashed capitalism, 167, 187, 189, 190

Sargent, T.J., 154, 161, 193
Sarkozy, Nicolas, 116
Say's law, 82, 85, 104
scala mobile, 165
Scandanavian countries, 97–98
    See also Nordic countries
Schumpeter: capitalism, flexicurity, and
    democracy, 66–142
    balanced reproduction, 82–86
    basic income guarantee (BIG), 75
    business administration elites, 120
    capacity utilization, 104
    capitalism
        decomposition of, 70, 112
        future of, 114–116
    career advancement for elites, 124–125
    central bank, 119
    children, education of, 98–100, 122–123
    citizenship education, 101
    commercial banks, failure of, 127
    competition in schools, 99–100
    consumption, 77–82
    corporate bonds, 104–107
    creative destruction, 110–114, 115, 137

credit, 86–88, 90–92, 111
cultural elites, 121
debt financing, 90–91, 108–109
demand driven output levels, 134–136
democracy, 67, 72
    education, 101
    social cohesion and, 76
economic development, 110
economic elites, 120
educational system, 67, 69, 93–104,
    115–116, 138–139
elites, 117–130, 138
    decision making, 117–120
    educational system, 121–123
    failures of, 126–127
    preferences, 125–126
    selection of, 67, 75, 118
employer of first resort (EFR), 68, 75,
    85, 138
employer of last resort (ELR), 69, 75
entrepreneurs, 110–111, 113
equal opportunities in education,
    97–102, 122–123
financial crisis, worldwide, 125, 127, 128
financial market reform, 67
firms
    price-setting, 130
    property rights, 119–120
fiscal policy, 119
flexibility, economic, 68, 76, 137, 138
flexicurity capitalism
    arguments for, 114–116
    basic principles, 74–77, 137–140
    benefits of, 92
    defined, 67, 74
    demand problems, 109
    Denmark, 73
    economic growth, 77–82
    elites
        remuneration of, 127–128
        role in, 128–130
    macrodynamic framework, 68–74
    social aspects, 113
full employment, 67, 74–75
government sector, 78–82, 119
growth model (Solow), 69
highly skilled workers, 78–81, 83, 93
    education of, 100
    growth rate of, 140

Schumpeter: capitalism, flexicurity, and democracy (*Cont.*)
  human rights, 70, 73, 97, 123
  education, 101
  incentives for elites, 117, 125–126
  income guarantee, 138
  industrial sector, 77–82, 85
  inflation, 132–134
  investment, 77–82, 87, 90–92
  job guarantee (JG) principles, 75
  labor market deregulation, 72–73
  labor market reform, 67, 139
  laissez-faire capitalism, 73
  law of value, 110
  lifelong learning, 100–101
  markup pricing, 130–136
  "no child left behind," 122–123
  pension funds, 84–85, 86–91, 141–142
  political elites, 119, 120
  political learning, 101
  price inflation, 108–109
  price-quantity dynamics, 139
  price-setting rules, 130–136
  primary labor market, 77–82
  profit maximization, 130
  profit rates, 133–134
  real wages, 82–83, 90
  recessions, 104
  reform, 67
  reserve-army mechanism, 114, 116, 139
  rewards for elites, 117
  second labor market, 77–82
  sectoral accounts, 77–82
  security, economic, 68, 76, 137, 138
  skilled workers, 78–81, 93
  social aspects of capitalism, 113–114
  social cohesion, 85, 115
  social status, 117, 129
  socialism, 67, 116
    competitive, 70, 117, 137–139
    Eastern states, 70, 72, 111, 113
    market, 66
    Western capitalism, emergence from, 72
  stability, 104, 109
    balanced reproduction, 82–84, 140–141
  steady state, 90–92, 109, 140–142
  "subnormal" workers, 112–113
  success, business, 131
  supply driven output levels, 134–136
  sustainability of balanced reproduction, 84–86, 141–142
  tertiary education, 100, 123
  unemployment, 82
    mass, 70, 113
    social consequences of, 70
  universities, 100–101
  wage-price spiral, 108
  wages of elites, 127–128
  wealth, accumulation of, 138
  welfare states, 68, 72, 130
  workers, types of, 69, 93, 95–97
Schumpeter, J., 1, 3–4, 197
  Capitalism, Socialism and Democracy (Schumpeter), 66, 72, 74, 113
  Theory of Economic Development (Schumpeter), 110
second labor market, 77–82
sectoral accounts, 77–82
security, economic, 68, 76, 137, 138
Semmler, W.
  full employment welfare capitalism, 61
  stability theorem, 204
  unleashed capitalism, 145–148, 158, 169, 174
skilled workers, 78–81, 93
Skott, P., 34, 43–45, 63
Smale, S., 14, 203
social aspects of capitalism, 113–114
social cohesion, 85, 115
social status, 117, 129
socialism, 1, 3, 67, 116
  competitive, 70, 117, 137–139
  Eastern state socialism, 70, 72, 111, 113
  market, 66
  Western capitalism, emergence from, 72
Socialism: An Economic and Sociological Analysis (von Mises), 66
Solow, R., 69
stability, 47–48, 162–168, 186–191, 196
  balanced reproduction, 82–84, 140–141
  flexicurity system, 104, 109
  theorems, 199–205
  See also instability
stagflation, 2, 12, 15, 19, 20, 72, 157

steady state
  flexicurity capitalism, 90–92, 109, 140–142
  full employment welfare capitalism, 32, 39–43, 48–50, 56–58, 60
  minimum wages, 22–24
  unleashed capitalism, 163–166, 179–181
stock market, 163–164
subnormal workers, 112–113
"subnormal" workers, 112–113
success, business, 131
supply, laws of motion, 37
supply driven output levels, 134–136
sustainability of balanced reproduction, 84–86, 141–142
Svarer, M., 75
Swedberg, R., 111

taxes, 153, 167
Taylor, L., 20
Taylor interest rate rule, 41, 59, 192–194
Tchernova, P., 75
tertiary education, 100, 123
Theory of Economic Development (Schumpeter), 110
Tobin, J., 5, 145, 151, 158–159, 167, 192, 196
Tobin's q, 184–185, 194

unemployment, 12–15, 82
  benefits, 17–22
  disciplinary aspects, 27–28
  mass, 1, 10, 25, 35, 65, 70, 113
  social consequences of, 70
United Kingdom, 92, 125
  wages and employment, 11
United Nations
  System of National Accounts, 137
  Universal Declaration of Human Rights, 16, 73
United States, 32, 75, 92
  economy, 144–145
  education, 123
  wage share/employment rate cycle, 70–71
universities, 100–101
unleashed capitalism, 143–196
  asset holders, 163, 175–176, 191, 192–193
  households, 148–150

asset prices, 158–159
bond price, 184
bond supply, 184–185
capital gains expectations, 159–162, 195–196
capital gains spirals, 144
capital markets
  gross substitutes, 158–159
  stability, 158–159
cascade of stable matrices approach, 162–168, 186, 190
central bank, 154
chartist asset holders, 150, 159–162, 191
comparative statics, 181–186
countercyclical fiscal policy, 164, 166, 190
damped oscillations, 168–170
eigenvalues, 169
equity demand, 163
equity prices, 193
financial crisis, United States, 143
financial markets, 176–177, 190–191, 195
firms
  investment, 150–152
  output adjustment, 152–153
  production, 150–152
fiscal authorities, 153–154
fiscal policy, 166–167
fundamentalist asset holders, 150, 161
goods market inflation, 165
government budget, 176
government services, 153–154
gross substitution, 158–159, 193
households, 147–150
inflation, 154–155, 169, 172
instability, 168–174
intensive form of long-term bonds, 177–179
interest-rate policy, 191–194
kinked wage PC, 168–169, 171
law of motion
  inflationary climate, 166
  inventories, 165
  labor capital ratio, 165
long-term bonds, 168–174, 174–191, 195
macrodynamics, 145–146

unleashed capitalism (*Cont.*)
    monetary authorities, 153–154
    monetary policy, 166–167
    money supply, 184, 192–194
    money wages, 196
    outcomes, 168–174
    period (cycle) doubling route to complex dynamics, 169, 173
    price inflation, 165–167
    profit-led goods market, 156–157
    public services, 153–154
    real markets, 195
    real wages, 164–165
        law of motion, 155–158
    real-financial market interaction, 144–147
    regime-switch induced viability, 168–174
    scala mobile, 165
    stability, 162–168, 186–191, 196
    steady state, 163–166, 179–181
    stock market, 163–164
    taxes, 153, 167
    "unleashed capitalism" model, 5–6
    wage-led goods market, 156–157
    wage-price spiral, 143–144, 154–160, 195
    wealth, 148–150, 175–176
    workers, households, 147–148, 175
upper turning points, 50–53
    Goodwin-type, 51–53
    Kalecki-type, 50–51

Viebrock, E., 75
von Mises, Ludwig
    Socialism: An Economic and Sociological Analysis (von Mises), 66
Voss, O., 9

wage-led economy, 49–50
wage-led goods market, 156–157
wage-management processes, rational, 6
wage-price dynamics, 32–36
wage-price spiral, 108, 143–144, 154–160
    interaction with aggregate demand, 195
    price inflation, 108
    real wage dynamic, 36
wages
    adjustment speeds, 55
    elites, 127–128
    regulation of, 7–10
    wage dynamics, 26
    wage inflation, 22–23
wages of elites, 127–128
Walrasian economy, 9, 110
Walrasian tâtonnement process, 159, 193
Walras's law, 210n13
wealth, 138, 148–150, 175–176
wealth, accumulation of, 138
Weisskopf, T.E., 16
welfare states, 1, 65, 68, 72, 130
    economic growth and, 28–29
    Nordic, 68
Wilthagen, Ton, 75
workers
    households, 147–148, 175
    types of, 69, 93, 95–97
workers, types of, 69, 93, 95–97
workforce utilization, 30
Wray, L.R., 75

York, J.A., 203
Yoshida, H., 205
Yunker, J.A., 66